MEN OF SOUTHOVER

The lives and deaths of
the sixty eight men named on Southover's two
War Memorials

1914 - 1918
and
1939 - 1945

by

Alison M. Benton

© Alison M Benton 1998

first published: March 1998

ISBN 0 9532833 0 5

Published by Moira Publications, 8 Egles Grove, Uckfield, East Sussex TN22 2BY

Printed and typeset by The Authors' Publishing Guild, Hadlow Down, Uckfield, Sussex
    01825 830319

Cover design: Moira Publications and The Authors' Publishing Guild

Front cover illustration: Southover Church with 1914-1918 War Memorial today.
(Alison Benton)

Back cover illustration: 1939-1945 Memorial Tablet, inside North Aisle, Southover Church.
(Edward Reeves)

CONTENTS

FOREWORD

On the past twenty Remembrance Sundays I have read out the Roll of Honour of the 68 men who are listed on the Southover War Memorials, but this year there was a significant difference for me.

Previously, most of the names meant little to me except for one or two names still familiar in the Southover area. However, after reading through this book by Alison Benton, Remembrance Sunday took

Southover Church exterior, c.1906
(Bob Cairns)

on a much greater importance for me. Being aware of the houses where the men had lived and learning something of their home life and their families made the events of both the World Wars much more meaningful than had previously been the case.

This book not only records the circumstances of the death of each of the men and gives us an insight into the terrible conditions in which they fought, perhaps particularly in the First World War, but it also gives us a picture of life in Britain at that time. I am sure that many who have either past or present associations with Southover, or who have a particular

interest in this period of our country's history, will find this book a fascinating record of past events.

It is obvious that Alison has taken a tremendous amount of time and trouble in gathering this information, both through talking with relatives still living in the Lewes area and also through her research of many different sources. One of the benefits already being felt from her work is that her enquiries have actually helped bring some families together again, and helped in the healing process of coming to terms with events that happened so long ago and yet which still affect lives today.

Southover Church interior, c.1906
(Bob Cairns)

She is to be congratulated on completing such an excellent project, and I am pleased to be able thoroughly to recommend this book.

November 1997

Peter Markby
Rector of Southover Church, Lewes

AUTHOR'S PREFACE

why and how this book came to be written

The seeds of this book were sown while in Southover Church during the summer of 1994. It was at the time of the eightieth anniversary of the start of the First War in August 1914, and the fifty-fifth anniversary of the Second War starting in September 1939. It seemed to me that even though all our lives in the rest of this century have been so profoundly affected by all that went on in those World Wars, we are in danger of losing sight of the real people behind those 'events', and perhaps some of the values they stood for.

When I looked at the names on Southover's two Memorials, forty six from the First War on the granite cross outside the north-east corner of the church, and twenty two from the Second War on the stone tablet inside the church at the back of the north aisle, I was struck by the enormity of the loss from such a tiny parish. (The population of Southover at the 1911 Census was little more than 1100 people, and 46 of them were killed by 1918.) It also occurred to me that those who have personal and family memories of the names on these Memorials must be a diminishing number, and must themselves have suffered greatly in losing these fathers, husbands, brothers and sons from their lives.

I decided that the best way I could contribute to honouring the sacrifices made by the men and their families was to record their individual stories and attempt to bring their memory alive to succeeding generations. I felt that recognition and acknowledgement are the best ways of honouring and valuing such sacrifice and loss. I have always believed that suffering can be redeemed, and that conflicts can be resolved. I also feel that, on many levels, commemoration can best be achieved by accepting and making use of the freedoms won for us. Those were my starting points in embarking on this book, and they have become my growing conviction.

This book has no claim to be a work either of history or of literature. It is rather an attempt to pay tribute to all those behind these Southover names, and to interweave the lives and deaths of them all with the world-wide and local events of the wars going on around them. The focus is therefore the individual biographies, but in writing them I have been struck by how much these few men seem to mirror in their lives and deaths so many of the main events and developments of the two World Wars, both nationally and internationally.

Southover has turned out to be more of a microcosm of the wider canvas than I was expecting to find. Among the sixty-eight there are both raw recruits and long-serving Regular soldiers, Territorials and Reservists; there are infantry and artillery, cavalry and their armoured successors; there are both the Navy as the 'Senior Service', and the earliest members of the Air Force; and there all ranks from Boy Sailors and Privates to NCO's and Captains, some were mentioned in despatches and a few were awarded medals. There are men who were killed in action and those who died of disease, those who died of their wounds and those who were killed by individual snipers, bombs or

Southover High Street looking east, c.1900
(Bob Cairns)

Southover High Street looking west, c.1900
(Bob Cairns)

shells; there are those who were gassed, and those who died as prisoners of war. There are those who were buried where they fell both in Europe and further afield, and those buried back home, and there are those whose bodies were never found. And yet all this breadth of later experience of life and death came to men who had in the main shared the same pre-war school and church life, and had lived mostly within a stone's throw of each other. There were young lads barely out of school, only sons and groups of brothers or cousins, and there were newly married men, and those with five or six children; all ages from 18 to 43 are represented.

A holiday visit to Lavenham Church in Suffolk and Geoff. Bridger's book about the men named on the Ringmer War Memorial, both in that same summer of 1994, showed me what could be done within one parish. My researches have taken me through Lewes, Chichester and Portsmouth to London , Ypres and the many battlefields, cemeteries and Memorials in the Salient, Normandy, and even Israel. These visits have been thought-provoking and enriching. Many people, libraries and archives have helped in this process; I have tried to give due acknowledgement to them all elsewhere in this book, but I apologise for the inevitable omissions.

My main regrets in ending this book where I have, after three years work, is that it is so uneven and so unfinished. Despite widespread publicity in local papers, shop windows, and the parish magazine, I have only been contacted by a minority of the families who were involved, so some men therefore have very much more detail than others. Nor have I been able to research as fully as I would have liked all the publicly available social and regimental records there are, both locally and nationally. I regret this very much, and hope that any readers who have further information about these men will contact me.

The presentation of the biographies
The risk of 68 consecutive biographies becoming somewhat repetitive and indigestible to read is great, so I have tried to break the text up into more manageable portions. Each separate biography therefore has its own boxed heading summarising the main facts of each man's life and death, followed by sub-headings which will hopefully help the text more readable.

The biographies are then grouped together chronologically, in year groups according to the dates of their deaths. In the First War, as only one Southover man was killed in 1914, I have put him together with those killed in 1915. In the Second War, where I have deliberately done less research as so much more is available from other sources (such as Bob Elliston's "Lewes at War"), I have divided the men into just two groups: those killed up to and including 1943, and those killed in 1944 and 1945. In both wars, there is a much greater number of fatalities in the last year or eighteen months of each war.

Each part has its own map to show battlefield and cemetery locations, as well as the map of Southover in the First War to show the men's home addresses. For the Second War, this map for home addresses has to be of the whole of Lewes rather than just Southover, because of the movements of families out to the new estates. Each part is also liberally illustrated with photographs taken both then and now.

There is then, by way of an introduction to each part of the First War, a selection of some of the main news items that hit the local headlines in each year. For the Second War, there is instead a linking passage entitled "Between the Wars", in which I have attempted to summarise developments in Lewes in the 1920s and 1930s, and identify some contrasts in the effects locally of the two wars.

I would just like to make explicit two of the emphases of the book which I trust will become clear to any who read the whole book.

One of these is about war itself:

There is no sense at all in which this book is glorying in war, or suggesting that it was only those who actually gave their lives who were brave or worthy of honour or commemoration. I am acutely aware of the suffering and sacrifice of both those who stayed at home, and those who went to war and came back damaged in mind, body or spirit. I am also very aware that the losses and damage inflicted on those who were then the enemy, and on those innocent peoples caught up between the hostilities of the 'great' nations, were unimaginably greater at least in scale than anything Southover suffered.

The other is about men specifically:

There is no suggestion in the title of this book, or in its contents in any way at all, that this book is viewing these 'men of Southover' as more important than anyone else, male or female, just because they went off to war. I have been trying to show throughout the close links between these men and the women who bore them, who bore their children, who did their jobs for them while they were away and since. I have also been trying to show that it was their womenfolk and their children who also lost and sacrificed much. We too, their successors, have lost so much that their lives and gifts could have contributed to our society today, had they survived. But we have gained the freedoms and honour they died for.

As the Second War Memorial Tablet says:

"See ye to it that they shall not have died in vain".

December 1997   Alison M. Benton

*The First War Memorial at the time
of the unveiling, c.1921*

ACKNOWLEDGEMENTS

1. Local Authors

Geoff. Bridger: *Valiant Hearts of Ringmer*, 1993

Robert Elliston: *Lewes At War*, 1995

Susan Rowland: *Lest We Forget: The Gallant Men of Hamsey*, 1995

It is these three to whom I owe a great debt of inspiration, encouragement and help; it was they who really got me started and gave me much help on the way. Geoff and Robert were able to fill in some puzzling gaps about Southover men for me from their great store of information, and steer me in the right research directions (see 'Helpful Places' listed below). Susan's encouragement, community interests, and in particular her mapping skills and resources have been invaluable.

2. Family Contacts

Without these people up and down the country who responded to my notices in local papers, shop windows, and the Parish Magazine, this book could not have been written. I thank them all most sincerely for sharing so much of themselves and their memories, often with pain as well as pride, and providing some of their precious photographs. Unattributed photographs are my own. I list the contacts with the serviceman they relate to:-

First War

6	Billy Hillman	Gillian Avis (great-niece)
8	Jesse Moore	Mabel Blaber (niece by marriage); Ray Moore (great-nephew)
33	Geo. Walter Moore	Jacque Blackmore (great niece)
13	George Fellows	Marjorie Attfield (daughter); Jacque Blackmore (grand-daughter)
		Peter Fellows (grandson)
16	Henry Neville	Mildred Nicholls (sister)
34	Joseph Neville	
17	Arthur Head	Sue Burley (niece)
37	Edward Steadman	Bill Steadman (nephew); Andy Steadman (great-nephew)
39	Alec Richardson	George A.(Tony) Richardson (nephew); Jean Davis (niece)
41	Frederick Pollard	Edie Pollard (daughter)

Second War

1	Walter Dunk	Patrick Dunk (brother)
2	Walter Raymond Beck	Brian Beck (second cousin)
4	Albert Webb	Elsie Larkin (sister)
5	Leonard Axtell	Margery French (sister); Terrance Axtell (son); Myles Axtell (nephew)
6	Ronald Olliver	Kathleen Newman (aunt)
8	Ronald Chas. Blythe	Kathleen Healey (sister).
10	Raymond Scrase	Joan Gurr (cousin)
13	Stanley Olliver	Kathleen Newman (sister)
14	Robert Wm. Kemp	Kenneth Kemp (son)
16	A.J.W. Stiles	Molly Stiles (widow); Janet Dawes (daughter)
17	Fredk. Moore	Ray Moore (brother); Mabel Blaber (sister); Jacque Blackmore (niece)
22	Harold Russell Grover	Phyllis Grover (widow).
	old schoolfriends	R.W.A. Brown, Bedford.

3. Helpful Places and People

East Sussex Record Office (ESRO), Lewes:

Southover Church Parish Registers (Baptisms, Marriages, and Burials); 1891 Census; maps; local newspapers of war years (*Sussex Express, Sussex County Herald, Sussex Daily News, East Sussex News*); details of Southover men as provided for the Lewes Town Memorial, 1921.

Lewes Public Library, Sussex Room: Lewes Street Directories etc.

West Sussex Record Office (WSRO) ,Chichester: Archives of Royal Sussex Regiment.

Public Record Office (PRO), Kew: Regimental War Diaries etc.

Commonwealth War Graves Commission (CWGC), Maidenhead: burial details of each man; booklets on each Cemetery and Memorial.

Holt's Tours: "Salient Points", tour of Ypres Salient battlefields, Cemeteries and Memorials, with Ted Smith and Christopher Throndsen, April 1996; also Steve Branch on the Royal Navy and its ships.

Imperial War Museum and Mrs Sylvia Anderson on Southover School First World War Project, 1985.

National Memorials: Merchant Navy, Tower Hill, London; Royal Navy, Portsmouth; Royal Sussex Regiment, Chichester Cathedral.

National Archive of Canada, Ottawa

Sussex Combined Services Museum, Redoubt Fortress, Eastbourne

Bob Cairns, Lewes picture postcard collection

Peter Markby, Rector of Southover; Jean Hebborn, Parish Visitor

Occupants of houses in Southover where the men lived, as acknowledged in the text.

Sussex Family History Group (SFHG)

Regimental Museums/Archives

The help of the following establishments is acknowledged with gratitude; they are listed following the numbers given in this book to the men concerned (all First War men):

Derby City Museum, Archives of the 9th Lancers (1 Turk D.F) The Royal Green Jackets Museum, Archives of The Rifle Brigade (5 Sandals); Maidstone Museum, Archives of the Queen's Own Royal West Kent Regiment (12 Glover); The Royal Hampshire Regiment Museum, Winchester (15 Williams); The Royal Regiment of Fusiliers, H.M. Tower of London (18 Suter; 22 Eade; 44 Selby); Royal Signals Museum, Archives of the Royal Engineers Signal Service, Blandford Forum (19 Coleman); Regimental Association of the Middlesex Regiment, New Malden (21 Wares; 38 Turk A.S.); The Royal Artillery Historical Trust, Old Royal Military Academy, Woolwich (23 Payne; 31 Compton; 41 Pollard); Soldiers of Gloucestershire Museum, Gloucester Docks (27 Anson) The Queen's Royal Surrey Regiment Museum, Clandon Park, Guildford (30 Thompson); The King's Own Royal Regiment Museum, Lancaster (32 French); The London Fusiliers Volunteer Museum, Balham, London SW17 (37 Steadman); The Tank Museum, Archive of Tank Corps & Machine Gun Corps, Bovington, Dorset (39 Richardson); Lancashire County & Regimental Museum, Preston, Lancs., for 14th Hussars (43 Cole); Regimental Museum, Royal Logistic Corps., for Royal Corps of Transport and RASC, Deepcut, Camberley, Surrey. (45 Putland).

I am most grateful for all the help I have had from all those above, and from many others, particularly my own family who have tolerated much and given much. But despite all their help, I alone must take responsibility for all errors and omissions, which I much regret.

4. Bibliography

Arnold-Foster, Mark, 1973: *The World at War,* Fontana/Collins.

Coate, Leslie D., 1983: *The Somme 1914 - 1918*, Tressell Publications.

Coombs, Rose E. B., 1976: *Before Endeavours Fade A Guide to the Battlefields of the First World War,* After the Battle Publications.

Churchill, W.S., 1951: *The Second World War*

Holt, Major T.& Mrs V.,1996: *Battlefield Guide to the Somme,* Pen & Sword Books.

Messenger, Charles, 1987: *Pictorial History of the Second World War,* Bison Books

Regimental Histories (as acknowledged in the text)

ABOUT THE AUTHOR

Alison Benton was born and brought up on the Surrey-Sussex borders. She lived mainly in old Crawley and on Cheals' Nurseries at Lowfield Heath. University at Nottingham and then London in the 1960s led on to her career in hospital social work in London and Bristol until the late 1970s. Marriage and raising a family (by adoption and by birth) followed this, in Bath first, then in Lewes from 1984. While in Lewes she belonged with the family to Southover Church, hence this book, but they now live in Uckfield.

Alison has already produced some histories of her Sussex forbears and the family nursery and Landscape Gardening firm. She is now able to devote more time to her interests in family, local, and oral history and reminiscence work, and to her voluntary work in the field of adoption.

MEN OF SOUTHOVER: THEIR CULTURAL CONTEXT

With great industry and skill Alison Benton has researched and interwoven a mass of biographical data to fashion a new memorial to the soldiers, sailors and airmen associated with Southover who died during the two World Wars.

That parish, though a suburb of Lewes had a distinct rural character in 1914. Many young men worked in the open air, in its gardens or at local farms and racing stables. Dennis Turk's knowledge of horses, shared by his brother Augustus, led him to the Queen's Royal Lancers. Edward Wares was a milk carrier for Uridge's Dairies, and James Crouch a cowman at Barcombe. Arthur Head tended Frank Verrall's shrubs at the Manor House, and another gardener, the emigrant Jesse Moore, returned 'home' with the Canadian infantry. And at least semi-rural in flavour amid the malt and the hops, was the labour at Ballards Brewery of William Martin and Ernest Payne.

By contrast, employment with the London, Brighton and South Coast Railway or its rivals, brought some men closer to the machine technology that lethally shaped the conduct of the Great War. Thomas Coleman was a telegraph clerk at Lewes Station; George Eade was a goods porter there, and Frederick Pollard a signalman at Eridge. William Martin and his brother Frank, and Alec Richardson were the sons of railwaymen. Others also worked amid machines and measurement, George Holder at the pumping station, Frederick Hillman as a dispenser at the Victoria Hospital, and William Hillman as a journalist with the East Sussex News. Two had trained in the County Surveyor's Office, Edward Sandals as a clerk and Lieutenant Brian Glover as an articled engineer, serving afterwards in the Royal Flying Corps - his brother, Captain Benjamin joined the Kent Regiment; their father owned the Portland Cement works at Cliffe. Arthur Blagrove was the son of a watchmaker.

The patriotism shared by these men had been in many cases strengthened by the parish school and the church choir, by football and rowing clubs, and by the Territorials who drilled in the parish. Thorold Stewart-Jones, a Captain in the Royal Sussex Regiment and resident at the Grange, had been a Territorial and a church-warden. Wilfred Anson's father was Rector of Southover till 1913. George Fellows, George Packham and Alfred Cole had served as professional soldiers, so had the fathers of Francis Green and Ernest Payne, both as sergeants in artillery units.

But as the casualty lists lengthened and Mons, the Marne, Ypres and the Somme became household words, the shared courage at the front and the shared anguish at home gave to British patriotism a deeper foundation, which a generation later in the Second World War fed the nation's resolve to defy Fascism. In that struggle, mercifully, fewer Southover men laid down their lives.

November 1997

Colin Brent
Lewes

First World War
The dedication on the Memorial

TO THE GLORY OF GOD
AND IN PROUD AND LOVING MEMORY OF
THOSE WHOSE NAMES ARE INSCRIBED THEREON ...

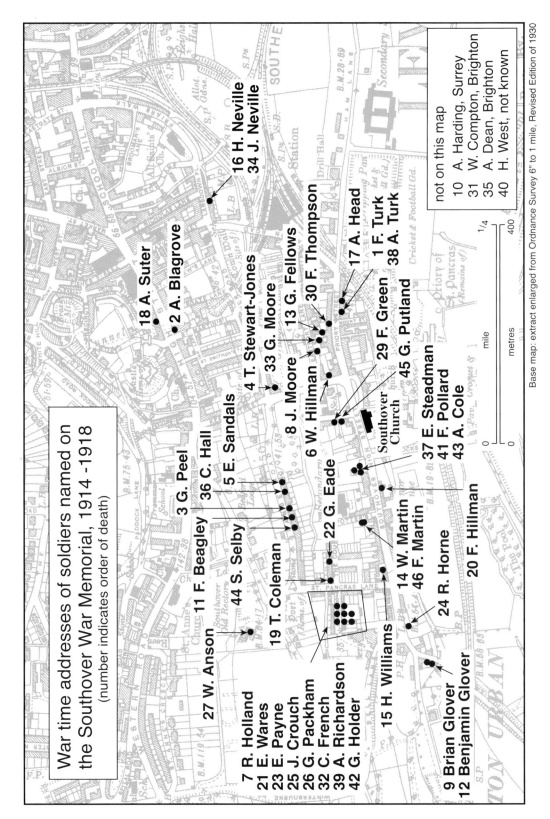

War time addresses of soldiers named on
the Southover War Memorial, 1914 -1918
(number indicates order of death)

not on this map
10 A. Harding, Surrey
31 W. Compton, Brighton
35 A. Dean, Brighton
40 H. West, not known

Base map: extract enlarged from Ordnance Survey 6" to 1 mile, Revised Edition of 1930

16 H. Neville
34 J. Neville
18 A. Suter
2 A. Blagrove
4 T. Stewart-Jones
33 G. Moore
13 G. Fellows
30 F. Thompson
17 A. Head
1 F. Turk
38 A. Turk
29 F. Green
45 G. Putland
8 J. Moore
6 W. Hillman
3 G. Peel
36 C. Hall
5 E. Sandals
37 E. Steadman
41 F. Pollard
43 A. Cole
Southover
Church
22 G. Eade
14 W. Martin
46 F. Martin
24 R. Horne
20 F. Hillman
11 F. Beagley
44 S. Selby
19 T. Coleman
27 W. Anson
15 H. Williams
7 R. Holland
21 E. Wares
23 E. Payne
25 J. Crouch
26 G. Packham
32 C. French
39 A. Richardson
42 G. Holder
9 Brian Glover
12 Benjamin Glover

Men lost in the First War

HOME ADDRESSES

Number	Street	First name	Surname	Number in book
2	The Course	Thomas Robert	COLEMAN	19
3	The Course	George Wm.Osborne	EADE	22
15	Eastport Lane	George	FELLOWS	13
20	Eastport Lane	Jesse	MOORE	8
20	Eastport Lane	George Walter	MOORE	33
12	Garden Street (his father)	Sydney James	*SELBY	44
2	Grange Road	Edward Roland	SANDALS	5
5	Grange Road	Charles Walter	HALL	36
10	Grange Road	George Ernest	PEEL	3
32	Grange Road (his mother)	Sydney James	*SELBY	44
36	Grange Road	Frank	BEAGLEY	11
72	High St., Lewes	Arthur John	BLAGROVE	2
174	High St., Lewes	Arthur John	SUTER	18
28	Lansdown Place	Henry Frank	NEVILLE	16
28	Lansdown Place	Joseph George	NEVILLE	34
53	Potters Lane	William Thomas	MARTIN	14
53	Potters Lane	Frank Harold	MARTIN	46
	Priory Place (see Southover High St.)			
9	Priory Street	Arthur Henry	HEAD	17
15	Priory Street	Dennis Frank	TURK	1
15	Priory Street	Augustus Stanley	TURK	38
20 and/or 48	Priory Street	Frederick Arthur	THOMPSON	30
Old Rectory	Rotten Row	Wilfred Gordon	ANSON	27
	Southover Grange	Thorold Arthur	STEWART-JONES	4
7	Southover High St.	William Norris	HILLMAN	6
15	Southover High St	Frederick Cecil	HILLMAN	15
Stable Cott., 24	Southover High St	Reginald Harry	HORNE	24
Brookside, 29	Southover High St	Brian Edward	GLOVER	9
Brookside, 29	Southover High St	Benjamin Hilton	GLOVER	12
36	Southover High St	Henry Douglas	WILLIAMS	15
40B	Southover High St	Frederick	POLLARD	41
40D	Southover High St	Edward George	STEADMAN	37
40E	Southover High St	Alfred	COLE	43
Gables Cott.,55	Southover High St	Frederick	JEFFERY	28
1	St.James' St.	Francis George	GREEN	29
3	St.James' St.	George	PUTLAND	45
2	St.Pancras Gdns.	George William	HOLDER	42
11A	St.Pancras Gdns.	Charles Henry	FRENCH	32
34	St.Pancras Lane	James	CROUCH	25
5	St.Pancras Place	(Ernest Victor	PAYNE born 1891)	23
5	St.Pancras Place	Edward James	WARES	21
3	St.Pancras Terrace	Alec	RICHARDSON	39
8	St.Pancras Terrace	George	PACKHAM	26
3	St.Pancras Villas	Reginald Jn.Edward	HOLLAND	7
	Canning St.,Brighton	Alfred Alexander	DEAN	35
	address not known	Alfred	HARDING	10
	address not known	William Walter	COMPTON	31
	address not known	Harry Spencer	WEST	40

OLD ST. PANCRAS GARDENS AREA

Men lost in the First War

IN ALPHABETICAL ORDER

Name		Home address (Southover, unless specified)	Number in book
ANSON	Wilfred Gordon	Southover Rectory, Rotten Row	27
BEAGLEY	Frank	36 Grange Road	11
BLAGROVE	Arthur John	72 High Street, Lewes	2
COLE	Alfred	6 Priory Place	43
COLEMAN	Thomas Robert	2 The Course	19
COMPTON	William Walter	29 Oriental Place, Brighton	31
CROUCH	James	34 St Pancras Lane	25
DEAN	Alfred Alexander	? Canning Street, Brighton	35
EADE	George Wm. Osborne	3 or 22 The Course	22
FELLOWS	George	15 Eastport Lane	13
FRENCH	Charles Henry	17 St Pancras Gardens	32
GLOVER	Benjamin Hilton	'Brookside', Southover High Street	12
GLOVER	Brian Edward	'Brookside', Southover High Street	9
GREEN	Frank George	1 St. James' Street	29
HALL	Charles Walter	5 Grange Road	36
HARDING	Alfred	? Warren Cottages, Tadworth, Surrey	10
HEAD	Arthur Henry	9 Priory Street	17
HILLMAN	Frederick Cecil	15 Southover High Street	20
HILLMAN	Wm. ('Billy') Norris	7/8 Southover High Street	6
HOLDER	George William	21 St Pancras Gardens	42
HOLLAND	Reginald Jas.Edward	3 St Pancras Villas	7
HORNE	Reginald Harry	'Stable Cottage', 24 Southover High St.	24
JEFFERY	Frederick	19 Friars Walk/Gable Cottage, 55 S'over High St.	28
MARTIN	Frank Harold	53 Potter's Lane	46
MARTIN	William Thomas	53 Potter's Lane	14
MOORE	George Walter	20 Eastport Lane	33
MOORE	Jesse	20 Eastport Lane	8
NEVILLE	Henry Frank	28 Lansdown Place, Lewes	16
NEVILLE	Joseph George	28 Lansdown Place, Lewes	34
PACKHAM	George	8 St. Pancras St./Terrace	26
PAYNE	Ernest Victor	5 St. Pancras Terrace	23
PEEL	George Ernest	10 Grange Road	3
POLLARD	Frederick	5 Priory Place	41
PUTLAND	George	3 St. James Street	45
RICHARDSON	Alec	3 St. Pancras Terrace	39
SANDALS	Edward Roland	2 Grange Road	5
SELBY	Sydney James	32 Grange Road	44
STEADMAN	Edward George	3 Priory Place	37
STEWART-JONES	Thorold Arthur	Southover Grange	4
SUTER	Arthur John	174 High Street, Lewes	18
THOMPSON	Frederick Arthur	20 Priory Street	30
TURK	Augustus Stanley	15 Priory Street	38
TURK	Frank Dennis	15 Priory Street	1
WARES	Edward James	5 St. Pancras Place	21
WEST	Harry Spencer	?	40
WILLIAMS	Henry Douglas	36 Southover High Street	15

Men lost in the First War

IN ORDER OF DEATH

No.	Rank and name	Regiment	Date of death	Place of death	Age
01	Private/Trooper Frank D. TURK	9th Lancers	21 Oct 1914	Flanders	22
02	Private Arthur J. BLAGROVE	1st/5th Royal Sussex	9 May 1915	France (Aubers)	24
03	Lance-Corporal George E. PEEL	1st/5th Royal Sussex	9 May 1915	France (Aubers)	24
04	Capt. Thorold A. STEWART-JONES	5th Royal Sussex	9 May 1915	France (Aubers)	41
05	Corporal Edward R. SANDALS	8th Bn., Rifle Brigade	30 July 1915	Ypres (Hooge)	26
06	Private William N. HILLMAN	2nd Royal Sussex	25 Sept 1915	France (Loos)	18
07	Private Reginald J.E. HOLLAND	9th Royal Sussex	27 Sept 1915	France (Loos)	18
08	Corporal Jesse MOORE	28th Canadian Infantry	8 Oct 1815	France (Loos)	22
09	2nd Lt. Brian E. GLOVER	8th Sqdn. R. Flying Corps	13 Mar 1916	Picardy, France	21
10	Private Alfred HARDING	9th Royal Sussex	10 Mar 1916	Flanders	20
11	Private Frank BEAGLEY	12th Royal Sussex	30 June 1916	France	30
12	Captain Ben H. GLOVER	7th Royal West Kents	1 July 1916	France (Somme)	19
13	Private George FELLOWS	2nd/3rd Royal Sussex	13 July 1916	London (Somme)	41
14	Private William T. MARTIN	2nd Royal Sussex	27 Aug 1916	Rouen (Somme)	19
15	Private Henry D. WILLIAMS	2nd Hanpshires	2 Sep 1916	Flanders	21
16	Lance-Corporal Henry F. NEVILLE	11th Royal Sussex	3 sep 1916	France (Somme)	19
17	Corporal Arthur H. HEAD	7th Royal Sussex	7 Oct 1916	France (Somme)	21
18	Sergeant Arthur J. SUTER	8th Royal Fusiliers	3 May 1917	France	36
19	Pioneer Thomas R. COLEMAN	47th Signals Coy, R.E.	28 May 1917	Ypres	18
20	Sergeant Frederick C. HILLMAN	Royal Garrison Artillery	27 June 1917	Hove (T.B. Hosp)	20
21	Private Edward J. WARES	12th Middlesex	3 Aug 1917	Ypres Salient	30
22	Private George W.O. EADE	26th Royal Fusiliers	5 Aug 1917	France/Flanders	19
23	Gunner Ernest V. PAYNE	Royal Garrison Artillery	12 Sep 1917	Flanders	26
24	Private Reginald H. HORNE	5th Royal Sussex	22 Sep 1917	Flanders	27
25	Private James CROUCH	1st/5th Royal Sussex	7 Oct 1917	Ypres Salient	26
26	Driver George PACKHAM	Royal Horse Artillery	22 Oct 1917	Ypres Salient	36
27	Private Wilfred G. ANSON	14th Gloucestershires	22 Oct 1917	Ypres Salient	27
28	Private Frederick JEFFREY	9th Royal Fusiliers	30 Nov 1917	France	38
29	Private Frank G. GREEN	13th Royal Sussex	11 March 1918	France	36
30	Private Frederick A THOMPSON	8th East Surreys	31 March 1918	France	26
31	2nd Lieut. William W. COMPTON	Royal Field Artillery	25 April 1918	Ypres Salient	26
32	Private Charles H. FRENCH	1/4 Kings Own R. Lancs	26 April 1918	France	20
33	Private George W. MOORE	11th Royal Sussex	27 April 1918	Ypres Salient	26
34	Signalman Joseph G. NEVILLE	RN, HMMS Blackmorevale	1 May 1918	North Sea	20
35	2nd Air Mechanic Alfred A. DEAN	R.F.C. (air balloon maint)	1 May 1918	Littlehampton	37
36	Saddler Sgt. Charles W. HALL	Royal Naval Division	11 May 1918	Lewes (gassed)	32
37	Private Edward G. STEADMAN	23rd London (R. Fusiliers)	22 Aug 1918	France (Somme)	18
38	Lance-Corporal Augustus S. TURK	23rd Middlesex	2 Oct 1918	Flanders	23
39	Pte/Driver Alec RICHARDSON	53rd Machine Gun Corps	10 Oct 1918	Palestine	31
40	Gunner Harry S. WEST	Royal Field Artillery	18 Oct 1918	France	
41	Corporal Frederick POLLARD	Royal Field Artillery	21 Oct 1918	France	30
42	Gunner George W. HOLDER	Royal Garrison Artillery	25 Oct 1918	France	30
43	Corporal Alfred COLE	14th King's Hussars	27 Oct 1918	India	29
44	Lance-Corporal Sydney J. SELBY	5th Royal Fusiliers	2 Nov 1918	Dover (Hosp)	19
45	Corp/Driver George PUTLAND	Royal Army Service Corps	8 Nov 1918	Ypres (Hosp)	36
46	Private Frank H. MARTIN	Queen's Royal West Surreys	9 April 1919	Norwich (Hosp)	20

Men lost in the First War

REGIMENTS/UNITS IN WHICH THE SOUTHOVER MEN SERVED

Regiment/Service.	Battalion/Unit	Name	Number in text
Canadian Expeditionary Force	28th Infantry Bn.	Jesse MOORE	8
East Surrey	8th	Fredk. THOMPSON	30
Gloucestershire	6th/14th	Wilfrid ANSON	27
Hampshire	2nd	Henry WILLIAMS	15
King's Own (Royal Lancs)	1st/4th	Charles FRENCH	33
King's Hussars	14th	Alfred COLE	43
Lancers	9th	Denis TURK	1
London	1st/23rd	Edward STEADMAN	37
Machine Gun Corps.	53rd	Alec RICHARDSON	39
Middlesex	12th	Edward WARES	21
Middlesex	23rd	Augustus TURK	38
Queen's Own (Royal W.Kents)	7th/50th T.M. Bty.	Ben GLOVER	12
Queen's, (Royal W. Surrey)	7th/50th T.M. Bty.	Frank MARTIN	46
Rifle Brigade	8th	Edward SANDALS	5
Royal Army Service Corps.	GHQ Troops Mech.Transp.Coy.	George PUTLAND	45
Royal Engineers	47th Signals Coy.	Thomas COLEMAN	19
Royal Flying Corps	47th Signals Coy.	Alfred DEAN	37
Royal Flying Corps	8th Squadron	Brian GLOVER	12
Royal Fusiliers	5th	Sydney SELBY	44
Royal Fusiliers	8th	A. John SUTER	18
Royal Fusiliers	9th	Fredk. JEFFERY	28
Royal Fusiliers	26th	George W. O. EADE	22
Royal Field Artillery	26th	William COMPTON	31
Royal Field Artillery	6th Bty.,40th Bde.	Fredk. POLLARD	41
Royal Garrison Artillery	6th Bty.,40th Bde	Fredk. HILLMAN	20
Royal Garrison Artillery	Anti-Aircraft Section	George HOLDER	42
Royal Garrison Artillery	152nd Siege Bty.	Ernest PAYNE	23
Royal Garrison Artillery	224th Siege Bty.	Harry WEST	40
Royal Horse Artillery	'B' Bty.	George PACKHAM	26
Royal Navy	HMMS "Blackmorevale"	Joseph NEVILLE	34
Royal Sussex Regiment	1st/5th Bn.	A. J. BLAGROVE	2
Royal Sussex Regiment	1st/5th Bn.	James CROUCH	25
Royal Sussex Regiment	1st/5th Bn.	Reginald HORNE	24
Royal Sussex Regiment	1st/5th Bn.	George PEEL	3
Royal Sussex Regiment	1st/5th Bn.	Thorold STEWART-JONES	4
Royal Sussex Regiment	2nd	George FELLOWS	13
Royal Sussex Regiment	2nd	W. N. 'Billy' HILLMAN	6
Royal Sussex Regiment	2nd	William MARTIN	14
Royal Sussex Regiment	7th	Arthur HEAD	17
Royal Sussex Regiment	9th	Alfred HARDING	10
Royal Sussex Regiment	9th	Reginald HOLLAND	7
Royal Sussex Regiment	11th/R.N.Divn.	Charles HALL	36
Royal Sussex Regiment	11th	George MOORE	33
Royal Sussex Regiment	11th	Henry NEVILLE	16
Royal Sussex Regiment	12th	Frank BEAGLEY	11
Royal Sussex Regiment	13th	Frank GREEN	29

PART ONE

1914 and 1915

The Death of Glory

The Great War came slowly to Southover. Only one of the men named on its War Memorial was killed in the first five months of the war from August to December 1914. There were seven men lost to Southover in the rest of this first part of the war, but it was not until May 1915 that casualties came to Lewes in any number. The whole town was hit hard then by the Aubers Ridge disaster of 9th May; so many Lewes men were in the same decimated Companies and Battalions of the Royal Sussex Regiment.

The three Southover men who were killed on that same day were in the same battle, and all belonged to the same Lewes Company of the 1st/5th (Cinque Ports) Battalion of the RSR. There is therefore an additional entry after the three individual biographies, on the activities of this Lewes Company from the outbreak of war in August 1914 up to and including the "Glorious 9th May". This follows the biography of Captain Stewart-Jones, no. 1.04.

Between May and October 1915, four more Southover men were killed. Apart from the first of the Southover casualties, Dennis Turk, who was given a decent burial in a country churchyard near where he fell in Flanders, none of the other seven were ever found so never had a burial at all. They are therefore commemorated on the Memorials to the Missing at Le Touret, Loos, and Menin Gate, as shown on the map below. By the end of 1915 Lewes as a whole had lost sixty men.

The following chart summarises Southover's eight losses in 1914 and 1915:

Home address		Name		Number in book
15	Priory Street	Dennis Frank	TURK	1
72	High Street, Lewes	Arthur John	BLAGROVE	2
10	Grange Road	George Ernest	PEEL	3
	Southover Grange	Thorold Arthur	STEWART-JONES	4
2	Grange Road	Edward Roland	SANDALS	5
7	Southover High Street	William Norris	HILLMAN	6
3	St.Pancras Villas	Reginald Jn.Edward	HOLLAND	7
20	Eastport Lane	Jesse	MOORE	8

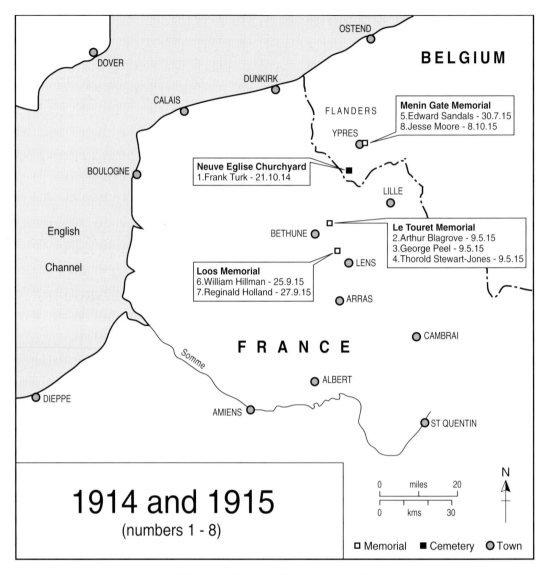

Where the first eight Southover men fell

Life in Lewes in 1914 and 1915

While these losses were being incurred in France and Flanders, the 'Home Front' in Lewes also saw massive troop movements. There were troops in transit, troops in training particularly on the Downs around Lewes, troops billeted with Lewes families, men enlisting, and men at Tribunals hoping not to enlist. Supplies were also being shifted about, particularly through Newhaven, and some scarcities began to be felt. But the rest of life carried on much as before, and the following extracts from some of the news stories of the year in the local papers illustrate:-

• Rolls of Honour were printed every few weeks, to record recruitment town by town across the county. There were also features on each town and local area, with photographs on all those who had "answered the country's call". 'Patriotic families' who had two or more sons at the Front were given special emphasis.

• Reports of Tribunal hearings in each town, with named outcomes of individuals' appeals against call-up, both as Conscientious Objectors, and on domestic or commercial grounds etc., and full details of some 'interesting' cases.

• Billeting arrangements, with list of payments that could be claimed by householders, i.e.:

lodging	9d. a night
breakfast	7½d.
dinner (hot)	1s.7½d.
supper	4½d.
stable & fodder	2s.7½d.
stable	9d.
Officer	3 shillings, plus rates for meals.

The *Sussex County Herald*'s Editorial Review of 1915 made its major items:-

• the 60 men lost from Lewes that year, and

• the horror of the Battle of Aubers Ridge on 9th May 1915 (when the three Southover men were killed), and its impact on the county and the county town :-

> *"The Lewes Coy. of the 5th Royal Sussex Territorial Regiment have paid a heavy price for conspicuous bravery… On the memorable 9th May, when the lambs were gambolling on the sun-kissed hills of Sussex, the Lewes Territorials were charging the German lines in France… Their brilliant though unsuccessful exploits cost them many men, Captain Stewart-Jones being amongst those who made the supreme sacrifice…"*

• the "general diminution of crime" all round the county. However,

> *"Sussex Discharged Prisoners' Aid Society reported a number of women were convicted for neglect of children… In most cases they were wives of men who had joined the Army, and had taken to drink…"*

• an escape from Lewes Jail in May, which was followed by an unsuccessful search by blood-hounds. The prisoner had four months' freedom, before joining the Army and finding himself in an Aldershot hospital, dying of spotted fever.

(With acknowledgement to the Editor of the Sussex Express *for permission to quote extracts from the* Sussex County Herald *and* East Sussex News, *also all quotations in the Introductions to subsequent years, and in individual biographies)*

Dennis Frank TURK   1.01
21st October 1914 aged 22
at Le Gheer, Flanders
4018 Trooper/Private
9th Queen's Royal Lancers, 'C' Squadron

HOME   15 Priory Street, Southover
BURIED   Neuvwekerke (Neuve Eglise) Churchyard, Flanders

Trooper Turk : link with the past and pointer to the future

Trooper Turk occupies 'pride of place' as the first Southover man to lay down his life in what was to become known as The Great War. He stands as it were at the watershed, between a bygone era and our present age. As a soldier, he was one of the last in an illustrious line of Cavalry regiments, who were horsemen even before they were soldiers. Among the men lost from Southover, he was almost unique in this. He was also in the very small minority who were already in the Regular Army by the time war was declared on 4th August 1914. His other great claim to military fame was the fact that he participated in both the last great lance-to-lance charge in history (7th September in the Battle of the Marne, see below), and within a month was involved in the first dismounted 'digging in' of a Cavalry regiment into trench warfare in Flanders, and the first issue of bayonets for fixing to Cavalrymen's rifles, in addition to their swords.

Family background

As a Sussex farm worker, Trooper Turk also stood astride the passing of the Victorian age and the dawn of our modern age, at a time when even farm labour was being mechanized. He was one of the last of these Southover men to have come from an itinerant farm worker family, who followed the harvests from parish to parish. His father, Spencer Turk, was an agricultural labourer who came from Buxted originally, and his mother Mary Ann was from Mayfield. Dennis Frank was the third of their five children. His older brother Frederic was born in 1888 while the parents were living at Rotherfield, then his sister Alice was born at Framfield in 1890. The Census of 1891 shows the little family living in three rooms at what was then 7 Garden Street, Southover (where the yard behind Messrs. Cheesmur's now is).

By the time young Dennis was born a couple of years later, the family had moved just outside Lewes to Kingston; he was baptised there on 3rd September 1893, as Frank Dennis George. His younger sister, Mona Irene, was also born there and was baptised on 10th October 1897. Between the two of them, there was another brother (Augustus Stanley - see no.38 below). He was born around 1895, and does not seem to have been baptised at either Kingston or Southover. This younger brother at least, and possibly Dennis, Frederic and their father as well, worked for some years at The Rise Farm, over the brooks from Southover, and possibly an Iford farm as well. Then by 1912, if not several years before, the family had moved back into Southover, and lived at 15 Priory Street

Trooper Turk's army service

Having grown up with horses on farms, and as farms had less and less work to offer, joining a Cavalry Regiment would have been a natural progression for the young Dennis. By 1912 when he was nineteen, if not some years earlier, he enlisted with the 9th Queen's Royal Lancers, who had newly returned from the Boer Wars. They had a series of recruiting drives across the whole of the country, including one at Chichester in 1912. Dennis was then based at Tidworth Camp on Salisbury Plain for the two years up to the outbreak of war, and was engaged in much training. The regiment started mobilising in mid-July 1914, and he had a short farewell visit to Lewes ending on 14th August.

He embarked with his Regiment from Southampton for Boulogne on August 17th. There were three Squadrons, 'A','B' and 'C', and they had 27 Officers, 523 'other ranks', and 611 horses between them. Once in France they were joined by 11 French interpreters, and together they formed part of the 2nd Cavalry Brigade in the 1st Cavalry Division. The whole British Expeditionary Force at that stage consisted of one Cavalry and four Infantry Divisions; the total B.E.F. manpower then was in the region of 88,000 men, as compared to 1,000,000 French and 1,500,000 German.

Retreat from Mons, and Battle of the Marne

They travelled from Boulogne overnight on the 18th/19th August by train down to Jeumont, a few miles to the south-east of Mons. These first few weeks of the war for the 9th Lancers involved a series of short marches, usually by night, sometimes billeted in villages, sometimes bivouacking in open fields, a logistical nightmare for the supply and veterinary support services. Up to 24th August they were advancing towards Mons, seeing action in support of the collapsing French forces, and suffering their first losses at Elouges and Audregnies. From about 25th August, they were part of the general retreat from Mons, and were moving south towards the Marne and the Aisne, in the defence of Paris. There was at least time on the afternoon of 3rd September for the whole regiment to bathe with their horses in the river, while on a rest day bivouacking in the woods at Gournay-sur-Marne.

These were desperate and daring days, when the war was still being fought very much on the move. But it was still a 19th century war, and one which everyone was expecting to be all over by Christmas. On 7th September, Trooper Turk's 9th Lancers played the lead role in one of the closing dramas of the 19th century part of the war, the only lance-to-lance charge in the

Lance against lance at the Battle of the Marne charge of Trooper Turk's 9th Lancers at Moncel, 7th Sept. 1914
(courtesy 9th Lancers Regimental Museum)

Great War, and the last in history. The 9th Lancers succeeded in routing the enemy in this charge at Moncel in the Battle of the Marne. (*Picture above reproduced by permission of the Regimental Museum, Derby).

Regimental H.Q. in Ploegsteert Wood

By 18th September the war had begun to change, and the 9th Lancers immediately had their first experience of trench warfare. The 'race to the sea' had started, and the remaining four years of the war were under way, fighting in the Flanders mud, backwards and forwards over the 'Ypres Salient'. On 16th October, the 9th Lancers established their Regimental H.Q. at the village of Le Gheer, between Neuve Eglise, Ploegsteert Wood ('Plugstreet' to the troops), Messines and Wulverghem, at the southern end of the 'Salient', in Franco-Belgian border country.

On 20th October, the 9th Lancers saw the enemy attack our trenches in the valley of the river Douve to the south of Messines. They were then able to dig themselves in to new temporary trenches, which they managed to hold until dusk, when they were relieved by the 11th Hussars. During that day, in among all its action and doubtless foreboding, knowing they were to be going into action again the next day, he was somehow able to write a Field Postcard to his mother back home in Southover, to assure her that he was "allright". Trooper Turk and his comrades in 'C' Squadron were then billeted in some farms to the north of Ploegsteert Wood. Back home in Southover, Mrs Turk received her son's card on 26th October. She had one week to feel relief and pleasure that he was "allright", before receiving on 2nd November the "official intimation" of his death the very day after he had sent his card.

Trooper Turk's death and burial

On the morning of 21st October, which was to be Trooper Turk's last, the regiment moved out of their farm billets at 5 am. They were very shortly under heavy enemy rifle fire while on the Messines to Ploegsteert road. Several casualties were sustained, and three men were killed. Trooper Turk was either one of those three, or was among a larger number killed later in the day. In this later action, the 9th Lancers were involved in successfully driving the enemy out of Ploegsteert Wood, and checking their advance on Le Gheer. To quote from Major E W Sheppard's "The Regimental History of the Ninth Queen's Royal Lancers 1715-1936" (quoted with permission):-

> "this counter-offensive was completely successful; the village was re-taken, over 100 of the enemy falling into our hands as prisoners, and some of the Garrison who had previously fallen into enemy hands were liberated."

Trooper Turk was laid to rest over the fields in the country churchyard of Neuve Eglise (now known as Nieuvwkerke). His grave is in the small military corner of this crowded French cemetery of ornate grey and black headstones. It stands out in a short row of three simple white headstones, uncluttered with only their grass surrounds and beds of English shrubs and daffodils, in restful contrast with those in the main Cemetery. The little military part of this cemetery is one of the smallest maintained by the Commonwealth War Graves Commission, with only 92 graves (now including 15 from the Second World War). It was used by Field

Ambulances and fighting units throughout the Great War, particularly cavalry units in the early part. The village of Neuve Eglise was again heavily fought over in April 1918. It fell at that time into enemy hands, but was regained by the Allies early in September 1918. By that time, the church itself was destroyed, and the graveyard would have been unrecogniseable from the peaceful spot it is today. Below the official inscription and regimental badge on Trooper Turk's headstone, his family had the following added:

"In Glorious Memory of our Loved One, from F.M.B.& S's".

 His doubtless hard-stretched "Father, Mother, Brothers and Sisters" would thus, by abbreviating, have had to pay only for seven rather than thirty four letters.

Dennis Turk's grave in Neuve Eglise Churchyard, Flanders (far left, with daffodils)

Thus passed the first of the Southover men to fall in the Great War, and with him passed a whole way of army life for the Cavalry. As one of his officers, Capt.Francis Grenfell (who had won the first VC of the 9th Lancers' war on 24th August at Audregnies) wrote in his diary of this October fighting:-

"I am afraid all the cavalry traditions are forever ended, and we have become mounted infantry pure and simple, with very little of the mounted about it. Our men look funny sights trudging along with spades and things on their backs, and when they are mounted they look funnier still; if you see a man carrying a lance, sword, rifle, spade and pick, he looks just like a hedgehog. But it is a jolly hard life for them to have to fight their way up to the line, then hold it, all the time cleaning and trying to look after their horses."

Arthur John BLAGROVE   1.02
9th May 1915 aged 24
at Festubert, Aubers Ridge
(T)2338 Private
5th Battalion (Cinque Ports), Royal Sussex Regiment

HOME   72 High Street, Lewes
COMMEMORATED   Le Touret Memorial, nr Bethune

Family background

The Blagroves were a well-established Lewes family, with several branches in various High Street businesses. Arthur John (who seems to have been widely known as John) was the younger of two sons born to Edwin and Jane Blagrove. The elder son was Archibald, and they all lived above the family watchmakers and jewellers' business at 72 High Street, Lewes (premises now occupied by Marston Barrett's and carrying on the same business). At least in the early years of the Great War, several of the wider family lived nearby along the south side of the High Street, between the main Post Office and Bull Lane.

There was Mrs E.M.Blagrove who lived next door at no.71 where she ran the tobacconist's shop (which is also still in business there as F.E.Hall's). On the other side of them at no.73 was Daniel Blagrove & Son, who were photographers. Across the road in Castle Precincts was Castlegate Villa (well known to later generations of Lewes school-children having School Medicals etc.), which was then the residence of Mr H. Gamble Blagrove. He was almost certainly an uncle of young Arthur John, as most probably also was Mr Edwin Ernest Blagrove, whose residence was "Melrose" in The Avenue.

72 High Street, Lewes
Marston Barrett's, jewellers, carrying on
Blagrove family business, with Blagroves'
flat above the shop, and St.Martin's Lane
beside it going down to Southover.

As a boy, Arthur John sang for many years in the Southover Church Choir. He then returned there on visits in later years, joining with his parents who were regular worshippers at Southover. Up to the outbreak of war he was working in Eastbourne, employed at Messrs. Hart's the Tailors.

Training and War service

Arthur John was one of the earliest of the Lewes men to enlist with the Royal Sussex Regiment in August 1914. He enlisted at Hastings, and shortly found himself in the same Cinque Ports Battalion of the Regiment as Cpl.George Peel and Captain Thorold Stewart-Jones (see 1. 03. and 1. 04. ff). The three of them were in training together at Dover Castle, and were also posted briefly to the Tower of London. John was in Room 21 while there, and played football in the Moat against the occupants of Room 20; those were the other Lewesians, who included George Peel (see photograph following). They then had a brief return in December 1914 for a week's field training in camp on the Downs above Lewes. They were back in Lewes again in mid-February en route for Southampton; they paraded up School Hill and along the High Street, right past the Blagrove's shop and home, and were given a rousing send-off with full military band playing. (See also the fuller details on their military lives and deaths with that Battalion, following Captain Stewart-Jones' biography, 1.04).

Commemoration

Pte.Blagrove and his Southover comrades, Lance Corporal George Peel and Capt.Thorold Stewart-Jones (see nos.1.03 & 1.04 following) were honoured together at Southover's own Memorial Service for them on 3rd June 1915. At that service, the Rector described Arthur John Blagrove as

> *"a young man who won many friends, and was justly beloved."*

After the War, when the Commonwealth War Graves Commision was faced with the magnitude of the task of commemo-rating all those whose bodies had never been found, or who were buried in unmarked graves, it built the Le Touret Memorial at Richebourg-d'Avoue near

Lewes Territorials Trench Digging
Pte. Blagrove is 4th from right in trench,
hatless and holding spade.
(ESN, 12th Feb.1915)

Bethune to commemorte those who fell in this northern part of the Front in France in the first year of the War, and whose bodies were never found. Pte.A .J. Blagrove's name is on it, together with the other two Southover men who fell in the same engagement (on Panels 20 & 21), and some 8,000 others on adjoining Panels.

The only picture showing Pte. Blagrove is reproduced here, from the *East Sussex News* of 21 May 1915. The local press and public were reeling for some months through 1915, from the catastrophe for Lewes and so much of Sussex that was suffered on 9th May. This photograph was taken some months earlier, of a group of Royal Sussex men while still in training on trench digging before leaving for France. Private Blagrove is hatless, slightly to the right of the centre, and is one of the three in the picture still missing three weeks after the battle. Of the other 15 others in the picture, one was known to have been killed, and six others wounded.

George Ernest PEEL   1.03
9th May 1915, aged 24
at Rue de Bois, Aubers Ridge
2496 Lance-Corporal
5th Battalion (Cinque Ports), Royal Sussex Regiment

HOME   10 Grange Road, Southover
COMMEMORIATED   Le Touret Memorial, near Bethune

Family background

George Peel was born in October 1890 at 10 Grange Road, Southover, and lived in the same street throughout his childhood. He was the youngest of three sons and one daughter of George William Peel and his wife Annie Elizabeth. George William had come from London, and was initially a clerk. He then took to bookselling; at some point he was Bookstall Manager at Lewes (Station), before taking over the Bookstall at London Bridge. His wife Annie had come from Portsmouth originally.

Pte. G. E. Peel
May 1915.

Childhood and youth

Young George Ernest was baptised at Southover Church on 2nd April 1906, but for some reason not till he was a lad of fifteen. His older sister, Mabel Eva, had been

10 Grange Road today
where George was born in 1899.

baptised also at Southover but as an infant on 28th April 1889. She was not much more than a year old when George was born. Before Mabel, there were the two older boys, Percy born in 1885 and Robert in 1886. At least when the children were little, their mother Annie had living-in help; young Fanny Christopher from Chichester was living with the family when George was born, and was herself only fifteen at the time.

George grew up widely known in the town. He played cricket for Lewes Priory and football for Lewes Town. He was also a member of St Anne's Church Choir, having been a boy chorister at Southover earlier on. He continued his Southover connections as Secretary to the Southover Men's Club up to the outbreak of war, though was not still living in the parish. It may be that he had already moved to the Shelley Terrace house that one of his brothers at least was in at the end of the war (see below: 'Aftermath'). George was

Grange Road in 1906, when George was 16
(Bob Cairns)

GRANGE ROAD.
Southover Road to St. Pancras Lane
(Left from Southover Road)

1 Morris, Mrs. Arthur
2 Sandals, William
3 Funnell, William Baker
4 Cresswell, David
5 Hall, Charles James
6 Martin, Mrs.
7 Goulden, Jesse
8 Verral, Herbert
9 Davey, Harold E.
10 White, D. W.
11 Boyes, William
12 Barrow, John
13 Harris, Alfred
14 Williams, W. H.
15 (Grange House) Green, The Misses
16 Chaplin, Arthur
17 Shrewsbury, Rev. H. J.
18 Bourner, Mrs.
19 Dowswell, F. J.
20 Channon, Charles
21 Weston, Henry
22 Richardson, Thomas
23 Beck, Mrs. A.
24 Dendy, Rev. A. S.
25 Severs, Charles
26 Sharp, Miss
27 Burstow, Abraham
28 Connell, Rev. James M.
30 Burbidge, E. G.
32 Selby, Thomas Henry
    Smith, S. H. nurseryman
33 Lamb, Mrs
34 Holman, Miss
35 Happold, A.
36 Tunks, Joseph
37 White, Frederick Sidney
38 Cheale, Mrs. D.
39 Safford, Arthur Herbert, Esq
40 Heather, Ernest
41 Glaisyer, Edward

(Left from St. Pancras Lane)

Wallington Villas—
    1 Davey, Miss
    2 Vinall, H.

(Elmdene) Goring, William
(Grantham Villa) Packham, Mrs. Kate
(Parkside) Patten, Thomas Albert, Esq

Street Directory excerpt for Grange Road in 1915.

working up to the outbreak of war, as a clerk in the East Sussex Education Committee's offices in Fisher Street, Lewes.

George's short war

George enlisted on 5th September 1914, and was a few days later attached to the 'D' Company of the 5th Battalion Royal Sussex Regiment. He was in training with them at Dover Castle through the winter, and then they all left for the Front in February 1915. It is likely he was involved to some extent in the action at Neuve Chapelle in March, as on 3rd April he was promoted to Acting Lance Corporal.

On 14th April he was referred to in a letter home from the Front from a comrade in the same 5th Battalion, Royal Sussex. I quote below just a short extract about George Peel himself.

(This comrade was Pte.W.G.Horton, who had been on the Editorial Staff of the *Sussex Daily News*; that paper therefore quotes much of many of his letters home to Offham in those early months of the war, which are most graphic and informative and full of the good humour and loyalty that kept these Battalions together in the face of such great odds).

> *"Two of our Section, Lance-Cpl. George Peel and Pte. H.S.Pullinger, went out on patrol close up to the German trenches, and in the course of their wanderings they suddenly spotted a prone figure just in front of them. Realising it was a German sniper, they separated and crept up to the spot and then found that he was dead. He was in a carefully dug trench and was leaning forward on his rifle as if about to fire. Close by were lying two helmets which of course were promptly bagged as souvenirs, and they got back to our trench in safety.*
>
> *After five days we were relieved on Monday night by the Gurkhas… and at six o'clock the next morning we set out on a 12 mile tramp back to the village where we are now resting. On the way down the German helmets and caps were worn, and were objects*

of much interest to the soldiers and civilians passed on the way. Quite a pathetic sight was a French laddie who followed us for some distance, offering our helmet wearers a franc for the trophy, assuring us that was all he possessed. I doubt very much if a hundred francs would purchase either of those trophies…"

Within a month George Peel was dead. He died on May 9th1915, with his friend and comrade-in-arms Arthur John Blagrove (see 1.02), and his near neighbour and superior officer, Captain Stewart-Jones (see 1.04), and a very great many other Lewes and Sussex men.

(Please see the fuller details on their wartime lives and deaths with the 5th Sussex, following the three individual biographies at page 16).

Aftermath

During or soon after the war, some of the Peel family moved to 10 Shelley Terrace, de Montfort Road. His eldest brother Percy was serving as a Private with the 11th London Fusiliers (Empire Battalion).

By the time of George's death, his parents had moved again and were living in South London. His death announcement appeared in the *Sussex County Herald* for 29th May 1915, and described him as the

"dearly loved youngest son of George W. and Annie E. Peel, of 34 Garfield Road, Lavender Hill, S.W., and late of Lewes."

Soon after that, George's father then died while relatively young, possibly even during the war.

In February 1916, just a year after George Peel had left Lewes for France, the *East Sussex News* had a piece about the Annual Meeting of the Southover Church Men's Club, of which he had been the Honorary Secretary. It reported that out of a total membership of 35, one Vice-Chairman and 12 members were currently serving with the Forces, and that:-

"practically every man of enlistable age has been attested under Lord Derby's Scheme. The Committee greatly deplore the loss of one Vice-President, Capt. T.A.Stewart-Jones, and two members, L/Cpl.G.E.Peel (late Hon.Sec.), and Pte.W.N.Hillman, killed while serving King and Country."

In each of the remaining years of the War, similarly fond 'In Memoriam' notices were placed by his grieving parents in early May. By the time the war was over and the Le Touret Memorial was built in the mid-1920's near where he fell, his mother had been widowed and had moved within South London from Lavender Hill to 10 St. Mary's Road, South Norwood. George Peel's name is inscribed with those of many hundreds of other Royal Sussex men whose bodies were also never found, on Panels 20 and 21 of that Le Touret Memorial near Bethune.

And so, with neither wife nor children to be left behind, and the rest of the family already moved away, George Peel passed from Southover's memory.

Thorold Arthur STEWART-JONES   1.04
9th May 1915 aged 41
at Richebourg
Captain, 'C' Co.y
5th Battalion (Cinque Ports), Royal Sussex Regiment

HOME   Southover Grange
COMMEMORATED   Le Touret Memorial, near Bethune

Captain Stewart-Jones was among the oldest of the Southover men to be killed in action. He was probably the most prominent and influential of them, in the parish and in the Lewes Territorials. He was certainly also one of those who left a large number of young children fatherless, and a young wife who had not yet given birth to the youngest.

His pre-war life in Lewes

He had moved down from London on getting married in the early years of the century, and took up residence in Southover Grange. His young wife was Eva Joan, nee Hammond, whose father was an Admiral. His own mother, who had herself been widowed by the time he moved to Lewes, lived with the growing young family at the Grange. His earlier life and work

Capt. Stewart-Jones, May 1915

had been in London, where he was a Barrister-at-Law with Chambers in the Inner Temple. He was also in business, with *"some considerable interest in shipping circles"*. His names suggest some Scandinavian and Scottish/Welsh connections, but nothing further has come to light about the family background.

The first of their five children was born at Southover Grange in 1909, and was baptised Diona Vere at Southover Church on 4th August. This was five years to the day before the outbreak of the War that was to leave her and her young brothers and sister fatherless. The others were born in quick succession, and were all baptised at Southover Church: Elizabeth Eva on 17th April 1910, Edward Thorold on 26th July 1912, and Richard Llewellyn on 9th April 1914.

Southover Grange, built 1572 with stones from ruins of Lewes Priory, and boyhood home of John Evelyn diarist, while attending Lewes Grammar School.

These little ones were all under five when they last saw their father. Their youngest brother, as yet unborn, was to be another of those war babies never to see their father. He was not born until 15th July 1915, two months after his father's tragic death, and was baptised Thorold Stephen Michael at Southover on 21st July, when barely a week old.

Captain Stewart-Jones had become closely involved in the life and worship of Southover

Territorials' Summer Camp on Downs above Houndean showing Lewes old mill and racecourse, and railway to Brighton along Hope-in-the-Valley. (Bob Cairns)

Church. He was Churchwarden for some years, and regularly read the lessons there. He became noted as a *"helper of causes that needed assistance"*. This led to a long involvement with the Red Cross, and he was the Treasurer of their Mid-Sussex Branch for some years. But perhaps his main involvement was with the Territorial Army locally. He became something of a figure-head there, but a very involved and active one, and for some years had commanded the Lewes Company of the 5th Battalion of the Royal Sussex Regiment. In that role, he regularly led his Company on parades and drills down on the Dripping Pan and along the High Street. He also took them each summer to Regimental Training Camps, usually on the Sussex or Hampshire Downs.

His war service

Immediately on the outbreak of war, Captain Stewart-Jones, despite his relatively advanced years, volunteered for active service. He was in part influenced in doing so, according to the Rector of Southover speaking less than a year later at his Memorial Service, by

> *"knowing that his example would lead others to do the same".*

By 7th August 1914 he had been posted, with the rest of the Battalion, to Dover Castle for Guard Duty and war training. By mid-October 1914 the 5th Battalion was moved to the Tower of London. Duties while there included escorting prisoners-of-war, and doing Guard Duty for the Maxim Gun Works at Erith. It must have been during that late autumn sometime that the Captain had a spell of home leave, as it was just nine months later in July the following year that the last of their babies was born back home in Southover Grange.

By mid-February they were in France, waiting for their first action or maybe recovering from their first taste of it at Neuve Chapelle in March 1915. It must at any rate have been a time of great stress for them all, and there was a lot of illness. Captain Stewart-Jones reported sick during this time, and was 'hospitalised' in Battalion sick quarters with 'general debility' from 7th to 11th April. Many of his fellow-invalids at that time were laid up with measles.

(for fuller details of his wartime service and death at the Battle of Aubers Ridge on 9th May

1915, please see details on following page about all three Southover men killed at this battle with the 5th Royal Sussex).

Captain Stewart-Jones was one of the first to be killed, at the very beginning of the charge. He was last seen by the men of his Company who held him in such high regard, leading them into action…

> *"with great gallantry, and was close to the German trenches when he fell… It was thought he was dead when the Black Watch brought him in."*

Southover's own Memorial Service

This was held in church, on Thursday evening 3rd June 1915, for Captain Stewart-Jones and his comrades Blagrove and Peel (see the two foregoing biographies, and the account of the service reproduced from the *East Sussex News* of 11th June 1915).

The parish had been hit hard in losing three of its men in one day, and the whole of Lewes and indeed Sussex, was reeling from the shock of its first direct involvement in one of the early disasters of the war. The service was conducted by the Rector, the Rev. Theodore Windle, and there was a large gathering of civic and Territorial dignitaries, as well as all the families involved. As the newspaper described it,

> *"Southover suffered a severe loss in the death of Capt. T. A. Stewart-Jones, of Southover Grange, formerly Churchwarden and a sidesman for several years; and in addition, the parish had lost two former choristers, Private G. E. Peel and Private A. J. Blagrove."*

Talking of the Captain, the preacher said he had

> *"received many testimonials of the regard and affection with which the men of his Company followed him. It was in answer and response to his own feelings of care for them… He died a soldier's death, for King and country and home…"*

The newspaper account makes mention of his mother's and his widow's involvement in the provision of the Tablet at the west end of the church, for the inscribing of the names of Southover's Roll of Honour, as follows:-

> *"It is a pathetic incident that his mother was responsible for the tablet, which is surrounded with laurel, being placed there, and that the second name on it was that of her son.'*

Her newly-widowed daughter-in-law was unable to attend the Memorial Service, being well advanced in her pregnancy, but was able to resume responsibility for keeping the inscriptions up to date for the rest of the war. It was also these two women who were prime movers in arrangements for the erection of the granite cross outside the north west corner of the church, and its dedication and unveiling on All Saints Day, 1921.

Mrs Stewart-Jones senior was also active in the parish as a School Governor, and was a regular visitor to Southover School, hearer of reading, checker of stocking darning and of needlework presented for the Grade exams, listener to poetry recitations, and accompanying on the piano for school assemblies and concerts. She is remembered to this day, eighty years on, by the last remaining daughter of another of the 'fallen comrades' (see 1.13 on George Fellows), playing the piano for assemblies.

A CALL TO ARMS!!

KITCHENER'S ARMY.

Your King and Country need you urgently.

A NEW REGULAR BATTALION

is being added to your County Regiment,

CALLED THE

7TH SPECIAL SERVICE BATTALION

ROYAL SUSSEX REGIMENT,

Forming part of the 35th Brigade of Lord Kitchener's 2nd Army.

Will you Come Forward

Or must Recruits be obtained outside the County?

We are confident you will help to uphold the honor of the County of Sussex.

Men are urgently required to enlist in the above regular Battalion.

Men between the ages of 19 & 30 can enlist for the duration of the war.

Men must be medically fit ; be 5ft. 3in. high and upwards ; have chest measurement of 34 inches.

Ex Regular N.C.O's and men, and men belonging to the National Reserve can enlist for the above Battalion ; conditions on application.

Married men or widowers with children will be accepted, and will draw separation allowances.

APPLY AT ONCE TO THE NEAREST RECRUITING OFFICE.

Owners of cars will greatly assist by driving intending recruits direct to the nearest recruiting office or to the Barracks at Chichester, where the above Battalion is being formed.

God Save the King.

RECRUITING OFFICES :

CHICHESTER The Barracks.	LEWES Drill Hall.	TUNBRIDGE WELLS 8, Neville Street.
HORSHAM - Drill Hall.	HAYWARDS HEATH - Drill Hall.	BRIGHTON 21, Windsor Road ; 8, Coombs
WORTHING—Drill Hall.	HURSTPIERPOINT—Drill Hall.	Terrace, Lewes Road.
UCKFIELD—Drill Hall.	BEXHILL Drill Hall.	HOVE 20, Church Road.
RYE—Drill Hall.	BATTLE Drill Hall.	HASTINGS 33, Brook Street.
PETWORTH Drill Hall.	CUCKFIELD Drill Hall.	EASTBOURNE Ordnance Yard.
ARUNDEL - Drill Hall.	LITTLEHAMPTON - 41, Gloucester Place	BOGNOR—Hambledon Chambers.

Printed by T. G. Willis & Co., Printers & Stationers, 21, East Street, Chichester.

A recruiting poster appealing to the men of Sussex to respond to Kitchener's call to arms, and to join the new 7th (Service) Battalion, at the beginning of the First World War, August 1914.

(reproduced from "The Royal Sussex Regiment. A Catalogue of Records." A.E. Readman, ed. WSCC 1985 (ref WSRO, RSR MS7/5) with permission from the West Sussex County Record Office)

The 5th Battalion (Cinque Ports), Royal Sussex Regiment, July 1914 - May 1915
The three men who perished at the Battle of Aubers Ridge, 9th May 1915

(with acknowledgements to the WSRO at Chichester for references from the War Diaries of the Battalion. WSRO RSR MS4/64))

Private Blagrove (1.02), Lance Corporal Peel (1.03), Captain Stewart-Jones (1.04).

These three, and a great many others from across Lewes and throughout Sussex, were all killed on the same day in the same action at Aubers Ridge. This was a few miles to the north east of Bethune, in the direction of Armentieres on the French border with Belgium. They all belonged to the Lewes Territorials, and they were part of the 'C' Coy. of the same 5th Battalion (Cinque Ports) of the Royal Sussex Regiment.

Training: Sussex and Hampshire up to August 1914

They had trained together before the war at their Drill Hall and at the Dripping Pan in Lewes, and on summer Territorial Training Camps on the Sussex Downs and on Salisbury Plain. They had in fact left Lewes on the 3.07 p.m. train on Sunday 26th July 1914 for what proved to be the last of these camps, at Bordon in Hampshire. They were with the other Lewesians in the sections under the command of Captain Stewart-Jones and the then Lieutenant Courthope (the latter was to return after the war, to his family who were involved in the eventual sale of their land for the new County Hall, with its Courthope Club now used as a staff canteen and for local community events).

What was to have been a fortnight's camp with a varied programme of route marches and training exercises, had to be cut short after a week with the declaration of war on 4th August. There was then a somewhat rushed issuing of further uniforms and kit (with difficulties in obtaining enough boots in the larger sizes) to those who were volunteering for active service.

Dover Castle: August to October 1914

The whole of their 5th (Cinque Ports) Battalion were then posted to Dover Castle for Guard Duty and further training. This consisted of Semaphore, Musketry, Night Ops., fire discipline, bayonet fighting, P.T., Squad Drill and Extended Order Drill. Ration Allowances for Officers living out were two shillings a day, and wives were allowed to visit on Sundays.

At the outset (7th August), Captain Stewart-Jones had just one Sergeant and a very small 'C' Coy. of only 24 men, under his own command, but numbers were soon swelled by new recruits flooding in from Lewes and other areas. Lord Kitchener was ensuring recruitment posters were everywhere.

Tower of London: October 1914 to February 1915

The Lewes men were then all transferred to the Tower of London, where they continued training and keeping fit. Football matches were played in the ancient Moat of the Tower between the various rooms or dormitories they were in. The Lewes men were mainly in Rooms 20 and 21, and the photograph (reproduced from an original found by Susan Rowland in an old attic!)

shows the triumphant team from Room 20. They also shared Escort Duty of German prisoners of war with the other Companies, as well as Guard Duty at the Maxim Gun Works at Erith on the Thames estuary.

In January, the Cinque Ports Battalion was one of those designated for service overseas. They became part of the 1st Army Corps. of the British Expeditionary Force (BEF)., and had to have the official course of innoculations before embarkation for the trenches. Then they were sent for one last Training Camp on the Downs above Lewes, and hopefully had some last opportunities for family farewells.

Football match in the Moat of the Tower of London
Lewes men of Room 20 (including George Peel seated 2nd from right in
front row) had just won match against Room 21 with A.J. Blagrove.
(Susan Rowland)

Ceremonial send-offs and embarkation for France, February 1915

On 15th February they marched with the whole Battalion up School Hill and along the main High Street, with their band playing. The official party stood on the steps of the steps of the Town Hall , and the salute was taken by the Mayor and the Lord Lieutenant of the County of Sussex.

The next day there was a similar ceremony in Hastings, including the temporary laying-up of the Colours in the Parish Church there prior to going into battle.

On 17th February, there must have been a troop train laid on to transport the whole battalion to Southampton for embarkation. They were the first British troops to cross the channel after the enemy's attempted blockade of our channel ports by mines and U-Boats had started. (They were also, I am told, the only battalion in the Royal Sussex Regiment if not in the whole British Army, to have its own cap badge, in addition to their Regimental badge; this apparently entitled the CWGC to use both on the headstones of all 'Cinque Ports' men of the RSR who were buried).

They crossed the channel from Southampton to Le Havre in safety but probably not in much comfort, in a cattle ship the S.S.Pancras (not inappropriately named for a bunch of Lewesians!), arriving on 18th February.

Early days in Fance: February to April 1915

On arrival at Le Havre they were entrained to Allouagne-par-Lillers in the environs of Bethune in the most north-easterly corner of France. It was snowing when they arrived, and they were dispersed to billets around Bethune. An outbreak of scarlet fever then started among them, but those who were fit were immediately put to trench digging work in support of the 2nd Battalion. In March they were behind the lines in Reserve, at the Battle of Neuve Chapelle. By April their sick lists were getting longer again, and sick bays filling up, as an outbreak of measles struck. General levels of resistance must have been much lowered by the cold and the first shocks of billets then trench life, not to mention seeing what happened to the 2nd Battalion and to so many other regiments as well, at Neuve Chapelle.

The Battle of Aubers Ridge: 9th May 1915

At 4 a.m. the 5th Battalion started their massive bombardment of the enemy front line trenches across a particularly narrow piece of 'no mans land'. At 5.40 a.m. it was assumed by higher command that the enemy's wire would have been cut and his trenches pulverized, ready for the 5th Battalion and others in support to charge forward in what was assumed would be an effective assault, and capture the whole position. The order was given to stop the bombardment, rum rations were distributed, and the order to charge was given. The Battalion's *Official War Diary* puts the next stage just as succinctly:

> *"'A', 'B', and 'C' Coy.s moved out with the 2nd Sussex to assault; the assault failed; very few men were able to retire till night; casualties were very heavy, particularly in' C' Co.y."*

Such was the carnage that day that there is some variation in Casualty Lists issued over the next few weeks. The final total seems to have been in the region of 119 wounded and 80 killed or missing, just for the 5th Battalion. The total Battalion strength had by the day before the battle already been reduced to 17 Officers and 682 Other Ranks. This was the first substantial, and the most catastrophic engagement of the whole war for the Royal Sussex Regiment.

Local newspapers of the time gave banner headlines in honour of "our heroes who in this gallant charge covered themselves with glory." Nothing like it, they said, had been seen since the Charge of the Light Brigade in the Crimean War. It was only later that the questions started being asked

THE GREAT CHARGE.

Something of the ordeal through which the 5th Royal Sussex, which included the Lewes Territorials, passed on the memorable Sunday—May 9—can be gathered from the letters received home and from the description by war correspondents of the unsuccessful attack. As was feared, last week's reports of a heavy casualty list are too true, and this week we have to record several additional losses to the town. The keenest and most heartfelt sympathy has been extended to all homes in Lewes where there are tears of sadness to-day, though the bravery with which the Lewes boys carried out the attack cannot but make the blood tingle of all who read their heroic, if unavailing, efforts. The correspondent of the "Times," speaking of the action, said it was unsuccessful owing to the lack of high explosive shells, and because of this deficiency the enemy's wire entanglements were not destroyed. This is a matter which has caused considerable comment in the country during the week, for it has been recognised by the general public that it is shameful to handicap our soldiers in this manner. It is also stated in some quarters that this is one of the things which has caused a crisis in the Government and the establishment of a coalition Cabinet. This, possibly, time will reveal.

Our soldiers in France, on the evening before the fateful Sunday received the news of the intended advance in the morning. The men handed in their packs and were served with extra ammunition. Then they went into the trenches and remained there during the night. Punctually at five o'clock in the morning the bombardment by the British of the German entanglements began.

Battle of Aubers Ridge, 9th May 1915: "The Great Charge", drawing & article (SCH 22 May 1915)

about uncut barbed wire, failing munitions supplies, lack of high explosives, and lack of machine guns which the enemy had used with such devastating effect that day. It was much later before the nation could bear to acknowledge the enormity of this tragedy, the first which gained absolutely nothing and lost a very great deal. But much the same was allowed to happen again over a year later on the first day of the Somme, when the uselessness of even days of preliminary bombardment shells filled with insufficient high explosive if not merely with shrapnel, was eventually realised to be no match for the superior fortifications of the enemy.

Tribute from Lewes Town Council

The *Sussex County Herald* for Saturday 5th June 1915 reported on the meeting of the Lewes Town Council the Wednesday evening two days earlier, under the title:

"PROUD OF THEM"

TOWN COUNCIL AND LEWES'S FIGHTING TERRITORIALS.

"... The Mayor [Councillor T. G. Roberts] *spoke of the official send-off of the Lewes Co.y on a memorable Sunday evening, and the sad news received since of some of those men fallen in battle. He thought it very fitting that the Town Council, as representatives of the inhabitants, should express their sympathy with the Company in the loss they had sustained and also send a kindly message to the wounded who were in hospital. They were proud of them for what they had done, and they had confidence that the Lewes boys of the 5th Sussex, now at the Front, would do their duty in whatever difficult position they found themselves, and uphold the traditions of the old Royal Sussex Regiment.*

The Deputy Mayor (Dr. Stott), as an old officer of the Regiment, spoke of the pluck and courage of the Lewes contingent in coming forward in the hour of danger to support the soldiers at the Front. He thought their gallantry ought to be a stimulus to recruiting in Lewes. He knew they had done a great deal, but they could do much more. He thought it was merely callousness and forgetfulness on the part of young fellows who did not take a hand in the work now before us. He also suggested a roll of honour for the fallen.

A resolution in the terms of the Mayor's remarks was then passed."

Southover's Memorial Service: Thursday 3rd June 1915

The same edition of the *Sussex County Herald* reported Southover's Memorial service to its three lost men from that May 9th battle. It was held on the Thursday evening, the night after the Town Council met as above:-

"A large congregation attended... to pay respect to the honoured dead... The

THE CONGREGATION.

Among those present at the service were Mrs. Stewart-Jones (mother of the officer), Admiral and Mrs. Holland (parents of the widow), Miss Holland, Earl and Lady Chichester, Admiral Pelham (treasurer of the Mid-Sussex Division Red Cross, of which Captain Stewart-Jones was a former treasurer), Dr. Lunn (Worthing Men's Detachment Red Cross), Mr. W. F. Ingram (commandant Lewes Detachment Red Cross), the Mayor and Mayoress of Lewes (Councillor and Mrs. T. G. Roberts), the Rev. H. S. Anson (former vicar of Southover), the Rev D. Pearce, Lieutenant Sutor (Lewes Company), Mr. F. B. Whitfeld, J.P., Councillor Verral, Colonel Alan Richardson (Lewes V. T. C.) and Mr. H. C. Hutton.

sermon was preached by the Rector, the Rev. T. H. Windle, and the lesson was read by the Rev. Prebendary Poole. The hymn "My God, my Father, while I stray" was sung at the commencement of the service; "There is a blessed home" before the address, and "Now the labourer's task is o'er" at the close. Then on the organ was played the "Dead March" from Saul, in which it seemed were the echoes of the guns of battle; and finally, Chopin's "Marche Funebre", so truly symbolic of sweet life after tumult."

Mass commemoration at Le Touret Memorial

After the war, the Commonwealth War Graves Commision was faced with the task of finding the unimagineable number of bodies, as yet unretrieved from the battlefields. Where it was still possible, these men had to be identified, and re-interred near where they fell in one of the many CWGC's War Cemeteries. Those who could not be identified were buried in un-named graves near their comrades. Those who were never found were commemorated by their individual name being inscribed on one of the stone panels on the appropriate Monument or Memorial.

These were architect-designed and publicly- funded memorials, sometimes within the borders of one of the cemeteries, and sometimes on their own as a focal point of the surrounding countryside. They were usually erected on land given by the people of France or of Belgium to the British Empire in perpetuity, in gratitude for the sacrifices made on their behalf. Most of these Monuments and cemeteries were created during the 1920's, just in the years that some of the less ravaged countryside was beginning to regenerate itself. Some were hardly completed before Europe began to prepare for its next great conflict. They all continue to be maintained by the Commonwealth War Graves Commission and their local nurseries, as places of great beauty, peace and dignity.

The Le Touret Memorial is at Richebourg-d'Avoue near Bethune, and it honours the memory of the 8,000 officers and men who fell in this northern part of the Front in France in the first year of the war, and whose bodies were never found. Panels 20 and 21 commemorate the names of the three men from Southover, together with the 443 others from the Royal Sussex who were also lost without trace in the same year and the same area.

The Le Touret Memorial, near Bethune
where the three Southover men killed on 9th May 1915 are commemorated (CWGC)

21

Edward Roland SANDALS   1.05
30th July 1915 aged 26
at Hooge, near Ypres
Z2668 Corporal
8th Battalion, Rifle Brigade

HOME   2 Grange Road, Southover
COMMEMORATED   Menin Gate, Ypres

Corporal Sandals had an even shorter war than the previous four soldiers. His lasted less than one month, as he did not leave for France till 29th June 1915, and this was just a month before his one and only battle. That action at Hooge, which decimated his Battalion and many others, has been described as "the night that Hell opened". It was that night when so many of our unsuspecting youth were enveloped and consumed in the enemy's first "Liquid Fire Attack", and paid a devastating price for the relative technological backwardness of our armies in both weaponry and communications.

Family background

Edward Sandals was the second son of William and Annie Sandals. Both his parents were Lewes people, and at the time of the April 1891 Census, they all lived at 18 Grange Road (later they moved along to No. 2 Grange Road). In 1891, William was 34 and a Solicitor's Clerk, and Annie was 31. She was at home with their two young children. Edward's older brother, Stanley, was three, and Edward himself was two.

School and work

Edward attended Castlegate School in Lewes, and then went to work at the East Sussex County Surveyor's Office also in Lewes. He would therefore have known Brian Glover (1.09) from his time at the County Surveyor's Office, and Billy Hillman (1.06) if not A.J. Suter (1.18) as well from their Castlegate School days. He later moved jobs from the Lewes to London, where he then worked at the

2 Grange Road, Edward Sandals' childhood home

headquarters offices of the British Bank of South America. This was presumably in the City, and within easy commuting reach from Lewes, possibly with a better train service than now. Or he may have had lodgings in the Battersea area, near the Rifle Brigade enlistment centre.

Either way, it was in Battersea that he enlisted in September1914, early in the first wave of patriotic recruits to Kitchener's "New Army". He took along some fifty fellow bank-clerks to enlist with him, which would have left the Bank somewhat short-staffed (and in the process would doubtless have helped to pave the way for the widespread entry of women into the job market from then on).

Edward Sandals' short war

Initially Edward joined the 5th Battalion of the Rifle Brigade as a Rifleman/Private, before being transferred for training and eventual posting with the 8th. When he arrived in Flanders at the end of June 1915, he found the rest of his Battalion had been rebuilding shell-shattered trenches around Ypres for a month or more. He was rapidly promoted from Private to Corporal,

"proof of his ability and keenness"

(*East Sussex News* of 13 August 1915).

It seems that by the time of his death a month later, further promotion was imminent, as he was already Acting Serjeant.

During the first week of his war in early July, Corporal Sandals was in the trenches at 'Railway Wood', just to the east of Ypres. There were one or two days under heavy bombardment and several losses were incurred. There followed a week in rest camp at Poperinghe to the west of Ypres. This was a popular place of rest and recreation for the troops, who knew it affectionately as "Pop", and flocked to its many lively bars and cafes. It was also home to the new 'Toc H' Rest Centre and Chapel, at which Edward may well have been one of the early visitors. They then had another week or so in Brigade Reserve billets back towards Ypres.

The last week of July was a somewhat confused time for the Battalion, with several changes of command as they were moved from one Division to another and then from the Vth to the VIth Army Corps. There were therefore several changes in plans about troop movements, which led to the inexperienced 8th Battalion having to take over at short notice front line trenches with which none of their officers, let alone the men, were familiar. It seems that the enemy, with his vastly superior field telephone systems and listening equipment, was only too well aware of this inexperience and unfamiliarity, and had determined to capitalise on it to the full.

On 28th July, the two Companies which had been billeted in tents in the town ramparts at Ypres, met up with the other two from 'Gingerbread Chateau'. Together they marched out to take over the front line and reserve trenches at Hooge, a couple of miles east of Ypres along the Menin Road in the general direction of Passchendaele. Corporal Sandals would thus have experienced at first hand the reputations of some of the danger points on that two mile march, such as 'Hellfire Corner', all well within range of enemy guns. The countryside they were occupying was a mile or two to the south of the break in our lines forced by the enemy in the disastrous first gas attack of 21st/22nd April 1915, in the 2nd Battle of Ypres.

The village of Hooge itself, and its Chateau, were already in ruins; underground tunnelling and mining activity was already going on under fields and woods in a wide area. The Hooge Crater itself, formed by some of this activity, and relentless shelling, was to be one of the major factors in the virtual annihilation of at least two companies of Corporal Sandals' battalion. The front line, having been cut in half by such a massive crater, proved impossible to hold.

Corporal Sandals' one and only battle

The Battalion was marched up to the front line, Company by Company, from 9 p.m. on 29th July until the relief was complete at 2 a.m. on the fateful 30th. The *Official War Diary* records that it was

"a dark night, with the moon in the third quarter".

The Battalion strength on taking over was 24 Officers and 745 Other Ranks, and they had a total of five machine guns between them. At 3.15 a.m. the enemy attacked, and the Diary continues:-

"There were two or three minutes of intense bombardment of the front trench, then suddenly sheets of flame broke out all along the front, and clouds of black smoke. The enemy had turned on 'liquid fire', from hoses apparently, which had been established just in front during the night.

Under cover of the flames, scores of bomb [throwers] appeared on the parapet and in rear of the line. The mass of them had broken through at the crater and then swung right and left. The fighting became very confused, and the Machine Guns were soon all out of action... The Battalion's extreme right and left platoons repulsed all attempts to bomb them out as they had not been affected by the flames... the enemy had pushed through the whole of the centre in spite of the most gallant fighting, and were established with Machine Guns in the ruins of Hooge on the south side of the Menin Road, commanding all the ground between there and Zouave Wood...

From 4 to 5 a.m. 'B' Co'y. counter-attacked, but were beaten back by machine gun fire... communications were cut, but reinforcements from the King's Royal Rifle Corps arrived at 9 a.m. The remains of the Bn. held the north edge of Zouave Wood. At 12 noon the order was received for another bombardment and counter-attack to begin at 2.45 p.m. 'D' Co'y. was the only one remaining. 'C' Co'y. was non-existent, and 'A' and 'B' Co'ys had suffered heavy losses.

At 2.45 the counter-attack started, with 'D' Coy. on the right advancing as if on

Hooge battlefield with gun on Menin Road and Hooge Crater Cemetery beyond.

parade. The enemy's machine gun and rifle fire had not been silenced by the bombardment. The whole ground was absolutely swept by bullets. The attack was brought to a complete standstill halfway towards its objective, and no reinforcements could reach it. The second counter-attack had failed.

The remnants of the Bn. held on to the communications trench till dark… and was finally taken out of action at 2 a.m. next morning."

The 8th Battalion's casualties for that one day were 6 Officers killed, 3 missing and 10 wounded, and among Other Ranks were 80 killed, 132 missing (most of whom were believed to be killed), and 267 wounded, in addition to 5 Other Ranks suffering from shock. All those were out of that pre-battle muster of 24 Officers and 745 Other Ranks. A telling post-script is added to the official record:-

"The men fought without rations or water throughout the day."

Crown copyright material in the Public Record Office is reproduced by permission of the Controller of H.M. Stationery Office, P.R.O. document reference W095/1896

Corporal Sandals' death and commemoration

It seems likely that Corporal Sandals survived the horrors of the initial 'liquid fire attack', only to fall in either the first counter-attack at dawn or the later one in the afternoon. It was to be many months before his family had final confirmation that he had been killed in action; the early reports of him being missing must have allowed them to cling to some hope. The *Sussex County Herald* for Saturday August 14th 1915, carried a brief item announcing that he had been reported missing in action a fortnight earlier. It quoted part of a letter written to his parents by his Commanding Officer, saying that he had been:

"… wounded in the course of a most gallant charge, and his wounds must have proved fatal. We can ill afford to lose men of his stamp. He is a very great loss to us. In the name of the officers and men, I send our deepest sympathy".

Much of the site of that battlefield is now maintained by the Commonwealth War Graves Commission as the Hooge Crater Cemetery, and is beautifully laid out on the south facing slope down from the Menin Road towards Zouave Wood. But there is no grave there for Corporal Sandals, for his body was never found. The family had to wait until 1921 to know that he had been commemorated, on the newly-erected Memorial at the Menin Gate in the restored town of Ypres.

Hooge Crater Cemetery, on site of battlefield

This sombre yet majestic

archway over the Menin Road was designed by Sir Reginald Blomfield to honour the memory of the first 55,000 dead of Britain and her Commonwealth who were lost without trace during the defence of the Ypres Salient, up to June 1917. Their names are engraved on stone Panels, in rank groupings and regiment by regiment, under the inscription:-

> *"Here are recorded the names of the Officers and Men who fell in the Ypres Salient, but to whom the fortunes of war denied the known and honoured burial given to their comrades in death."*

Carved in stone above the central arch are the words:-

> *"To the armies of the British Empire who stood here from 1914 to 1918 and to those of their dead who have no known grave"*

Since 1928, the people of Ypres pause in silent commemoration of these 55,000 under the Arch every night at sunset, while two buglers play the Last Post.

Menin Gate Memorial to the Missing, Ypres.

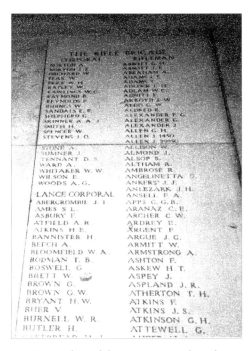

Corporal Sandal's name engraved on the Memorial (top left of tablet) with other Corporals of the 8th Battalion Rifle Brigade.

William Norris HILLMAN   1.06
25th September 1915 aged 18
at the Battle of Loos
G/1488 Private
'B' Co'y, 2nd Battalion, Royal Sussex Regiment

HOME   Southover Post Office, 8 Southover High Street
COMMEMORATED   Loos Memorial at Dud Corner British Cemetery,
                    Bethune-Lens Road

Southover childhood

'Billy' Hillman, as he was widely known, grew up in and above Southover Post Office and grocer's shop. At that time, around the turn of the century, this was at Nos. 7 and 8 Southover High Street (this is where The Gallery and the house between it and the King's Head now are). He and his immediate family lived in one part, next door to his grandfather, his Uncle Norris (after whom he was named), and two aunts, who all shared the other part. It was in the part of the High Street to the north of the church, opposite 'Fairholme' and between the King's Head and Eastport Lane. Between them, the Hillmans ran both the Post Office and the grocer's shop, known as "Shaw's Stores" , all under the same two roofs. Billy was born there on 18th October, 1896, and was baptised at Southover Church six weeks later on 29 November. He was the only son of his parents, and his younger sister Dulcie was born a few years later.

His father, William Alfred, spent his whole life in Southover, as grocer and later Postmaster, living in the same two houses all the time. He sang in the Southover Church choir (as did his son after him), and later became one of the Churchwardens there. Southover Bonfire Society, and later the Lewes Cycling Club, were the other big things in his father's life, besides all his wider Hillman family activities. There were many branches of Hillmans all over Lewes, going back many generations, and two or three others in Southover as well. Young Billy would therefore have had plenty of cousins all around to play with (it was almost certainly one of them, Frederick Cecil Hillman who died later in the war - see no. 1.20). His grandfather next door had tales to tell of his own childhood where "The Snowdrop" now is in the Cliffe, when he was nearly lost in the Lewes Avalanche of 1836; he had

Southover Old Post Office with Hillmans' home above,
7 Southover High Street

apparently had to be carried out as a young child, and ferried to safety on a barge across the river.

Lewes youth

Billy's school-years were spent at Castlegate School, near the Barbican Gate of the Castle. He would have been there at the same time as some of the other young Southover men who were also to lose their lives in this war. He was only fourteen when he left school, and he went straight into his first and only job. This was as a Journalist at the Lewes office of the *East Sussex News*; he worked for three years on their editorial staff, becoming well-known to many in Lewes and the surrounding villages.

Private Hillman's war

He had enlisted while he was still only 17, in September 1914 before the war had run a month. He was with the 3rd Battalion initially, and had his preliminary training with them, before he embarked for France in the first week of January, 1915. He was then transferred to the 2nd Battalion, another of the original Battalions of the Regiment in the 'old Army'. Many re-arrangements were having to be made in all these old Battalions, to accommodate the great influx of new young recruits responding to Kitchener's appeals, and after so many units of the Royal Sussex Regiment were decimated in the Richebourg and Festubert disasters of May 1915.

Pte. Hillman saw action himself over there in May, and was also at Aubers Ridge. His parents had a letter from him just after the so-called "Glorious 9th May", re-assuring them that he had been there but had "escaped unhurt". He came through that catastrophe unscathed, only to fall at the next one, as the Front advanced four or five miles on to the south in as many months. He had barely nine months in France, and all of those without any home leave.

He wrote to a colleague at work early in September 1915, saying how much he was hoping to have a few days leave very soon. He mentioned that he had been with the

Prvt. W. N. Hillman

Regiment since September 1914 without a break, apart from a few days in hospital with bronchitis, from which he had now completely recovered.

His death at the Battle of Loos

That eagerly awaited leave was never to happen, for big moves were afoot in that part of the Front. All leave was cancelled in anticipation of another big 'set-piece' battle when all possible troops would be needed. It was a new thrust planned, in support of the new French offensive in Champagne. The build-up to it was particularly chaotic, due to last-minute changes in the weather and the military command. The logistics alone must have been something of a nightmare for them all; unprecedented numbers of British (and also now Commonwealth troops returning in eager support of their mother-country), old armies and Kitchener's 'New Armies', all had to be got across the Channel, uniformed, equipped and fed, armed, trained and led. They then had to be marched scores of miles still sea-sick from the crossing, or moved from previous positions nearby, into new positions among the slag heaps and colliery towns of north-eastern France.

It would be known as the Battle of Loos, and was to run on through fog and rain, un-cut wire, clouds of poison gas, and more chaos, from 25th September to 19th October 1915, with the loss of 50,000 lives. Private Hillman was then killed just as this great battle was launched. It began before dawn on 25th September, with several hours of intense bombardment of the enemy front line. Our forces first released gas at 5.50 a.m., and the infantry 'went over' at 6.30 a.m. Nearly half of its casualties were never found, lost without trace in the shellfire and the mud, and have no known grave. That includes all the four from Southover. Needless to say, it took many weeks for any firm information to reach the families.

The anguish of the family back home was made the more poignant once the grisly facts of the battle were known. They had known the reason for leave being cancelled, but then had several more weeks to wait before receiving any official information. Their suspense must have been heightened by an extraordinary letter they had out of the blue on 29th October. This was from an unknown Sergeant in the Northumberland Regiment, newly returned home on leave from the Front at Loos. He enclosed in it a mud-stained photograph of the Hillman family, which he had found lying on the battlefield a few days after the end of the battle a month earlier. As their address was on the back of it, he decided to forward it to them. It was a photograph they would have recognised, as it was taken of them all at home before Billy went to the Front. Billy had written all their names on the back of it and had, they knew, gone off to war with it in his tunic pocket. It must have been a very bitter-sweet letter to receive, on the one hand warning them of the virtual certainty that he was already dead, but on the other offering a last tangible link with their beloved boy.

It was well into November before they had any official confirmation of his death. As Billy's last employers, the *East Sussex News* gave the sad story full coverage in their issue of 12th November 1915, and included much of the information already quoted above:-

> *"Prvt. Hillman was well known in Lewes and the surrounding district. He was an old boy of Castlegate School, and for three years prior to enlisting he was a member of the editorial staff of this paper at the Lewes office, and his duties brought him into touch with many in the county town and the surrounding villages… Had Privt. Hillman lived till October 18th, he would have reached the age of 19.*

> *He is the first member of our staff to give his life for his country, but some of his former comrades have been wounded, and have returned to duty."*

The paper goes on to list ten other members of their Lewes staff alone "who are serving with the Colours." Other local papers carried the news too; one of the *Sussex County Herald's* front page items next day was headed: "Lewes Journalist Killed".

National and local commemoration

Private Hillman's name is one of four from Southover to be inscribed on the Loos Memorial. They are each commemorated with their respective Battalions on their different Panels of the Loos Memorial, built during the twenties as part of the wall of the Dud Corner Cemetery. This is on the north-east side of the main road from Lens to Bethune, on the top of a low ridge, with some mine buildings across the road a little to the north-west. There are some 1,800 actual graves in the Cemetery; the remaining 20,712 names are inscribed on the Panels. Private Hillman's name is with 531 others from the Royal Sussex Regiment, on Panels 69 to 73. It is again some of the Scottish regiments whose losses were greatest; the Black Watch alone have 829 names on the Memorial. As the CWGC writes in its booklet on the Cemetery and the Loos Memorial:

> *"The graves in this area are for the most part those of men who died in 1915; the Le Touret and Loos Memorials record mainly the names of those who first tried to break the German line, and died three years before it was finally broken."*

Long before 1929, when the Loos Memorial was finally completed, Southover's own granite cross had been unveiled, with Billy Hillman's name inscribed on it as one of the forty six 'men of Southover'.

For many of the intervening years, Mr & Mrs Hillman put entries in the "In Memoriam" columns of the *East Sussex News* at the end of each September, as follows:-

> *"In ever-loving memory of Billy, killed in action at Loos, 25th September 1915.*
> > *'Rest quietly, best beloved,*
> > *Thou who fellest asleep in thy youth,*
> > *And thy beauty, and thy strength,*
> > *Rest quietly in the long slumber.'"*

Soon after the war, Billy's only sister Dulcie (whose photo had been in his pocket on that battlefield) married a local man called Harry Avis. Her parents continued to run the Post Office for many years, and lived on there in retirement. Billy's and her mother, Beatrice, had come from Croydon and had an aunt, Emma Goldsmith, who was for many years the popular licensee of the King's Head on the corner of the High Street next door. Mrs Hillman also became quite

Loos Memorial.
(CWGC)

a local figure, as one of the founder members of the Southover W.I. and its choir, and was in the Southover Mothers' Union, as well as helping in the Post Office.

Then, some thirty years further on, Mr and Mrs Hillman's Golden Wedding was celebrated in September 1943. The celebration was master-minded by their daughter Dulcie, and was marked by a long write-up in the *Sussex Express* (from which much of the family detail above has been acquired, and the following photograph of them in their early eighties is reproduced with permission). Their wedding had been on 26th September 1893; thus, Billy was killed just one day before their 20th wedding anniversary. The last line of the long write-up about them at their Golden Wedding, in the middle of the second world war, is: *"Mr & Mrs Hillman lost their only son William Norris Hillman on active service in the last war."*

Pte. Hillman's parents at their silver wedding anniversary, September 1943

After the death of the elderly parents in the years shortly following the Second World War, Dulcie and Harry moved in to the old Post Office themselves. Many years later, they were in turn to leave it to their niece Gillian Avis. Gillian and her mother Freda Avis live on there, and are glad to have been able to keep the property in the family. They have restored it delightfully, and live in the same front room that had the Post Office counter in it.

Reginald John Edward HOLLAND   1.07
27th September 1915 aged 18
at Battle of Loos
3122 Private
9th Battalion, Royal Sussex Regiment

HOME   3 St Pancras Villas, St Pancras Gardens, Southover
COMEMMORATED   The Loos Memorial, Dud Corner Cemetery,
                    Bethune-Lens Road

Private Holland survived just two days longer than his fellow 18 year old, Billy Hillman (No. 1.06 above) from Southover Post Office. The carnage that was Loos claimed them both in the same week. They had grown up within a quarter of a mile of each other in Southover, they had joined the same regiment, fought in the same actions, and were then to be commemorated on the same Loos Memorial in Flanders.

His pre-war life in Lewes

Nothing is known of any other family members, or where Private Holland grew up. He does not seem to have been baptised in Southover Church, but he and his mother were established in Southover well before the war. She was Mrs. Emla (sic.) Holland, and the two of them lived, apparently on their own, at 3 St Pancras Villas. This little row of houses seems to have been part of St Pancras Terrace, but neither Villas nor Terrace still exist. They were likely to have been part of the original St Pancras Gardens between the Winterbourne Stream and the old Southover Brewery, all demolished during or soon after the Second War. The new St Pancras Gardens, with the flats and the St Pancras Stores, have been built in their place.

Pte. R.J.E. Holland

The young Reginald's first job on leaving school was being a Post Office Messenger for two years, though whether for the whole of Lewes or just Southover we do not know. He then became a motor mechanic at the Lewes County Garage, 170 High Street (next door to the Barbican House Museum), in the spring of 1912. This would doubtless have been a much sought after job among the lads of Lewes in those early days of motoring and mechanised farm machinery. He stayed there for eighteen months, right up to the outbreak of war, and for the first month of its course.

His war

It was in the second week of September 1914 that he enlisted with the Royal Sussex Regiment, just three months before his eighteenth birthday. He then had nearly a year of training, before embarking for France with them in September 1915. His batch of newly trained recruits would have been rushed down to the Front in anticipation of this great new offensive planned for the end of the month. This became known as the Battle of Loos, and young Reginald only lasted the first two days of it. He was killed three weeks after arriving in France, just three months before his nineteenth birthday.

The last letter home

Private Holland last wrote to his mother on 25th September, the day the battle started. His Battalion would have been in Reserve, knowing their turn to go forward would come the next day. Amazingly, despite those battle conditions, that letter got through, and was delivered to Mrs Holland in St Pancras Villas on the evening of 28th September. The post-boy that delivered it was probably well known to Billy Hillman's parents at the Post Office, and may well have delivered a similar letter to them from their son just a few nights earlier. The soldiers would all have been given a suitable form of words in which to alert their next of kin that a big action was imminent, but without divulging details that would not pass the military censors. Mrs Holland would have been left in no doubt that her son's life was hanging in the balance, and that the next day or two after he mailed the letter would have been critical.

The prolonged suspense

With every day that then passed for Mrs Holland, and indeed Mrs Hillman, without further news of their sons, their hopes must have dropped a little more. It may well be that they could be of some comfort to each other in the anguish they shared, as the days became first weeks then months. As we have already seen, Mrs Hillman could read some unofficial 'news' of her Billy into his returned photograph of the rest of the family on 29th October, forwarded by a Sergeant returning on leave from the Front, where he had found it in the mud.

Mrs Holland had a similarly distressing contact from some of her son's friends at the Front, telling her that he had been wounded and taken prisoner-of-war. Her attempts to get this confirmed or denied by the War Office achieved nothing.

Then on Wednesday 3rd November, Mrs Holland received a letter from Pte. B. Jackson, another of her son's friends at the Front. In it he said how sorry he had been to hear of her Reginald's death several weeks earlier. This naturally prompted Mrs Holland to make immediate enquiries through the various War Office channels, who had still sent no information at all. She must then have contacted the *Sussex Express*, who printed his photograph on Friday 5th November, Bonfire Night but without the Bonfire that year, under the heading

    "A Lewes Soldier Missing".

It confirmed that Private Holland was indeed missing, and that "in regard to [his] safety, the gravest of fears are entertained."

The *Sussex County Herald* had a fuller story the next day, quoting at length from a letter Mrs Holland had by then received from the Sergeant Major of her son's Company.:-

Photo from article "A Lewes Soldier Missing", ESN 5th Nov.1915

"You must, I am sorry to say, steel your heart for the worst. Your son was shot about midday on 27th September in the chest. He was reported as being wounded and missing. I naturally thought you had received official information some time ago. [Since receiving your recent enquiry] I made enquiries of those who saw him last, and they are quite sure he was dead. On behalf of his comrades and myself, I offer you our deepest sympathy. He was a good lad, and I was very much attached to him. He acquitted himself like a hero in the most trying ordeal that man could be called upon to endure. He laid down his life in defence of his home and womenfolk, to save them from cruelties far worse than anything Belgium has had to endure."

Unbelievably, it was not until the end of the next June that Mrs Holland heard anything official from the War Office. She then put the standard Death Notice in the Personal Columns of the *East Sussex News* on 27th June 1916, confirming the death of her "beloved only son" at Loos at the end of the previous September. She also put a brief notice in the 'Return Thanks' column thanking all friends for messages of sympathy etc.

The *Sussex Express* reported it on 15th July 1916, with a pre-war photograph, saying merely that:

> *"official intimation had now reached Mrs Holland that her only son, Pte R J E Holland, had been killed in action at Loos on the previous 27th September".*

This had of course been just the day before she had read his last words to her.

The Loos Memorial

Reginald Holland's name remains today, along with those of the 20,500 other British soldiers who perished that same autumn in the mud and mines and slag-heaps around Loos, and who like him have no known grave. There are over 500 names of other Royal Sussex men, all on Panels 69 - 73. Many of the other names are from the five Scottish regiments, who sustained the highest losses in those early days of the Battle of Loos.

The Memorial has been built in part of the 'Dud Corner' Cemetery, on that dismal road between Bethune and Lens-en-Gohelle. That latter village was by then an obliterated community; its name in English is grimly suggestive of the very window into hell there must only too vividly have been in the whole area around it. It would also have been in the shadow of the infamous 'Hill 70', before it was exploded out of existence. It stands almost exactly where an enemy strong point, the Lens Road Redoubt, had stood and was captured on the first day of the Battle, which was two days before Private Holland was killed.

Floods at junction of old St.Pancras Gardens and the Course, opposite Holland's home.

Jesse MOORE   1.08
8th October 1915 aged 22
at the Battle of Loos
74019 Corporal, 'D' Coy.
28th Infantry Battalion (Saskatchewan Regiment), C.E.F.

HOME   20 Eastport Lane, Southover (parents) and
910 Avenue 'G' North, Saskatoon, Saskatchewan, Canada (wife)
COMMEMORATED   The Menin Gate Memorial, Ypres

Returning emigrant

This young man was the third of the Southover men to fall at the Battle of Loos; but he was by then also a Canadian. Alone among the forty six Southover casualties, he had emigrated in the closing years of Empire, and then came back in support of the old country in its time of need. He had gone out to the Canadian far west, to make a new start where space and opportunities abounded, but he was still willing to 'come home' when the call came, despite having just got married.

Lewes childhood and youth

Jesse Moore was the third of five sons (and one daughter) born to Harry and Mary Ann (Polly) Moore, of 20 Eastport Lane, Southover. His father Harry was Southover born and bred, from one of the many branches of the Moores in and around Lewes. Harry was porter to a tallow-chandler initially, then became the tallow-chandler himself (?perhaps at the Old Candlemakers, or even nearer to home at the Cattle Market). His mother Polly, nee Hughes, came from Firle. While her six children were all very small, she had the benefit of her younger sister Emily moving in with them from Firle to help out. The house they lived in was behind the old Bell Inn which fronted Eastport Lane; it occupied some of the space now used for the yard between the Priory Flats on Priory Street, and the rear of Eastport Lane. (His two older brothers, Charles and George Walter, also went off to the war, but only Charles returned; for George Walter, see 1.33; his younger brother Fred came back with the Military Medal for "exceptional bravery in bringing in wounded men under fire".)

Jesse Moore

Jesse was born on 4th February1893, and was baptised at Southover Church a month later on 7th March. For the whole of his Southover childhood he had numerous brothers, sisters, cousins and neighbours all around Eastport Lane and Priory Street. He attended Southover School, and sang in Southover Church Choir for many years. He also became firm friends with a lad of his own age called Stanley Killick, whose father the Revd. H. Killick was the Pastor of the Providence Baptist Chapel in Lancaster Street, Lewes. It was with this Killick family that Jesse was to emigrate shortly before the war, and it was Stanley's sister Fanny Irene who was to become Jesse's wife and very shortly his widow as well. Neither Stanley nor his brother were to return from the war either, so the Killick family was particularly hard hit.

After leaving school in Lewes, Jesse worked with some of his brothers, for Mr F. Holman, Solicitor, at his garden and residence off the High Street. This was at no. 86 & 87, between St.Swithin's Lane and Bull Lane. While there, he was also for three or four years a trumpeter in the Lewes Company of the Sussex Royal Garrison Artillery, and an active member of the local Militia.

Jesse's emigration to Canada, and his marriage there

There are few further details as to why, how and when he emigrated. It seems he settled in Saskatoon, capital city of Saskatchewan, with or near the Killicks, and that he was working as a tailor, but there is no indication of how long he had been over there when war broke out.

On 26th October 1914, Jesse and Stanley enlisted "for the duration of the war" in the 28th North Western Battalion of the Canadian Infantry. Not yet being married, he gave his mother back in Southover as his next of kin. He swore the Oath of Allegiance to King George the Fifth, passed his Medical and was considered "Fit for the Canadian Overseas Expeditionary Force". He is described as being 21 years 8 months, and having "brown eyes, dark hair, dark complexion, 5ft.7ins.in height, with a girth of 36 ins., and a scar on the inner side of left leg."

Jesse had presumably got to know Stanley's sister Irene back home in Lewes, and it may be that she was the reason for Jesse following the Killicks over there in the first place. Whether or not the young soldiers then brought their wedding plans forward because of the likelihood of going off to war in the next few months, they had a grand double wedding just two months after they both joined up. It was held at the home of Stanley's parents, the Revd. & Mrs. H. H. Killick, in Saskatoon on Christmas Day 1914. The Saskatoon Daily Star reported the wedding thus:-

> "The contracting parties were their son Pte. Stanley S. Killick and Miss Annie Scott Hill, daughter of George Campbell Hill, MRCVS, Glasgow; and Pte. Jesse Moore, son of Henry Moore of Lewes, England, and Miss Irene Kathleen Killick, only daughter of the Revd. & Mrs H.H. Killick. Both brides wore becoming costumes of grey silk eolienne, with swansdown and oriental trimming…
>
> … Following the ceremony, an enjoyable wedding breakfast was partaken of by the guests. The two bridegrooms left the following day to re-join their regiments in Winnipeg."

Jesse's short war

History does not relate whether those regiments in Winnipeg granted the young soldiers any longer wedding leave in the next few months, merely that they embarked for England on SS Northland on 29th May 1915. (But the National Archives of Canada have been able to provide all the following details of his war service.) The fears of all concerned about torpedoes and U-Boat activity in the North Atlantic must have been considerable, but they arrived safely. Training began in earnest at Otterpool, Kent; and then there were two promotions for Jesse: on 1st July he was made Lance Corporal, and then on 28th July this was up-graded to Corporal. They then had a brief spell of leave early in September, when the brothers-in-law Jesse and Stanley were able to visit family and old friends in Lewes. Included in that time for Jesse was a farewell service at Southover Church, in which he occupied his old place in the choir, before setting off for France. The Canadians disembarked in Boulogne on 18th September 1915, and then began the long march across to Loos, as so many of the Royal Sussex Regiment had done just before them.

Sadly, Stanley Killick was only to survive a week or so. He was killed on 26th September, just the day before Private Holland, the previous entry at no.7 above. Jesse somehow heard of Stanley's death while in a different sector of the Front, and wrote to Canada to commiserate with Stanley's bride of less than a year. Then, less than two weeks later, on October 8th, it was Jesse's own turn. He was killed in action during the Battle of Loos, at the age of 22. His own young widow thus lost both her husband Jesse and her brother Stanley, both within three weeks of their arrival in France in that early autumn of 1915, just nine months after their far-off Canadian wedding day.

It was Stanley's remaining brother, Private F. Killick, who was serving with the same regiment in France, who first broke the news of Jesse's death to his widow Irene Kathleen, and to his parents Harry and Polly. He described how there had been a mine explosion in Jesse's trench, which had killed him. The parents had to wait till 22nd October before they heard officially from the Major in charge of Jesse's Company, who then wrote to them as follows:-

" Cpl. Moore was not only one of the best soldiers, but one of the most consistent and cheerful Christians I have ever met. He died at his post, and has gone to his sure reward."

The aftermath

Apparently the Chaplain of the Canadian 6th Infantry Brigade was responsible for Jesse's interrment on what had been the battlefield, when his remains were found on 20th December 1915.

Jesse's widow had to wait until July 1920 to receive her "War Service Gratuity to Dependents of Deceased Soldiers"; it was $180, less the $64 already paid as a Special Pension Bonus. Shortly after that, she moved from their previous address in Saskatoon out further west to New Westminster, British Columbia. Perhaps she was putting the past further behind her.

By 1921, the arrangements for all the inscriptions on the Menin Gate Memorial at Ypres were finalised. It had been decided to record the names of a proportion of the missing from all the Empire forces on the Menin Gate, and Jesse Moore's appears there with some 260 others of his 28th Battalion alone, on Panels 26 and 28

Menin Gate Memorial to the Missing, Ypres.

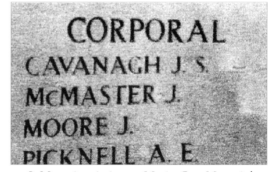

J. Moore inscription on Menin Gate Memorial

P.S.

Originally from Beddingham, Jesse's grandfather Henry married Eliza Stanford at St Nicholas Church, Brighton, in November 1864. By the time their firstborn, Harry (who would become Jesses's father), arrived in 1865 the family had moved to Southover and lived at 15 first then16, Eastport Lane. (It was one of their other sons, Daniel, who was to marry Edith Satcher from Hamsey. Daniel and Edith were to become the parents of the other large Moore 'clan' along the road at 15 Eastport Lane, after moving round the corner from 52 Priory Street. One of the eldest of their children, Mabel, still lives in Lewes and has provided much of my information on the Moores and the families they married into. One of the youngest, Raymond, has also been a great source of information on them all a generation later, particularly on the youngest, Frederick, was to give his life in Italy in the Second World War.)

PART TWO

1916

The Year of the Somme

There are nine men named on the Southover Memorial who were killed in 1916, one more than in 1914 and 1915 together. Six of these nine were killed at or in the direct aftermath of the Battle of the Somme. Seven of these men were buried at the battlefield, or in one case back home in Southover Churchyard after unsuccessful treatment in a London military hospital. The remaining two were never found, so are commemorated on the Loos and Thiepval Memorials.

Eight of the nine were single men, but two of them were brothers. Three of them had brothers who were also to be killed in action before the end of the war, and one was a family man who left a widow and five children. The ages of these men covered the whole range from 19 to 41.

Six of them were killed in action, and one by a sniper. The remaining two died of their battle wounds, one safely behind the lines in a Rouen hospital and the other further behind the lines in London. They included the first of the Southover men to be gassed, and the first to be killed in aerial combat.

The nine men are listed here

HOME ADDRESS		NAME		NUMBER IN BOOK
Brookside, 29	Southover High Street	Brian Edward	GLOVER	9
	Address unknown	Alfred	HARDING	10
36	Grange Road	Frank	BEAGLEY	11
Brookside, 29	Southover High Street	Benjamin Hilton	GLOVER	12
15	Eastport Lane	George	FELLOWS	13
53	Potters Lane	William Thomas	MARTIN	14
36	Southover High Street	Henry Douglas	WILLIAMS	15
28	Lansdown Place	Henry Frank	NEVILLE	16
9	Priory Street	Arthur Henry	HEAD	17

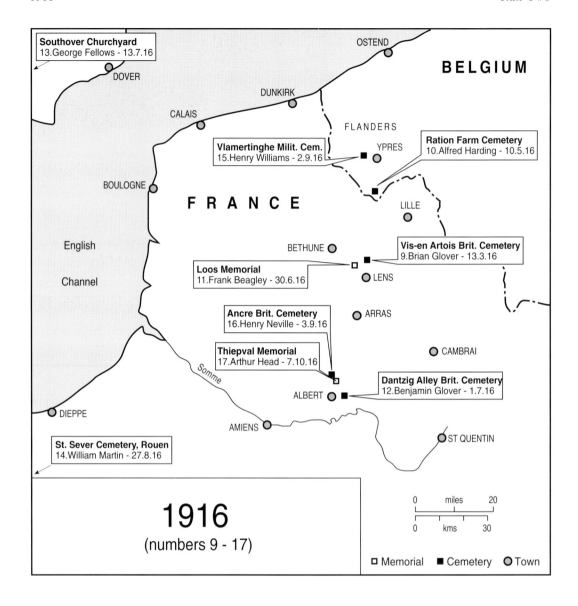

Southover Churchyard
13.George Fellows - 13.7.16

OSTEND

BELGIUM

DOVER

DUNKIRK

CALAIS

FLANDERS

Vlamertinghe Milit. Cem.
15.Henry Williams - 2.9.16

YPRES

Ration Farm Cemetery
10.Alfred Harding - 10.5.16

BOULOGNE

F R A N C E

LILLE

English

Channel

BETHUNE

Vis-en Artois Brit. Cemetery
9.Brian Glover - 13.3.16

Loos Memorial
11.Frank Beagley - 30.6.16

LENS

ARRAS

Ancre Brit. Cemetery
16.Henry Neville - 3.9.16

CAMBRAI

Thiepval Memorial
17.Arthur Head - 7.10.16

Somme

Dantzig Alley Brit. Cemetery
12.Benjamin Glover - 1.7.16

ALBERT

DIEPPE

AMIENS

ST QUENTIN

St. Sever Cemetery, Rouen
14.William Martin - 27.8.16

1916
(numbers 9 - 17)

```
0        miles        20
|————|————|————|
0        kms          30
```

□ Memorial   ■ Cemetery   ◉ Town

The extracts of newspaper items for 1916 show that the war was beginning to bite at home too. There were increasingly strict lighting restrictions for fear of attacks and reconnaissance from enemy Zeppelin airships. Army training camps all round Lewes continued, and there were civilian preparations for invasion possibilities.

Floods at The Course/St.Pancras Lane (with Mrs Holland at top window of St Pancras Villas on R.)

Yet again Southover had winter floods to contend with as the Winterbourne Stream burst its banks, and much hardship was suffered. Much of this was in the old St Pancras Gardens area, from which so many of the First War soldiers came but which has now been re-developed.

Jan 1st & 2nd 1916, and Dec 31st 1915:
National days of Intercession "in connection with the war";
Large services at Cliffe and St John sub Castro churches.

Jan 1st-8th:
Southover floods bad all week; 50 residents of The Course and Spring Gardens had to live upstairs; main road blocked at Newmarket;
Rector of Southover wrote letter of Appeal to public via Editor of *Sussex County Herald*; Petition drawn up by W. Burfoot of 18 Garden Street and residents of Garden Street, The Course and St Pancras Gardens, asking the council for compensation and prevention.

Jan 15th:
Wounded soldiers were entertained at St Michael's Social Club, while convalescing at School Hill House and St Anne's Hospital.

Feb 25th:
Southover Bellringers rang a Quarter Peal of Grandsire Triples before the Evening Service, being the Sunday nearest to the tenth anniversary of the re-hanging and re-constituting of the bells in 1906. There was a band of eight ringers, including W Moore, Tenor, who is shortly joining H.M. Forces. The Peal was also rung as a birthday compliment to him.

Feb 26th:
Deep snow all week.

Lighting regulations continue to be disregarded; summonses this week to the Minister of Eastgate Baptist Church, and Miss Eleanor Poile, Matron of Victoria Hospital.

Easter:
Volunteer Corps in training on the Downs for a week.

Apr 15th:

"Instructions to be followed in the unlikely event of an invasion: On hearing the jangling of church bells, residents of Southover are to take all their food, wear warm clothes, and collect up in Winterbourne Lane where onward arrangements will be made. Everyone should have a pot and saucepan and a rolled up blanket with them, and should leave their front door unlocked."

September:

Fear of Zeppelins leads to more strict Lighting Regulations, to ensure less light at night.

November:

Advertisements for Christmas presents for soldiers:-

e.g. T Lawson of Old Steine, Brighton, were advertising wrist watches with radium dial and hands for 30/-. "It is not an extravagance to give a soldier a luminous wrist watch; it is a necessity", and Wm. Hill were offering boxes of Christmas presents for soldiers for 5/-, containing 2 towels, 2 tablets of soap, 2 handkerchiefs, 1 tube of toothpaste, 1 toothbrush, notepaper and envelopes, and 1 pencil.

Dec 16th:

Sinn Feiners to Lewes Prison from Dartmoor; "only those who had promised no disturbance or escape attempts could be in civilian dress; the others would be in convicts' clothes and chains."

Dec 23rd:

Southover School Annual Prize Distribution was attended by the Rector and Mrs Windle, Alderman Miles, Councillor Verrall and Miss Verrall, and the Revd. A S Dendy, Curate.

Training Camp at Kingston

Brian Edward GLOVER
13th March 1916 aged 21
in air combat over Picardy
Second Lieutenant
Royal Flying Corps (8th Sqdn) & General List

1.09

HOME "Brookside", Southover High Street
BURIED Vis-en-Artois British Cemetary, Picardy

Double loss for the Glover family

1916 was a very black year for the Glover family of Southover. Lt. Brian Glover was the second of three soldier sons of Councillor Edward Arthur and Mrs Gertrude Glover, of 'Brookside', Southover High Street. All three went to war, but only one survived to return, the eldest Eric who was in the Machine Gun Corps. The Turk family in Priory Street had already lost one of their two sons who were not to return, and before the end of the war, three further families from Southover were each to lose their two sons. In another way, too, was the Glover family particularly hard hit. Although they had known from mid-March 1916 that Brian was missing in action, they had no definite news for three long months, and then it was final – that he had actually been killed in action, rather than taken prisoner of war. They had less than a month to come to terms with that loss, before news of their youngest son's death then reached them (see no.1.12). The other families with double losses had in the main several years between their deaths.

Early days of aerial reconnaissance and combat

Brian Glover's service career and tragically premature death, also marked the important shift in military tactics and technology that came with advances in signalling, aerial reconnaissance and combat. He was the first of the only two Southover men to be killed in action with the Royal Air Force, and that in its earliest days while it was still known as the Royal Flying Corps. He must have been one of the earliest soldiers to be transferred in action to an aerial squadron, while also remaining on the 'General List'.

"Brookside", Southover High Street

The Glover family's house is still there, still called 'Brookside', and stands prominently at the far end of Southover High Street on the bend after The Swan Inn. It is on the corner with what was the Juggs Road to Kingston, earlier known as Mill Road, on the west side of the road after the Swan Inn. The house was used as a Barracks in the 19th century, and was connected with the Depot and

Brookside House"
Southover High Street/Juggs Road.

Drill Ground of the East Sussex Artillery Militia, further on towards Kingston where Saxonbury now is. There is still a little gap in the old wall up behind 'Brookside', which leads to 'Artillery Cottage'. The present owners had heard that a gun battery was put in place in or near the house during the First War, to command the Ouse valley towards Newhaven.

Thanet College, Lewes Cement Works, and Lewes Town Council

The three Glover soldier boys were all educated at Thanet College, Margate. This was possibly where they hailed from, or maybe they boarded there, coming back to Southover for the holidays. The family did also have connections with Ringmer, which seem to have been only short-lived and before they settled in Southover. There were also two other younger Glover boys, born shortly before the outbreak of war, also at 'Brookside'. Both were baptised at Southover Church, Alan on 8th May 1910, and Denis on 30th July 1913. They would have been devastated at six and three respectively when they lost the first of their big brothers, but were doubtless some consolation to their grieving parents.

Their father was a prominent local businessman, and ran the town's Cement Works in South Street, Cliffe, on the way out to Beddingham. He was proprietor of the Lewes & Portland Cement and Lime Co., Ltd., as it was then called. They were cement manufacturers, and white and grey stone lime-burners, and would have been one of the larger local employers of the time. Cllr. Mr. E. A. Glover obviously had sufficient staff under him to be able to spend much of his time helping to run civic affairs, and sat as a member of several different Committees of Lewes Town Council over the years. Once the War started in 1914, he was frequently to be found chairing the various Tribunals that sat locally to hear appeals from those challenging their call-up papers, either as Conscientious Objectors, or for family or family business reasons.

Brian Glover's youth and army career

When he left Thanet College around 1912, Brian Glover continued with both his sporting interests and his plans to become a Civil Engineer. He was a "very popular young man", according to the *County Herald* of the time, and was playing hockey for the Sussex County team. On leaving school, he became articled to Mr F. J. Wood, the County Surveyor at County Hall, Lewes. When war broke out in August 1914, he had just heard the successful results of his Studentship exams. for the Institute of Civil Engineers.

It was thus something of a natural progression for him to move into the Royal Engineers, once his initial Army training was completed with the 5th Royal Sussex Regiment. He and his older brother Eric had joined up together in the first week of the war, and had gone to Dover Castle together with the other 5th Royal Sussex volunteers from Lewes for training. Eric then transferred into the Royal Fusiliers, and later the Machine Gun Corps., and Brian then joined the Royal Engineers. He trained with the 47th Signalling Division, and eventually embarked for France as a Motor Cycle Dispatch Rider with them.

No sooner had Brian been promoted Corporal early in 1915, than he had to be sent home for five weeks' convalescence following an injury. He continued as Dispatch Rider on his return to the Front, and was kept very busy through the autumn in relaying information between the Allies in the run-up to the disastrous Battle of Loos in north-western France.

His medals and further promotion

On Saturday November 20th 1915, the Lewes edition of the *Sussex County Herald* carried a brief announcement about a medal award to Corporal Glover, under the following heading:-

> *"Honours for Lewes Dispatch Rider: DCM and MM*
>
> *For conspicuous gallantry from Sept. 21st to October 1st, during the operations between Le Brebis and Loos , when he was constantly employed in carrying dispatches and operation orders over roads under heavy shell-fire, and never failed to deliver his messages… Cpl. B. E. Glover, of 'Brookside', Southover High St., has been awarded both the Distinguished Conduct Medal, and the French 'Medaille Militaire'."*

Photo of Corporal B.E.Glover, awarded DCM, ESN 19th Nov. 1915

A later posthumous report gave further details of this French battle honour

> *"The proud tribute of the French to this plucky young officer was the awarding of the coveted Medaille Militaire, for volunteering to take a verbal message to Gen. Castlenau, over roads constantly shelled by heavy artillery. By the getting of this message through, the French General was able to withdraw two battalions of infantry from a wood which the Germans had almost surrounded."*

In February 1916, a further brief news item in the local paper reported that on January 30th he had received his Commission:

> *"Cpl. (M / Cyclist) B. E. Glover of Lewes has been gazetted Second Lieutenant on probation, in the General List and attached to the Royal Flying Corps."*

His professional and technical interests in signals and dispatches were now extended into the new fields of aerial reconnaissance, and the earliest ventures into aerial combat. He was attached to the 8th Squadron Royal Air Flying Corps, and was based on the French/Belgian borders in the northernmost parts of the Western Front in Picardy.

Second-Lieutenant Glover's death in air combat

By the middle of March 1916, news had reached Brian Glover's parents in Lewes that he was reported missing in action. His mother would then have had much in common with Mrs Holland round the corner at St Pancras Villas, who had still heard nothing of her only son, R.J.E. Holland (see no.7), missing since the Battle of Loos in late September 1915. For both these grieving mothers, there was to be no official War Office confirmation of their sons' deaths until June 1916.

For the Glovers, it came early in the month, and confirmed that Brian had been killed on 13th March 1916, in an air engagement over Vis-en-Artois. He had been returning from a reconnaissance flight over enemy lines, as an observer in a plane (B2 'C' 4197) piloted by a Lt. Grune of Southwick, near Shoreham. According to the article in the *Sussex County Herald* on Saturday June 10th 1916,

> "… the machine was the target for a fusillade of German anti-aircraft shellfire at an altitude of 7,000 feet. Both the intrepid airmen were killed, and they fell with their machine into the German trenches…"

This article was under the heading:

"The Great Sacrifice:
Lewes Airman-Hero's End.
How Second-Lieutenant B. E. Glover Died"

and it continued, after giving much of the detail quoted above, as follows

> "When the war drum rolled… the patriotic spirit was strong within him…",

reiterating that it was on the very first day of the war that he and his older brother had first enlisted with the 5th Battalion, the Royal Sussex Regiment. It then added:

> "In the midst of their great sorrow, Mr & Mrs Glover have been cheered by the many messages of sympathy from a host of friends, and by the proud knowledge that their son died bravely, meeting his death fearlessly as a gallant soldier and gentleman should, not counting the cost in the moment of the Great Sacrifice".

The previous week, the *East Sussex News* had carried the family's announcement in its 'Deaths on Active Service' column. In the next week's issue, Mr & Mrs Glover put the following announcement in the much-used 'Return Thanks' column

> "Cllr. & Mrs A E Glover desire to express their sincere thanks for the many kind enquiries and expressions of sympathy with them on the loss of their second son."

Public recognition and condolences in Lewes

Several local dignitaries also gave more official voice to the town's shock and distress, at meetings of various public committees in Lewes that first week of June. The Lewes Tribunal, on which Cllr. A. E. Glover regularly sat, was chaired by Cllr. T. J. Farncombe that week, and he made a formal expression of sympathy to Mr & Mrs Glover on behalf of himself and all members. Following this,

> "Captain Selby Ash, on behalf of the military representatives, feelingly associated himself with the expression. Speaking with emotion, Cllr. Glover then thanked the members for their expression of sympathy. He had, he said, lost one of the best boys who ever breathed, but while he and his family felt it very deeply, they thought of other parents who, perhaps, were suffering more than they were, and he felt proud that he had been able to give a son to serve his country for eighteen months."

Lewes Town Council held its next meeting a few days later, with Cllr. Glover representing Priory Ward as usual, at which:-

> "…touching reference was also made by the Mayor, who proposed that in the name of

the Council, a letter of sympathy and condolence should be sent to Mr & Mrs Glover."

Second-Lieutenant Glover's Burial

It is likely that Brian Glover's body was for some years laid to rest in one of the many little local cemeteries, or possibly even initially a German military cemetery, given the circumstances of his death. After the Armistice in 1918, when the Commonwealth War Graves Commission began its long task of identifying, recording, grouping together, and honouring the Commonwealth war dead across all the battlefields, it absorbed into its own Cemeteries the military graves from the many small local cemeteries in each area. As part of that process, the Cemetery where Second-Lieutenant Glover now lies, was created.

B.E. Glover's grave in Cemetery.

It is known as the Vis-en-Artois British Cemetery, Haucourt, in the Pas-de-Calais. It is situated on the north side of the straight main road between Arras and Cambrai, about seven miles south-east of Arras. It now contains 2,335 War Graves, of which 1,736 are of U.K. soldiers and airmen. The majority of the remainder are Canadians, who liberated the area in August and September 1918, and a large proportion of them all are un-named. The cemetery is surrounded by a low wall on a gentle slope rising from the Sensee valley, and has been planted with poplars, yews, and other trees and shrubs. Brian Glover is buried in Plot XI, Row A, Grave 2.

Vis-en-Artois Cemetery, Picardy.

ROBIN STEADMAN

> **Alfred HARDING**   1.10
> **10th May 1916 aged 20**
> **near Messines, West Flanders**
> **G3180 Private**
> **9th Battalion, Royal Sussex Regiment**
>
> HOME   ? Southover, ?East Grinstead
> BURIED   Ration Farm (La Plus Douve Annexe) Cemetery
>   near Ploegsteert

The Harding family: Seaford to East Grinstead, via Lewes

Alfred Harding was the eldest of three brothers, who all enlisted in East Grinstead in the first few days of the war. He himself started out with the 3rd Battalion of the Royal Sussex Regiment, but was then transferred to the 9th. The next brother down, Albert, stayed with the 3rd Battalion; and the youngest, Edgar, became a Gunner with the Royal Field Artillery. It seems that the younger two survived the war, and only Alfred did not. They all seem to have been well known in Southover, but it is not clear when or where they lived there.

The family seems to have come from Seaford, where Alfred was born in 1895. It is likely that they then moved into Lewes, or that Alfred's work took him there, but it has not been possible to trace any Lewes address for them. Their parents were Alfred and Louisa C. Harding, and although the address given for them as next of kin on Alfred's War Graves Commission papers after the war was: 2 Warren Cottages, Tadworth, Surrey, it seems likely they only moved there via Southover then East Grinstead. His brother Albert must also have had some Lewes connections, as the *East Sussex News* for 4th December 1914 (when the war was barely four months old and everyone still thought it would be over by Christmas), printed some paragraphs of a letter from his brother Albert written from France, to family or friends in Lewes, as follows

"Lewesians Meet at the Front"

"I am getting on all right. We are having some fine sport out here… but we get in some tight corners sometimes. I should like to have the job of sticking Kaiser Bill. I don't think myself this war will last much longer, as we keep making big captures, but when they get the range of us with their 'coal box' guns, they roast us a bit… We are having a lot of goods sent from Sussex, and the boys thank the people very much for them… Tell them at home it is better sport than being at a rough football match in Lewes. I must tell you that I met W. Escott* out here, and he is looking well. He was quite pleased to see me. We have had it very cold out here, snow and rain, but it is warmer now."

* (H. Escott was a horse trainer who lived in Spital Road opposite The Gallops during the War, and this lad was probably his son.)

Alfred Harding's war: Loos to 'Plugstreet Wood' and Messines

Once he had transferred to the 9th Battalion, Alfred was in the same Battalion as R. J. E. Holland from Southover (see 1.07), who was killed at the Battle of Loos. It is therefore quite likely that Alfred too saw action in the mud and gas at Loos in late September 1915. In the winter months following that disaster, the Regiment would have been re-grouping, and moving with the Front directly to the south of Ypres, the south-western part of the 'Ypres Salient'. It was at that time, and throughout 1916, that tunnelling under the low hills of the Messines Ridge began. Much use was made of tunnelling and mining, and several major operations right through 1917 were launched by the simultaneous detonating of enormous amounts of explosives deep underneath many key enemy strong-points.

In the weeks just before Private Harding's death in the spring of 1916, when he may well have been involved in some of this mining activity, some of the first big British mines had been blown. These were notably around St. Eloi and in the Warneton-Messines-Wytschaete area, and continuing on down through Hill 60 to Ploegsteert and its famous 'Plugstreet Wood'. The craters thus caused were fought over and over, not always leading to the battle successes hoped for. Many of them are still visible today and are used as fishing lakes, but some have been built over.

Apart from the prolonged mine warfare in this area, and the eventual triumph of the New Zealanders and the Ulstermen on Messines Ridge in June 1917, each with their beautiful Memorial Parks remaining in honour of the tunnelling and the surface assaults, there was another major claim to 'fame' of this area. This was the presence through 1914/1915 of a young German Infantryman by the name of Adolf Hitler, who was allocated a billet at that time in the crypt of Messines Church.

Private Harding's death and burial

Alfred Harding was 20 when he was killed on 10th May 1916. The corner of West Flanders in which he last saw action, was, as already described, fought both over and under for over two more years. It is therefore inevitable that his first burial place was not where his grave now is, unlike Trooper Turk who was buried from the outset in Neuve Eglise Churchyard just a few miles down the road (see 1.01).

Private Harding's grave is now in a spot of utmost pastoral tranquillity, with brown and white Flanders cows grazing peacefully just over the cemetery wall, and for miles around. The countryside around is more undulating and leafy than much of the 'Ypres Salient', and the spire of Wulverghem Church is just a mile or so away down the valley. It is very much in Franco-Belgian border country, with Ypres just 13 kilometres to the north in Belgium, and Armentieres 10 kms. to the south in France.

Alfred Harding's grave in Ration Farm Cemetery
(La Plus Douve Annexe), West Flanders.

Ration Farm Cemetery
with Wulverghem Church in distance.

He and a dozen or more Royal Sussex men, who all died around the same time, are laid side by side in the Ration Farm (La Plus Douve) Annexe to the La Plus Douve Farm Cemetery near Ploegsteert. The main cemetery and its Annexe are within a stone's throw of each other, down a farm track in the valley of the river Douve, between Ploegsteert and Wulverghem. The two sets of farm buildings, La Plus Douve and La Petite Douve, were razed

to the ground between 1914 and 1918, but have now been impressively reconstructed. La Petite Douve Farm was the object of a celebrated raid by the 7th Canadian Infantry Battalion in November 1915. La Plus Douve Farm (also known to the troops as 'Ration Farm' because Battalion transport could approach it at night with rations), was generally within the British lines, and was used at times as a Battalion Headquarters.

Cross of Sacrifice at Ration Farm Cemetery

The Annexe has only 202 war graves in it, nearly all of them U.K. men; while the main Cemetery has 336 war graves, of which over two-thirds are Canadian, Australian and New Zealanders.

The grave reference for Private Harding in the Annexe is Plot II, Row A, Grave 7. Below the official Regimental inscription on his headstone, are the words aptly chosen by his family

"Peace Perfect Peace".

Ration Farm now rebuilt, was rations supply dump.

Frank BEAGLEY   1.11
30th June 1916 aged 30
at Richebourg/"Double Crassier"
SD2058 Private
12th Battalion, Royal Sussex Regiment

HOME   36 Grange Road, Southover
COMMEMORATED   Loos Memorial, Near Bethune

Family background

Frank Beagley was born and brought up at 34 Western Road, Lewes, nearly opposite the Black Horse Inn. When he was born in 1887, he already had two older brothers (George who was seven, and Herbert who was five), and two older sisters (Jessie who was three, and Eleanor who was two). Two younger brothers were then born in quick succession, Henry in 1888 and Percy in 1889.

That was the family at the time of the Census in April 1891. Their parents were George Beagley, a Solicitor's Clerk, and his wife Annie (nee Darvill). Their father George was 34 at the time, and had come from New Alresford, Hampshire, originally. Their mother Annie was a year younger, and she was a farmer's daughter who had come from Tring, Bucking-hamshire, originally.

Frank Beagley's birthplace in 1887
and his childhood home: 34 Western Road.

The Tunks connection

Frank's father died young, sometime during Frank's childhood or youth. By the time Frank was 20 in 1907, his mother had fortunately met a widower willing to marry her and take on the remaining children. She had by then moved from Western Road to 22 St. Anne's Crescent, Lewes.

On 13th July 1907, as a widow of 47, she re-married at Southover Church. Her new husband was 56, and a commercial traveller by the name of Joseph Tunks. He was living at 36 Grange Road, which then became Frank Beagley's wartime address, and Joseph his stepfather. By the

51

time the war started, Joseph had retired and was becoming a local figure of some importance; he was Assistant Secretary to the Lewes Victoria Hospital and Dispensary, and Assistant Overseer & Collector of Poor Rates for Lewes and for the parish of South Malling Without.

(Frank had acquired at least one step-brother, William V. Tunks, by his mother's re-marriage. This William had been to Castlegate School, Lewes, and had become involved with Army Chaplains helping to run summer camps at Eastbourne and Portsmouth. He then went off to the war as did Frank at the outbreak of war, but was soon discharged as medically unfit. He, William, then began working towards the ordained ministry, and from October 1916 was a Lay Reader in Eastbourne. A year later, just before Christmas 1917, he was ordained Deacon at Lichfield Cathedral, to serve his first curacy in the parish of Dresden, Staffordshire).

Frank Beagley's war

Frank himself was 27 by the time the war broke out, but nothing is known of his life then. It seems he was still single, as his mother remained his next-of-kin. He enlisted in the Royal Sussex Regiment and served with the 12th Battalion. On 30th June 1916 he was reported missing in action at Richebourg. This was the same day as two Ringmer men were killed in the same area, at the 'Battle of Double Crassier', among the colliery villages and mining heaps around Lens. It was also the last day of the build-up to the start of the Somme offensive, a little further to the south.

Frank's body was never found, and his grieving mother had no further news of him for nearly a year. Like Mrs. Glover, Mrs. Holland, and Mrs Hillman, she had many agonising months to wait in suspense; and when she did hear from the War Office in May 1917, it was only to notify her officially that he was now classified as "Missing, Presumed Dead".

He is commemorated with three other Southover men on the Loos Memorial, Panels 69 - 73. By the end of the war, or at least by the time both the Southover and the Loos Memorials were unveiled in 1921, his bereaved mother had left Lewes and moved to South London. For several years she put "In Memoriam" notices in the local Lewes papers in memory of her son Frank, from her new address, 58 Kay Road, Stockwell.

36 Grange Road
Frank Beagley's home after his mother's re-marriage in 1907

Benjamin Hilton GLOVER   1.12
1st July 1916 aged 19
Maricourt, Somme
Captain
7th Battalion Royal West Kent Regiment
(attached 50th Trench Mortar Battery)

HOME   "Brookside", Southover High Street
BURIED Dantzig Alley British Cemetery, Mametz, Somme

Second son killed within four months

Ben Glover was the youngest of the three soldier sons of Cllr. and Mrs E A Glover of 'Brookside', Southover High Street (for home and family details see 1.9, B. E. Glover). He was killed on the first day of the Battle of the Somme, perhaps the most appallingly evocative day in the whole history of the British Army. The day he died was in fact less than a month after his sorrowing parents had heard War Office confirmation of the death of his next eldest brother, Brian, over three months earlier back in mid-March 1916.

Ben Glover's own death was then reported in the columns of the local papers in mid-July 1916, somewhat surprisingly within only a fortnight of the event, despite the massive numbers of casualties suffered that first day alone. By contrast, it was in the very same issue that there was reported the much-delayed official confirmation of the death of Reginald John Holland, 1.6, at Loos, a full six months earlier still.

School, work and early days in the Territorials

Like both his older brothers before him, Ben Glover had been educated at Thanet College, Margate. On leaving school at 15, he became an Articled Pupil to Mr. D. Cronin at the Southdown and East Grinstead (Ballards) Brewery, Lewes. This was situated between St Pancras Gardens and the Swan Inn, (where Boehringers now is), a stone's throw from his home.

Early days at the Front

Then at just turned 16, he joined the 1st/5th Bn., Royal Sussex Regiment, as a Territorial. He was with several other Southover recruits in training at Dover Castle during 1914. He was among those in billets, presumably without easy access to canteen facilities, who were each paid the princely sum of two shillings

Lt. B. H. Glover

53

(10p.) a day in lieu of rations. He would have arrived in France with them in February, in billets in the Bethune area, awaiting deployment for the big offensives at Neuve Chapelle and Aubers Ridge. He in fact escaped that latter disaster all together, as he was off sick with measles from 4th to 24th May 1915. Back in February 1915, the *Sussex Express* printed a letter it had received from Private Horton, one of its pre-war journalists; Ben Hilton and his treasure-hunting in abandoned German trenches had quite a mention, as the following extract shows:-

> The actual trenches we were in were made by the Germans, and held by them till they were driven out. Our fellows were very soon on the track of interesting German souvenirs. Several found German rifles, while German bayonets and Mauser ammunition were quite common finds. More interesting souvenirs were German caps, a pipe, bandoliers and a couple of gorgeous German helmets. At least one German soldier (if he is alive) is mourning the loss of a treasured possession, for one of Private Ben Glover's finds was nearly a foot of German sausage! Between our trenches and the Germans were far more serious relics in the shape of dozens of dead bodies, the majority of them German. Of course, it is impossible to get to them, so there they lay—victims of the greed and avarice of their devilish Emperor. How much richer would the world be were he among those silent figures.

Extract from letter to ESN referring to Ben Glover:
from Pte. Horton, 19th Feb. 1915.

Commission in the West Kents

On Christmas Day 1915, at the age of 18 years and six months, he obtained a Commission in the Royal West Kent Regiment, and was gazetted Second Lieutenant in their 7th Battalion. A month later, in January 1916, he was transferred within that Battalion to the 50th Trench Mortar Battery, a Battery which had the "latest pattern" Trench Mortars. By March 1916, he was promoted full Lieutenant and given command of the Battery. He was involved in particularly heavy fighting early in June, by the end of which engagement he was the only officer remaining out of five in his battery. June 13th 1916 was his nineteenth birthday, and he wrote to his parents that he had celebrated it actually in the trenches. This was at the height of the build-up to the 'Great Push' to be launched on the Somme.

The first day of the Battle of the Somme

Ben Glover's 7th Battalion West Kents were 'holding the line' in the far south east of the British sector in the last few days of June. They were positioned between Mametz in the far south-west of the British sector, and Maricourt in the north-east of the French sector. Shortly after dawn on the long-awaited 1st July, the time had come to attack rather than defend. As part of 18th Division, their task was to take the low ridge that runs from Montauban two or three miles westwards to Mametz, and their neighbouring 30th Division was to take the village of Montauban itself.

By dawn, there had again been some two or three hours of heavy artillery bombardment which, as at Aubers Ridge and many other battles, served as little more than a useful 'advance warning' to the enemy. Its intention, of course, was to cut the German wire and destroy their preliminary defences, before the command to charge. Tragically, intelligence and reconnaissance had failed to comprehend the enormity of the German underground defences and troops' accommodation and supply lines.

A survivor from that day in the 7th West Kents, Frank Bastable, takes up the story (as quoted in Leslie Coates': "The Somme 1914 - 18" p.28):

> *"It was a misty morning, but this soon cleared when the sun came right up - lovely day it was later on. Yes, we felt tense, but this is what we'd waited for - for a year now. To know we were at last 'going over the top' was a sort of relief. In a way we were frightened and excited at the same time. That last barrage was terrible – just before zero, I'd never heard a noise like it.*
>
> *Montauban our objective was, you could see it on the ridge, We had a drop of rum – Dutch courage, I suppose.*
>
> *Well, they really had us pinned down at first, you couldn't stand up, you had to crawl. You could hear the rattle of the machine guns. Our Sergeant- Major, Button his name was, he stood up – I remember because I was right next to him – and put his stick up for us to follow, but he didn't stand a chance. He got killed almost straight away; he should have got a medal, that bloke.*
>
> *Anyway, we got forward by crawling – we were surprised to find that the Germans had gone when we got to their trenches. We got on better after that. I remember it being hot, lying there and getting really thirsty. Well, we got through in the end and took our objective – I don't think many did that day, we were one of the few. I was lucky really."*

With every succeeding wave of gallant British, Commonwealth and French soldiery that went 'over the top' that morning, there was another wave of freshly supplied and rested German machine -gunners waiting to mow them down. Total losses on that day alone were so colossal that details needed to be released in small doses only, and over many months. There were 21,000 British dead alone at the end of that first day. There were no Allied gains anywhere else along the whole Front apart from Captain Glover's Montauban and Mametz. The rest of the First Battle of the Somme was waged on for three and a half months, at the end of which there were over a million dead, and three times as many wounded and taken prisoner.

Captain Ben Glover's death

Captain Glover was the only man named on the Southover memorial to be killed actually in the horrors of that first day. It was just two weeks after his 19th birthday, and he had just been promoted Captain. He was killed early on enough in the war, and was from a well-known enough family, for the local paper to wax fairly eloquent in describing it. The *Sussex County Herald* for 15th July 1916 reported his death thus (his latest promotion to Captain had not yet been Gazetted, so he is still referred to as Lieut.):-

> *"The hand of sorrow has fallen heavily on Mr & Mrs E. A. Glover, of 'Brookside', Southover, Lewes. Five weeks ago, it was our reluctant task to tell the sad but splendid story of how their son, Lt. B. E. Glover, DCM., of the RFC, gallantly went to his death. And now with a sense of personal sorrow, we have to announce that their third son, Lt. B. H. Glover, who was serving in a Trench Mortar Battery, was killed near Maricourt on July 1st…*

He was but a lad as years go, but he had the heart and spirit of a man, the stuff that heroes are made of. In the desolation of their grief, his parents will find solace in the knowledge that he went to his death bravely, as his brother did before him...

Feeling reference was made to the death of the gallant young Lieutenant at Tuesday's sitting of the Lewes Tribunal, when Mr F B Whitfield expressed the deep sympathy of the members. Mr Glover acknowledged the kindly expression on behalf of Mrs Glover and himself, saying it was some satisfaction to the family in their bereavement to know that his son had been able to spend nearly two years of his short life on active service for his King and country."

It must also have been "some satisfaction" to the sorrowing family that their one remaining soldier son, Eric, was able to be home with them for a while. In August 1916, the *Sussex County Herald* reported that he was

"...home on leave, looking very fit, before being attached to a training company in the north of England."

Eric had started the war with the 11th (Empire Bn.) of the Royal Fusiliers, but was then transferred to the Machine Gun Corps. as an NCO. Training soldiers in the north of England was presumably a somewhat safer and more congenial role for a man who had already lost his two brothers, and preferable any day to the trenches of the Somme.

Burial at Dantzig Alley British Cemetery

This cemetery where Ben Glover was eventually buried is at Mametz, eight kilometres east of Albert, and a mile or two north of the river Somme itself at Suzanne. It lies on the north side of the road from Mametz to Montauban, the very ridge which Captain Glover's 7th West Kents fought for and won the day he died. The name "Dantzig Alley" refers to a German trench just to the east of Mametz, where there was particularly heavy fighting on that day. Ben Glover's grave is in Plot VIII, Row T, no.3.

After the Armistice, this cemetery was greatly enlarged to contain its present complement of nearly 2000 British and Commonwealth soldiers and airmen. Most of them, including Captain Glover, were originally buried in smaller battlefield cemeteries used by Field Ambulances and fighting units, in that far south-eastern corner of the British sector, particularly in those early days of the Somme campaign. Much of that same ground was again fought over in the last German offensive in the spring of 1918, and some of the original graves were then destroyed by shell-fire. There are to this day a dozen or more War Cemeteries in as many kilometres between Albert and Maricourt.

George FELLOWS   1.13
13th July 1916 aged 40
died of wounds after Somme
14991 Private
2nd/3rd Battalion, Royal Sussex Regiment

HOME   15 Eastport Lane, Southover
BURIED   Southover Churchyard

Family from Hastings

George Fellows came from an old Sussex family in the far east of the county. His parents were Jesse and Eliza Fellows from Fairlight and Brede. He was born on 14th October 1875, the youngest but one of five brothers and three sisters, all born between 1861 and 1878. (family tree available)

George's wife, Hephzibah Elizabeth nee Collins, came from Warbleton and Cackle Street near Hastings. (Hephzibah's maternal grandfather Bridger is still remembered by George's youngest daughter Marjorie for the dahlias he grew in his garden at Ore; and grandmother Bridger is remembered for the ironing she took in, by pony and cart from the laundry in Hastings, to the upstairs ironing room where they had the stove surrounded by flatirons.)

Like his parents before them, George and Hephzibah also had eight children, and again three girls and five boys, who were all born over there in Ore between 1895 and 1913. They did have a fourth girl, but she died in infancy. (It is the youngest of the girls, Marjorie, who has been one of my main sources of information. She was born in 1905, and lives on in Landport in her nineties. Also, the son and daughter of Marjorie's younger brother Thomas, who was born in 1907, have also provided photographs and much background information. Thomas Fellows' son Peter has newly retired to Seaford, and fortunately saw my request in the *Sussex Express* for information on the Southover men in 1995; he put me in touch with his sister Jacque who lives in Norfolk and has amassed a great deal of family tree details. I am much indebted to them all.)

Army in India to construction work in Lewes

George was a carpenter by trade, but had for some eight years served as a regular soldier with the Royal Sussex Regiment, including a tour of duty in India from about 1900-1904. He then came out of the Army (but stayed in the Reserve), in search of more lucrative local work having a large family to support. He found building and construction work in Lewes, and for the last year or so before the war was involved in the laying of sewers along Friars Walk.

Family in Eastport Lane from January 1914

In January 1914 he brought his wife and family from Hastings to Lewes to be with him. They lived at 15 Eastport Lane, at least for the duration of the War. The house was reached by an alleyway beside The Bell Inn, between it and Mr. Urry's coal-yard. Where that yard was, there is now the yard behind the block of flats on Priory Street that the council built between the wars; 'The Bell' was then turned into a private house.

George and Hephzibah's three eldest children (Charlotte Alice born 1893, Hephzibah Elizabeth born 1895, and George Frank born 1899) had all finished their Elementary Schools in Hastings and were away 'in service'. The next one, Marjorie, was nine but had already had five years education in Hastings (where children could start school at 3) so was too advanced to join Southover School, yet still too young to start her secondary education at Central School. So for a year she was attached to Southover School as a classroom assistant, helping the little ones with counting their beads etc., as well as continuing her own lessons, till she could move on to the Central School. She can clearly remember Mrs Stewart-Jones from Southover Grange (mother of Capt. T. A. Stewart-Jones, 1.4 above) coming in to Southover School, where she was also a Governor, to play the piano for assemblies, and to help the older children prepare for their Grade exams.. The next three Fellows boys (Thomas born 1907, William born 1909, and Frederick born 1911) were at Southover School until they were 10, then Tom at least went to the Pells Junior School. That just left the baby, Albert, at home with mother.

Rejoining the Colours at the outbreak of war

As soon as war broke out in August 1914, George re-joined the colours from the Reserve, and was then sent to the Front in the summer of 1915. His own brothers, Harry and Edgar, were also serving with the Royal Sussex Regiment. The two of them came through the war unscathed and lived on for many years, in Chichester and Hastings respectively. George however was not to be so fortunate.

On Outpost Duty" George Fellows is 3rd from left (no gaiters), 1st Nov. 1914/?1915.

In May 1916 he was summoned home urgently when his youngest son, Albert, became critically ill with meningitis. This had developed following a fall on to his head, from his high chair on the stone-flagged floor of their kitchen. George was given some days compassionate leave from the Front, but was not able to reach Lewes in time. He arrived home on June 1st to find the child had already died on May 14th, just two days after his third birthday, and had been buried in Southover Churchyard. George then had eight days' leave with the sorrowing family, before returning to the Front for the last three weeks of his war. He little knew that was to be the last time he would see them, or that within two short months he too would be buried in the very same grave as his young Albert.

Battle of the Somme: build-up and aftermath

Throughout June 1916, the Royal Sussex, along with countless other Regiments, was heavily involved in the preparations for the 'Big Push' on the Somme. It was on that fateful first day, 1st July, which saw the slaughter of so many tens of thousands of men, and also took the life of George's fellow-Southoverian, Benjamin Glover (see 1.12), that George Fellows was himself mortally wounded.

After emergency treatment at a Casualty Clearing Station, he was transported back behind the lines towards the Channel ports, as it became clear he would need major surgery if he was to survive. He may have been one of the lucky ones, and been transported smoothly by hospital barge down the Somme to the Seine and the sea, or he may have had to endure the further hardship of a very rough ride in horse-drawn or early motorised 'ambulance'.

Military hospital in London

George's wife in Lewes was informed by military telegraph of her husband's critical injuries and his imminent embarkation in a hospital ship bound for Newhaven, on 4th July. Wartime travel restrictions meant she had to obtain a special 'passport', in order to be allowed to travel, whether to Newhaven or to the destination Military Hospital in London. There would then only have been time for the most fleeting of contacts, either on the quayside before the wounded men were despatched by hospital trains to the various military hospitals allocated to them, or at the bedside once they got there.

George's train took him to the City of London Military Hospital at Clapton, N.E. Once he had been seen by the doctors there, it was found necessary to amputate both his left hand and his left leg. Sadly he was not to survive that massive trauma, on top of the injuries themselves, not to mention the rigours of ambulance transport across both France and the Channel, and he died there in the Military Hospital in north-east London on Friday 13th July. The hospital released his body to the family immediately, and it was brought by train to Lewes Station on Monday 16th July.

Military Funeral at Southover

This was a very special occasion for Lewes, as its very first wartime funeral with full military honours, and it was in fact the only such funeral to be held at Southover. From the photographs the family have provided, it can be seen that the coffin was draped in the Union Jack and Regimental insignia, and mounted in a horse-drawn

Last stage in journey home from the Somme. Pte. Fellows' funeral at Southover, 16th July 1916: Military procession passes "King's Head" in Southover High Street.

Hearse in procession from Lewes Station to Southover church.

glass sided hearse. Comrades from the Royal Sussex Regiment marched in close formation with reversed arms surrounding the hearse on its short but sombre march from station to church.

The *East Sussex News* on Friday 21st July carried the following account:-

"…the service was conducted by the curate, the Revd. A. S. Dendy. The family mourners were Mrs Fellows (widow), the Misses Alice and Hephzibah Fellows (daughters), Mrs Fellows (mother, Hastings), Pte. Harry Fellows, Royal Sussex Regt. (brother); Mrs Leeson, Mrs Marchant, Mrs Morley of Hastings (sisters), Mrs H. Fellows of Chichester (sister-in-law), Miss Lizzie Leeson (niece).

A detachment of the 3rd Bn. Royal Sussex Regiment attended under Lt. J. J. Burdett with the firing party, and also Regimental Band under Bandmaster Patrick. Lt.-Col. W. H. Dewe of the Royal Defence Corps, and Captain and Adjutant H. Andrews of the 2nd Battalion Sussex Yeomanry also attended, together with a number of NCOs and men of 8 Protection Coy. Royal Defence Corps.

Burial in Southover Churchyard
Rev.A.S.Dendy, curate, officiating

Amongst those at the graveside was Sgt. H. Bunce, Sussex R.G.A., who is home on special leave from the Front.

The coffin was covered with the Union Jack and was borne to the grave by men of the 3rd Royal Sussex. At the close of the service, three volleys were fired and two buglers sounded the Last Post. There were several floral tributes, which bore the following inscriptions:-

"With Love to my Darling Husband, from his Loving Wife and Family"
"To my Darling Father from his Loving Daughter Alice"

"To my Darling Father from his Loving Daughter Dolly"
"In Loving Memory from Mother, Liz and Pat (sister & brother-in-law)"
"In Ever Loving Memory of my Dear Brother. Eliza."
"To a Brave Hero from Mr & Mrs Todd and Daughter"

Marjorie (nee Fellows), George's youngest daughter, who has filled in so much of the above detail for me, remembers being considered too young to attend her father's funeral. She was called home from school to look after her young cousins instead, while the aunts and uncles went to the service. She also remembers hearing that her father's coffin was buried in the same grave as that of her young brother Albert, laid there in Southover Churchyard just two months earlier. She remembers the Todd family who gave one of the 'floral tributes'; they were their neighbours in Eastport Lane, and Mr. Todd was the landlord of the Bell Inn.

It seems that none of George's remaining sons were present at the funeral, presumably either away from Lewes by then serving abroad, or also thought too young to attend. But when his son Thomas, (who would have been just nine at the time), died some seventy years later, that newspaper cutting above was found folded in his wallet.

War widow dies three years after George

When Private Fellows died, his eldest son George Frank who was then 21, moved back with them all, having been brought up by grandparents. George's widow, Hephzibah, having already lost both husband and toddler during the War, was then herself found to have cancer. She died in July 1919 and, unlike husband and toddler son, was buried in Lewes Cemetery. The remaining family had moved across Lewes with their mother to 8 Edward Street, and thus from Southover into St John's sub Castro parish, and George Frank then took over the tenancy.

Orphaned children in post-war dispersal

The remaining children were thus all orphaned, and doubtless relied heavily on George Frank as they grew up. In the autumn following their mother's death, it was realised that the three youngest boys (Thomas 12, William 10, and Frederick 8) had never been baptised. They were therefore all baptised together at St John's sub Castro on 11 October 1919, together with Marjorie, then 14 (although it was later discovered that she had in fact been baptised in infancy at Ore on 1 February 1906).

Big decisions then had to be made about the care of the children. It was decided that the three young boys should be taken into the care of Dr. Barnardo's Homes in Stepney.

Marjorie remembers her older brother George being

c.1922: his three youngest sons with Dr. Barnado's at Watts Naval Training School, Norfolk. L to R: William James (10 in 1919), Frederick (8 in 1919), Thomas (12 in 1919).

appointed her guardian, and staying on at Edward Street with him while going into service locally to begin with. She was unhappy with her very strict local employers, so moved into service at Leytonstone, not very far from her young brothers. The three boys were soon moved on by Barnardo's from Stepney to the Dr. Watt's Naval Training School at North Elmham, near Dereham, Norfolk; it was while there that the photograph of them in sailor suits was taken. Marjorie was back in Lewes by the early thirties, raising her two children from her first marriage to Charles Richardson. During World War Two she was widowed and went to work at the Lewes Iron Foundry (see photograph in "Between the Wars" section). At the end of the war she re-married; her new husband was Alfred Attfield, a widower whose two children she then raised. She and Alfred still live in Lewes, in their nineties and in pretty good health, and celebrated their Golden Wedding early in 1996.

Thomas was the first of George's boys to be moved on again; he became part of the Barnardo's assisted emigration scheme for youngsters leaving care. He was sent to Canada and worked on farms in Saskatchewan and Alberta for some years.

Charlotte Alice was George's older sister and she too was to emigrate to Canada. She had got married in Lewes to Walter Gartley at the end of the First War. The last of her three children was born in 1921 in Vancouver, and she herself lived on out there till her death in 1982.

William and Frederick were the two youngest of George and Hephzibah Fellow's children. They both joined up with the Royal Navy from the Naval Training School in Norfolk. William finally retired back to Norfolk, having attained the rank of Lieutenant Commander, and lives near his daughter Audrey outside Norwich, and in the same county as his brother Thomas's daughter Jacque as above. Frederick remained a bachelor, and sadly was to lose his life during the Second World War, when his ship HMS Bleen was torpedoed off the coast of Algeria on 17 December 1942.

The Moore connection

Thomas, meanwhile, had returned to the 'old country', and in 1929 he joined the RAF. He served there for a total of 24 years, reaching the rank of Warrant Officer. In 1937 he married a Southover girl, Irene Rose Moore, who had grown up at 20 Eastport Lane, across the coal-yard from the Fellows family. (Her cousins Jesse and George Walter Moore are also named on the Southover War Memorial; Jesse was killed at Loos in 1915, see 1.08 in this book, and George Walter at Ypres in 1918, see 1.34.) Thomas, like his mother before him, was to lose his life to cancer, but lived on in Lewes till a year before he would have celebrated his Golden Wedding in 1987. There had been a big family celebration for their Ruby Wedding in 1977, before he died in Victoria Hospital. His widow Irene then moved up to Norfolk to be near her daughter Jacque, my other main source of information, and lives on in a residential home up there.

George Fellows' grave in Southover Churchyard today.

William Thomas MARTIN   1.14
27th August 1916 aged 19
at Rouen, died of wounds
G/1685 Private
2nd Battalion Royal Sussex Regiment, from the Somme

HOME   53 Potters Lane, Southover
BURIED   St Sever Cemetery, Le Petit Quevilly, Rouen

William and his younger brother Frank were another pair of Southover brothers who both lost their lives in the Great War. They both died in hospital, from some combination of wounds and disease.

William was the third Southover man to fall at the Somme, but survived long enough to be transported only to base hospital behind the lines at Rouen, not to be shipped back across the Channel.

His family background

He was born in 1897, the elder of two sons born to Thomas and Ruth Martin of the Cliffe. William was only three when his mother died, possibly in giving birth to his younger brother. By the time he was four, his father had met and married a new wife, and they all moved to 55 Priory Street, Southover. Their wedding was at Southover Church on Boxing Day 1901, and the new bride was Mary Anne Tulley, a spinster of 46. Her father George had been a labourer, and she would have had her hands full taking on two motherless infants. Their father Thomas was by then 37, and a plate-layer on the railway.

When William left school, he joined Ballards Brewery, where he would have been contemporary with Ben Glover (1.12). He enlisted at the outbreak of war, by which time he and his father, step-mother and brother had moved to 53 Potter's Lane. This was nearly at the top end of the Lane, just off Southover High Street, where the garages now are.

Potters Lane as it was in William Martin's childhood. These children are standing just outside where the Martin family's home was at no.53. (Bob Cairns)

His war

On August 19th 1916, six weeks after the start of the Somme offensive, and two years since William had joined up, the *Sussex County Herald* referred on its front page to

> "…*an avalanche of Royal Sussex men, who swept forward after nine sleepless nights, and took two hundred prisoners… They had advanced from Pozieres on August 4th and 5th, with the Anzacs and the Kent & Surreys…*"

William Martin was very probably part of this great advance, for it was on 20th August that he was mortally wounded in action. He was taken out of the battle zone by Field Ambulance, and maybe was then put on one of the many small railways to connect up with the main lines to the Channel ports.

At Rouen, he was admitted to the 9th General Hospital, and died of his wounds there on 27th August.

The news of his death seemed to reach Lewes in record speed, for on Friday September 1st the *East Sussex News* carried the following brief news item

> "*Lewes Soldier Killed.*

> "*Information has been received that Pte. W. T. Martin of the Royal Sussex Regiment died in the 9th General Hospital at Rouen on Sunday last from wounds received in action. A son of Mr. Thomas Martin of 53 Potters Lane, he enlisted two years ago.*

> *He went to the Front several months ago with the big batch of men who, it will be remembered, had an enthusiastic send off at Lewes Railway Station…*"

His burial at Rouen

Rouen is an old cathedral town on the River Seine. During the war, British base camps and hospitals were placed on the southern outskirts of the city; a Base Supply Depot and part of General HQ were established there, and its railway sidings were greatly increased to deal with the British supply and troop trains which passed through the Rouen stations or were despatched from them.

Rouen's many hospitals almost all remained there throughout the war, and the great majority of the dead from them all, including William Martin, were buried in the City's own St. Sever Cemetery. This is just outside the city wall, in the commune of Le Petit Quevilly, about 3 kms. south of the Cathedral. By September 1916, there had been over 3000 British and Dominion burials in it, and 700 more of the hospital dead had been buried in smaller local Cemeteries. As the casualties continued to rise from the Somme battle alone, it was found necessary to begin using the St. Sever Extension from September onwards.

Private Martin's grave reference in the original cemetery is Plot B, Row 26, Grave No.14.

Henry Douglas WILLIAMS   1.15
2nd September 1916 aged 20
near Ypres
21311 Private
2nd Battalion, The Hampshire Regiment

HOME   36 Southover High Street
BURIED   Vlamertinghe Military Cemetery
            between Ypres and Poperinghe

Henry Douglas Williams was born in Eastbourne in 1896 or 1897. He was the eldest son of Henry and Lizzie Williams, who seem to have moved to Southover around the turn of the century. Their next child, a daughter Lilian, was baptised (privately) at Southover Church on 13 January 1902. Henry senior had already retired from the Royal Artillery as a Sergeant Major, and was starting up in business as a grocer.

Growing up above the grocer's shop

Henry's father bought the Leasehold of the Stores that were then at 36 Southover High Street, on 30th June 1902, and the young family lived above the shop. Eighteen months later, young Henry's next brother, Harold George, was born and was baptised at Southover on 27 September 1903. Two more sons were born to the family, John Edward Norman (baptised 29 March 1908), and Charles Gordon (baptised 27 March 1910).

The shop was on the north side of the High Street, between the junctions with St Pancras Lane and Potters Lane. It was known in the area as 'The Gob Stopper Shop', and must have been a focal point for the spending of any pocket money there was in those years. With the Leasehold, the Williams family also had the use of the pump and the well in the garden behind no. 35 next door, and a right of way across the bottom of the garden and out into St Pancras Lane. It seems that for some years they owned both properties anyway, and the rent on them both together was £24.14s.0d. p.a. Mr. Williams was also liable for a District Rate of £1. 1s. 5d., and a Poor Rate of £1. 3s. Hopefully this was only half-yearly or yearly, as his trading figures were not too substantial, his average takings being only

Pte. Williams' boyhood home, 36 Southover High Street: the steps remain up to what was the front door of his father's shop. The house next door, no.35, at junction with St.Pancras Road, was the birthplace of Arthur Head in 1895 (see 1.17)

in the region of £12 to £14 a week.

The present owners of no. 36, Mr and Mrs C. W. Hodges, have beautifully renovated the cottage. In so doing, they uncovered an old Accounts Book kept by Mr. Williams in 1907, but unfortunately not before the mice in the wainscotting got to it. I am much indebted to him for letting me see the old Accounts Book and quote the above details

By 1910 when his youngest brother Charles was born, Henry Douglas would have been 13 or 14, and well into his education at Brighton Grammar School, if not nearly finished. On leaving school, he started commuting to London, and became a Civil Servant at Somerset House in the Strand.

Going off to war

When war broke out, Henry Douglas was 18. In March 1915 he enlisted with the Royal Sussex Regiment, with the number G/5446. Later in 1915, he was transferred into the 2nd Hampshires, with whom he immediately went to Egypt, possibly a more pleasant wintering-place than the trenches of northern France. By February 1916, "they proceeded to France" (as the *East Sussex News* put it in their report of his death some seven months later). On Friday 22 September 1916, they reported the above details, under the heading:

"Pte. H. D. Williams Killed"

adding only that he *"had seen a good deal of fighting"*. The newspaper and his family at the time reported that he was killed in France, but he was in fact buried in Belgium though very near the French border. It was in that same south-western corner of the Ypres Salient that had already claimed the lives of two Southover men, Trooper Turk (1.01) and Alfred Harding (1.10).

The Hampshire Regiment's Honorary Archivist has kindly provided the following details (quoted with his permission):

> *"The 2nd Battalion had re-entered the Ypres Salient on the night of 30/31st August, and went into Brigade Reserve near Ypres - leaving two Platoons of 'Z' Company remaining in Vlamertinghe as escort to Artillery. The War Diary* [for the 2nd Bn,] *for 1st September shows 3 wounded, and for 2nd September 2 wounded...*
>
> *Henry Douglas Williams was (therefore) wounded on either 1st or 2nd September, and died on 2nd September from his wound(s). He lies at rest in Vlamertinghe War Cemetery.*
>
> *Obviously, the nature of his wound(s) precluded any rearward medical evacuation. In World War 1, the Regiment's losses in killed/missing totalled 7,541."*

Vlamertinghe Military Cemetery

The Cemetery where he was buried is now in the middle of the village of Vlamertinghe, two or three miles west of Ypres towards Poperinghe, and is only six or seven miles from the French border at Bailleul. In 1916 it was on the outskirts of the old village, near a station on the troops' railway in and out of Ypres, near several of the large military hospitals, Casualty Clearing

Vlamertinghe Military Cemetery, near Ypres.

Stations and camps in the hop fields behind the lines. Vlamertinghe itself was almost totally destroyed in artillery barrages, with only its battered church tower remaining by 1918. The Cemetery was used by fighting troops and Field Ambulances up till mid-1917, when it reached capacity (and the New Cemetery had to be started a mile or two further out). The Commonwealth War Graves Commission describes it as being

"…remarkable for the care with which men from the same Unit were buried side by side if they fell at about the same time, (and) for the very high proportion of graves of Territorial units…"

It now has 1176 British and Dominion graves, all from 1914 till June 1917.

The village has been rebuilt right up to the walls of the Cemetery, and Private Williams' grave (Ref. No. Plot IV. Row C. Grave no. 4) can be seen in the picture as appearing to be almost in the back garden of a little West Flanders house. Despite the large number of graves, their rows go in many different directions and seem less military than many cemeteries. It gives much more the impression of being in a kitchen garden or orchard; there are gnarled old fruit trees among the graves, reminiscent of the Williams' family's own back garden between Southover High Street and the back of The Course, where Henry grew up. And on his headstone, under his name and number and the Hampshire Regiment crest, and the date of his death, is the family's chosen inscription:

> *"In Sure and Certain Hope.*
> *Southover, Lewes, Sussex."*

A year later, the family put the same words in the *East Sussex News'* "In Memoriam" column.

Within five months of the Armistice, Mr Williams had sold the dwelling house at no. 35, and a year after that he sold the remaining lease on the grocer's shop and rooms above at no. 36, to another grocer, one John Pettit.

Pte. William's grave at Vlamertinghe.
The family's inscription can be seen
at the bottom
"In sure and certain hope.
Southover, Lewes."

Henry Frank NEVILLE   1.16
3rd September 1916 aged 19
at the Somme
704 Lance Corporal
11th Battalion Royal Sussex Regiment

HOME   28 Lansdown Place, Lewes
BURIED   Ancre British Cemetery, Beaumont Hamel

Henry Neville was one of only a few named on the Southover War Memorial who did not grow up in Southover. It is in fact unlikely that he himself ever lived in Lewes at all, as his family did not move to 28 Lansdown Place until after the war had started. They came from South East London and its borders with Kent, and when Henry was born in 1897 they were living in Beckenham. He was the younger son of Henry William and Jane Neville, who also had an older son and three younger daughters. The Nevilles were another of the Southover families to lose both their sons in the war. Henry was the younger and the first to be killed, and his older brother Joseph was then killed eighteen months later in May 1918 (see 1.34).

Henry William, their father, was employed by the Gas Board. While the children were young, he was transferred from Beckenham to Woking, where the boys spent much of their childhoods. Their father was moved again before the war, this time to Bognor. Young Henry had by then left school, and had himself been able to get a job in the Gas Board there.

When the war broke out in August 1914, he was just 17. He and his father went to the Enlistment Centre together, but only he was accepted. His father was turned down as being too old. Not long after that, the remaining family moved to Lewes; it was parents and daughters alone, as both boys were by then in the Forces, young Henry with the Royal Sussex Regiment, and Joseph in the Navy.

Last survivor of the Nevilles in Lewes

Their sister Mildred, who was the eldest of the family moving to Lansdown Place at the beginning of the First War, has been my main 'informant' for her family's story, since returning to Lewes in the 1980s. She had stayed on till shortly before the Second War, but then spent the middle years of her life away from Lewes, mainly in Brighton and working in the fashion departments of some of the big stores. She then returned to Lewes in her later years, and resumed contact with Southover. After having to give up her home and move eventually into Barons Down Nursing Home, she was visited there by the Rector of Southover, who took Communion to her through her recent frail years.

So it was that he was able to put me in touch with her once I started researching this book. She was almost the first person I met who was a surviving close relative of one (and in her case two) of the "Men of Southover", and I felt privileged to be able to sit at her bedside in her 91st year and hear her talk about her beloved brothers. Although her recent memory had left her by the time I met her in 1995, she still had very vivid memories of those First War years and the loss of her two brothers.

It is almost entirely thanks to her that anything much can be known about this family at all. She is also visited by a niece, one of her sister's children, but unfortunately it has not been possible for me to have contact with her.

Talking about Henry's enlistment, Mildred said with evident pride: "no. 704 he was - that shows he was one of the earliest ! He was one of 'Lowther's Lambs', you know." (These were the men and boys of the three Southdown Regiments, raw recruits under General Lowther to the Royal Sussex's contribution to Kitchener's 'New Armies' of untrained volunteers. Many thousands of them were to perish in the carnage of that war, for example 366 of them in the one disastrous Richebourg action alone, in May 1915).

She was particularly proud that he had not only joined the Royal Sussex Regiment, but that it was on the Somme itself that he had been killed in action. When I asked where it was he had been killed, she retorted with some vehemence: "The Somme, of course !", as if nowhere else would have counted.

3rd September 1916

The day Lance-Corporal Neville died was the day of the second "titanic clash" in the prolonged Allied assault on the Picardy village of Beaumont Hamel. The first one, on the disastrous 1 July, had achieved nothing but a massive casualty list. The village is in the chalk uplands and ridges north of the River Ancre, in the northern part of the whole Somme battlefield. It was not finally captured until mid-November 1916, and then not without great loss to the Royal Naval Division. By then, the marshy ground on the banks of the Ancre was full of lakes and swamps, and success then was even more crucial before the winter rains made the whole area impassable. It was that final battle for Beaumont Hamel that saw the advent of

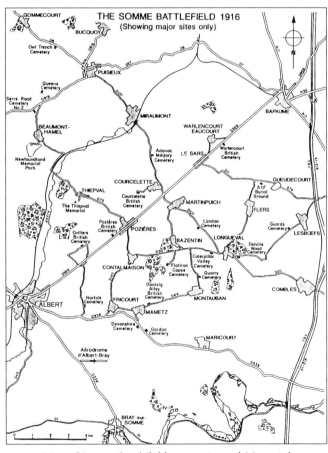

Map of Somme battlefields, cemeteries and Memorials.
(CWGC)

the tank. On one side of the River Ancre at Hamel, there is the Newfoundland Memorial Park, with its famous Caribou statue 'baying for its young', in honour of the Canadians who fought there so valiantly. On the other side is the Ulster Tower and the Thiepval Memorial to the Missing.

On 3rd September, Henry Neville's 11th Southdown Battalion of the Royal Sussex was part of the 39th Division. He had a particularly illustrious comrade in the same Battalion that day, though was probably not aware of it - the war poet Edmund Blunden. Blunden's task was to establish an ammunition dump across the river Ancre at Hamel, in which he succeeded. He survived the experience, and returned to the river later in the war, writing "The Ancre at Hamel: Afterwards", in evocative memory of his lost comrades:-

> *"The struggling Ancre had no part*
> *In these new hours of mine,*
> *And yet its stream ran through my heart;*
> *I heard it grieve and pine,*
> *As if its rainy tortured blood*
> *Had swirled into my own,*
> *When by its battered bank I stood*
> *And shared its wounded moan."*

quoted from Major and Mrs Holt's "Battlefield Guide to the Somme" with permission

The Ancre British Cemetery, Beaumont Hamel is where Lance-Corporal Henry Neville was finally laid to rest. Originally this cemetery contained only 500 or so Allied graves, but after the Armistice nearly two thousand further graves were concentrated into it. The great majority all fell on the same three days (1st July, 3rd September, and 13th November), and over half of them lie in unmarked graves. They are nearly all British soldiers, sailors and Marines, but there are also nearly fifty from the Dominions, particularly

HEROES OF THE 'BIG PUSH'

THE PRICE THE GALLANT SUSSEX PAID.

The Men Who "Did Their Bit."

Newfoundland. The cemetery covers some 7,400 square metres, and is surrounded by a low red brick wall above the road, from which it is reached by a flight of steps. There are sweeping views over the valleys of the Ancre and the Somme.

Henry's grave is in Plot III, Row D, Grave 33.

His sister Mildred's grief at the loss of first Henry then Joseph was still very real, even eighty years on. She felt Henry's death perhaps more as she was closer to him, since Joseph had already left home when she was only seven or eight, and she remembered more of her childhood with Henry. She also very much shared her parents' concern at being told during September 1916 that Henry was missing, and having to wait many long months for War Office confirmation that he should then be 'presumed dead', and very much shared their devastation then.

Even to this day, there are no known details of the circumstances of his death. Mildred did remember having been shown a photograph of the cemetery with his regimental memorial in it (or she may possibly have been thinking of the regimental insignia on the CWGC headstone). She does not remember there ever having been any thought of the family visiting the cemetery after the war.

The Cenotaph

But she does have vivid memories of the day, in 1920, when the Cenotaph in Whitehall was unveiled. Her parents were allocated tickets, but with an actual seat for her mother only. All the fathers had to stand further back and travel from home at their own expense, but her mother had her train ticket paid and was particularly thrilled to have a seat very near the Cenotaph and with a good view of all the dignitaries.

Arthur Henry HEAD   1.17
7th October 1916 aged 21
on the Somme
1667 Corporal
7th Battalion Royal Sussex Regiment

HOME   35 Southover Street, then 9 Priory Street, Southover
COMMEMORATED   Thiepval Memorial, Somme

His home and gardening family

Corporal Arthur Head was another of the Southover men who came from an old Lewes family with many different branches all over town, and further afield (details available). Arthur himself was born early in 1895, and was baptised in Southover Church on 30 June 1895. His parents were William and Annie Head, who lived at the time at 35 Southover High Street. This was near the corner of St Pancras Lane, and next

9 Priory Street, where the Head family moved later in Arthur's childhood from 35 Southover High Street (see 1.15 above)

door to where Henry Douglas Williams grew up at the grocer's shop from 1902 (see 1.15). Arthur's father William was a gardener, and had come from Mayfield; and his mother Annie came from Glynde. Arthur was their third child, and had an older sister (Kate) and brother (William Horace). He also had two younger brothers, Alfred Ernest and Walter George, and a younger sister, Rose Elizabeth.

During Arthur's childhood, the family moved along the street to 9 Priory Street. He then started work, following in his father's footsteps as a gardener. His employer was Mr F. Verrall (whose home was the old Southover Manor, with his offices opposite it at 47 Southover High Street), so he would have had no distance to walk to work. He became good friends with another Southover casualty, Reg. Horne, whose home was along Southover High Street at Stable Cottage, next door to the Brewery Stables.

Militia-man wounded, then returns to Front among first tanks, but killed by sniper

At the outbreak of war, Arthur was already in the Sussex Militia, so was immediately called up in August 1914. Initially he was with the 3rd Royal Sussex, but later changed to the 7th Battalion, probably on returning to France in February 1916. For some weeks up to that point he had been having a convalescent break back home in Priory Street after being wounded in action. On his return to the Front he would have quickly become caught up with all the preparations for the 'Big Push' on the Somme, but ironically in the event was 'merely' killed by a single sniper in the middle of the third phase of this 'Big Push'.

One of the main battles going on around 7th October, the day he was killed, was in the Gueudecourt trenches just south of Bapaume. The other was the final Battle for Thiepval Chateau and village (which had in fact been the Allies' original objective on that infamous 1st July). The CWGC summarises the autumn of 1916 on the Somme as follows

> *"September 15th saw the start of the third phase of the battle, and the first use of tanks in war. The churned-up ground and the mechanical limitations of the small number of tanks available hampered their effectiveness, however, and the slog forward by the infantry continued. The end of September finally saw the capture of Thiepval, an original objective of the first day of the battle.*
>
> *Throughout October and the first half of November, the north and eastward attacks continued in increasingly difficult weather conditions, until finally with the onset of winter and exhaustion, the Battle of the Somme ended on 18th November 1916."*

His commemoration on the Thiepval Memorial

Whichever part of the battlefield Corporal Head fell in, there must have been much more fighting going on over the same ground after his death, for his body was never found.

His memory is honoured on the Thiepval Memorial (Pier and Face 7 C), on the actual site of the old chateau. There are over 72,000 other British names on the Memorial, over 90% of whom fell between July and November 1916. It is the largest of the Memorials built by the Commonwealth War Graves Commission, and was designed by Sir Edwin Lutyens, being begun in 1928 and finished in 1932. It stands in its own grounds of 40 acres on a ridge overlooking the battlefield, about eight kms. north-east of Albert.

As the CWGC own text explains:

> *"The Thiepval Memorial bears witness to the fact that a high percentage of those who died in the Battle of the Somme have no known grave. Many bodies (have) been lost entirely in the pulverised battlefield, and many others not found until battlefield clearance took place after the war, by which time all traces of identity had disappeared in most cases."*

Thiepval Memorial   SUE BURLEY

In addition to being a Memorial to the Missing, the Thiepval is also a Battle Memorial commemorating the joint Anglo-French offensive on the Somme in 1916. Beneath the dedication to the French andBritish armies, are inscribed the simple words:

"THE MISSING OF THE SOMME"

Those he left behind

Corporal Head's parents put the 'killed on active service' announcement in the local paper on 21st October that year, as soon as they received the 'official notification'. They had already had an 'advance warning', when their Arthur's friend, Sergeant Arthur W. Horne of Stable Cottage, 24 Southover High Street (brother of Reg. Horne, see 1.24), wrote them a letter of condolence, having heard the news of their Arthur's sniper's bullet out there before they did back home.

Arthur Head's name on the Memorial

A year later, when they put in an 'In Memoriam' notice, they had already moved away to "The Cottage" at Barons' Down. It may be that the elderly parents then died, for the next-of-kin given in the CWGC papers is no longer them but Arthur's brother, William Horace Head, instead. His address was then 144, High Street, Lewes. He was also a Corporal in the war, with the Highland Light Infantry, and he survived despite being wounded twice.

This brother William Horace, went on to father a daughter Phyllis, who has been very helpful in compiling the very last biography in this book - that of her own late husband, Harold Grover, right at the end of the second World War (2.22). Until my researches and advertisement in local newsagents' windows, this Phyllis had lost contact with a cousin living in Lewes, namely Sue Burley (nee Head).

Sue Burley is the daughter of another of Arthur Head's brothers, Alfred Ernest, and grew up in Landport. She remembers her grandmother's glass cabinet, which contained the Death Plaque sent by the War Office after the Armistice in memory of Corporal Arthur Head. She used to call it her "big penny" when her grandmother brought it out on special occasions.

(They all now have a further mutual connection, who made contact with me after seeing my entry under "Head" in the Sussex Family History Group list of Members' Interests; this man, Frank Hull from Worthing, has many Head family relatives, though none as yet with any proven link with any of Arthur Head's family. That is, apart from the shoemaker and boot repairer William Thomas Head, who lived in North Street, Lewes, up to about 1866 when he moved to Dartford. There does seem to be a possible link with Arthur Head's forbears in Lewes, but more research is needed to prove that.)

Dedication Tablet on Thiepval Memorial.

PART THREE

1917

Attrition in Mud and Gas

Eleven of Southover's men were killed during 1917, and it must have been the darkest year of the war to live through for those at home. For some months the Rector had a period of extended sick leave, leaving the parish in the hands of the Curate. It was the Curate who led Southover's own Memorial Service in November 1917 in honour of those lost from the parish up to that point. (This is fully described at the end of Part Three).

More of the action which killed these Southover men in 1917 was around Ypres than in France as had been the case. Perhaps surprisingly, there were only four of these eleven men who were never found, and so are commemorated rather than buried. Three of the men died of their wounds in military hospitals behind the lines in the Ypres Salient, and a further man died of disease in hospital at home.

1917 was the first year in which Southover artillery-men were killed. Two of the eleven lost were under 20 and three were well over 35. Two of them were young fathers; three children were left fatherless in one family, and two in the other.

Southover men lost during 1917

Home address		Name		Number in book
174	High St., Lewes	Arthur John	SUTER	18
2	The Course	Thomas Robert	COLEMAN	19
15	Southover High St	Frederick	HILLMAN	20
5	St.Pancras Place	Edward James	WARES	21
3	The Course	George Wm.Osborne	EADE	22
5	St.Pancras Place	Ernest Victor	PAYNE	23
Stable Cott., 24	Southover High St	Reginald Harry	HORNE	24
34	St.Pancras Lane	James	CROUCH	25
8	St.Pancras Terrace	George	PACKHAM	26
Old Rectory	Rotten Row	Wilfred Gordon	ANSON	27
Gables Cott., 55	Southover High St	Frederick	JEFFERY	28

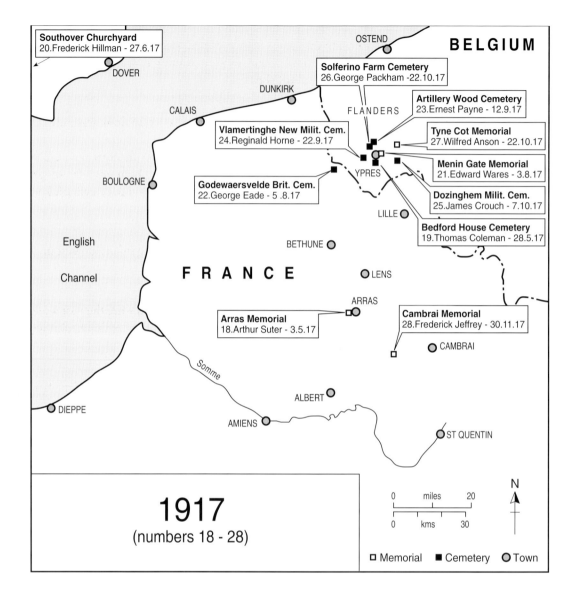

Southover Churchyard
20.Frederick Hillman - 27.6.17

OSTEND

BELGIUM

DOVER

Solferino Farm Cemetery
26.George Packham -22.10.17

DUNKIRK

Artillery Wood Cemetery
23.Ernest Payne - 12.9.17

CALAIS

FLANDERS

Vlamertinghe New Milit. Cem.
24.Reginald Horne - 22.9.17

Tyne Cot Memorial
27.Wilfred Anson - 22.10.17

BOULOGNE

YPRES

Menin Gate Memorial
21.Edward Wares - 3.8.17

Godewaersvelde Brit. Cem.
22.George Eade - 5 .8.17

Dozinghem Milit. Cem.
25.James Crouch - 7.10.17

LILLE

English

Bedford House Cemetery
19.Thomas Coleman - 28.5.17

Channel

BETHUNE

F R A N C E

LENS

ARRAS

Arras Memorial
18.Arthur Suter - 3.5.17

Cambrai Memorial
28.Frederick Jeffrey - 30.11.17

CAMBRAI

Somme

ALBERT

DIEPPE

AMIENS

ST QUENTIN

1917

(numbers 18 - 28)

0   miles   20

0   kms   30

N

□ Memorial   ■ Cemetery   ○ Town

Some local newspaper items from 1917

Jan 5th:
Appeal for Side Drums: Lewes men of the Royal Sussex Regiment at the Front are in need of two small side drums, as they are forming a Mouth Organ Band to while away the winter nights…

May 3rd
Royal Proclamation on Food Economy: official reading at Main Entrance to Lewes Town Hall, by the Town Clerk surrounded by the Mayor, Aldermen and Councillors, and the High Sheriff of Sussex… "The King's Charge": Eat Less Bread… Bread Ration is now 3lbs. per week per person, that is 3 slices a day per person, or 3 x half loaves.

May 26th:

German P.O.Ws are being seen working on local farms and road works; they work an 8 hour day for 1d. an hour. Objections are being raised about them attempting to fraternise with local children when marching to and from the Naval Prison…

June 2nd:

Organ repairs at Southover Church are now completed. Whit Sunday collections and previous donations to the Rector covered the whole cost of £25.

Lewes Communal Kitchen opened on Whit Tuesday… 250 servings on the first day… The menu being offered is: Thick Soup @ 3d per quart, Stewed Beef & Dumplings @ 4d per portion, savoury rice (as veg.) @ 1d per pint, cold ham @ 6d, roast beef @ 6d, boiled salt beef @ 6d, rice cream @ 2d, "transparent pudding" @ 2d.

June 8th:

Big storm in Lewes on Wednesday night… washed allotments away, and gardens at bottom of Station Street were ruined…

July 21st:

… guns on the Belgian coast have been heard in many parts of the county during the past week. … girl Munitions Workers (from factories in London) are on holiday in Lewes this week; they are the overflow from Brighton, where every available lodging has been taken.

July 27th:

Southover Sunday School had a war-time treat on Wednesday. Messrs. Ballard & Co.'s field (beside the Brewery) had been lent for the occasion. About 100 children assembled there after a tea in the Church Hall, and spent a happy time in various games and sports.

Aug 10th

Bank Holiday Fete was held last Monday at Priory Fields, to raise funds for the Lewes War Hospital Supply Depot on School Hill… it was very successful, and a total of £262. 9s. 6d. was raised.

Aug 18th:

Limbless Soldiers in Stoolball Matches in Lewes… part of general revival of stoolball in Sussex.

Sept 28th:

Choristers' Entertainment: adult members of Southover Church Choir and the Organist were entertained to dinner at Southover Grange on Friday evening. A most enjoyable evening was spent, and the hospitality of Mrs Stewart-Jones was much appreciated. The Choirboys had been entertained at Southover Grange on a previous occasion.

HIGH STREET

Oct 26th:

A second Communal Kitchen has now opened in Lewes, at the premises in Cliffe High Street previously known as Fox's Toffee Shop. An impromptu concert was held at School Hill House, on the occasion of its third anniversary as a hospital for wounded soldiers.

Nov 17th:

Rations: for men on heavy industrial and agricultural work are now 8lbs. bread per week,
for women on heavy industrial and agricultural work   5lbs bread per week

for all adults
$\left\{\begin{array}{l}\text{10oz. butter,}\\\text{12oz. other cereal,}\\\text{2lbs. meat,}\\\text{8oz. sugar.}\end{array}\right.$

for men on ordinary industrial work   7lbs bread
for women on ordinary work or domestic service   4lbs bread
for men on sedentary work or un-occupied   4lbs. 8oz. bread
for women on sedentary work or un-occupied   3lbs 8oz. bread.

This compared to Compulsory Rations for Germans as follows:
4lbs 4oz bread, 8$^1/2$oz meat, 10oz butter, 5$^1/2$oz sugar, 3$^1/2$oz cereals, 2oz fats.

Nov 24th:

Red Cross Hospital for Wounded Soldiers has now opened at The Shelleys (lately The Vine)

Dec 1st:

Three months' off duty for Rector of Southover: The Rev. Theodore Windle M.A., announced on Sunday evening that, acting under medical advice, he was about to take three months' rest from duty in the hope of regaining his health… The time would be spent in travelling. During his absence the Rev. A. S. Dendy, Curate, would be in charge of the parish, helped by the Rev. E. Griffiths, Headmaster of the Lewes Grammar School.

Our readers will join with us in expressing the hope that the Reverend gentleman, who has been suffering for some time from sleeplessness, will return fully restored to health so as to resume the good works he has done for the parish of which he has charge.

Dec 15th:

The bells of Southover Church sounded a joyous peal on Tuesday at midday to celebrate the surrender of the city of Jerusalem… the ringers being Messrs. Hide (captain), Turner, E. Hill, Steadman, Moppett, Sgt. Moore, C. Errey (hon. sec.), and Miss Ward.

Dec 22nd:

A Memorial Service at Southover Church was held on Sunday evening for those who have fallen in the war… It was a memorable service and the church was crowded, notwithstanding the icy storm raging outside… The troops present occupied the south aisle, and included the Lewes Company of Volunteers, under the command of Lt. Glover… many of those present were in mourning, including the Mayor and many Councillors. … All 23 names were read out from the Roll of Honour, as tended with such loving kindness by Mrs Stewart-Jones, and an interval was set apart for private prayer… (for details of the service itself, please see the report from the *East Sussex News*, dated 21st December 1917, at end of Part Three).

The Christmas Editorial of the *East Sussex News* in 1917, included the sentence:

"The berries of Christmas are very red this year, and the holly leaves sharp to the touch…"

Arthur John SUTER   1.18
3rd May 1917 aged 36
near Monchy, France
60704 Sergeant
8th Battalion Royal Fusiliers, 'B' Coy., V Platoon
(previously 6th Royal Sussex)

HOME   174 High Street, Lewes
COMMEMORATED   Arras Memorial to the Missing

Family background and family firm

Sgt. Suter was one of three soldier sons of George and Sarah Ann Suter. They lived at 174 and 176 High Street, Lewes (either side of where the Bow Windows Bookshop now is). They all ran the family business there, Suter & Sons, General & Fancy Drapers. By the time the war started, it seems that George senior had died, and Arthur John and his mother together were running the Ladies Outfitters and Milliners part of the business at 174 High St., next door to the Westminster Bank. This was also the address throughout the war year for the Lewes Chamber of Commerce, and A. J. Suter was listed as its Secretary. His older brother George E. had married Alice, and moved two doors along into 176 High St., where they ran the drapers and haberdashers part of the business.

The other two soldier sons, Arthur John's younger brothers, were both in the Artillery. Charles Henry was a Gunner, and Quartermaster-Sgt. H. N. Suter was a gun-carriage/leading horse Driver with the Royal Field Artillery (19th Battalion, 7th London), and both seem to have survived the war. There were also two daughters, who possibly were able to step into their absent brothers' shoes and help run the two shops. Their sister in law Alice had two young children, so would perhaps not have been able to do so much to help; her daughter Alice Mabel was baptised at Southover on 28th December 1913, and her son Frederick on 23rd May 1916 (both at about six weeks old).

Although they lived in the parish of St. Michael, Lewes, the family's links were more with Southover. Arthur John had been a boy chorister at Southover, was prepared for confirmation there, and was regarded by the Rector as "a true son of the church". He went to school just round the corner at Castlegate School, as presumably did his other brothers as well.

174 and 176 High Street, Lewes, where Suter's the Drapers had their two shops, and where the family lived above.

Sergeant Suter's war

When Arthur John enlisted in Brighton, he was perhaps older than the average recruit, but it must have been quite early on in the war, as he had a very low number, 448. He was with the 6th Royal Sussex initially; this had been formed in 1908 as a Cyclist Battalion of the new Territorial force, serving in coastal defence in England and overseas in Ireland and India, before being disbanded in 1919. Arthur had become a Lance-Corporal with them, and was then in some way "attached to" the Royal Fusiliers (though whether this was instead or as well as, is not clear). It was anyway with the Fusiliers that he went to France, and was promoted Sergeant in 'B' Coy. (V Platoon) in the 8th Battalion.

The spring of 1917 was a time of important changes and new developments, both for the British Army on the Western Front starting a major new advance at Easter, and for the Suter family back home in Lewes. At the very end of March, Arthur's widowed mother, Sarah Ann Suter, died aged 71. She was buried in Lewes Cemetery, with the funeral service being taken by the Rector of Southover. The Sussex County Herald for 7th April 1917 reports on the occasion, and gives a long list of the mourners. Two of her four sons were there, George the eldest and Gunner Charles Henry the youngest, with their wives. The other two were of course away at the Front, Sgt. A. J. and Sgt. H. N., but the two daughters were there, Miss M. K. and Miss A. Suter. Her eldest son, George, had been named as her Executor, and the Will she made in July 1914 left an estate of £3,552 gross.

His last battle

A month after his mother's funeral, Arthur John himself was reported missing near Monchy on 3rd May (or at least, it was later realised that that was the last date on which he had been seen). There were many actions during April and May 1917 during the battle for Arras. This was all in much the same area as that in which the first of the Glover sons to die had been shot down over Vis-en-Artois a year earlier. The village of Monchy-le-Preux, built on high ground about 5 miles to the east of Arras just off the road to Cambrai, had provided the Germans with a commanding view of the Allied lines. It was captured by the 37th Division on 11th April 1917, during a blizzard. It was a costly capture because of its protection by wide bands of barbed wire. Despite many German counter attacks over the following weeks, Monchy was held until the final German offensive in March 1918, when it was lost again till August 1918.

Arthur's little niece next door, back home in Lewes High Street, would have been only three at the time of his death, so probably grew up with no abiding memory of her uncle. He would have died not knowing that his sister's new baby was a boy, born on 30th April. He might possibly not even have heard of his mother's death, given the extremes of weather and fighting in which his last few weeks were spent.

His death and commemoration

It was 1st June 1917 before the East Sussex News reported that Sgt. A. J. Suter was

> "unofficially reported missing, and believed to be a prisoner of war. He has been serving in the great advance on the Western Front since it began at Easter."

Six months later, on 16th December 1917, there was a Memorial Service at Southover Church in honour of those of its sons who had already died. (see *East Sussex News* article at end of Part Three) The names of all 23 known to have died at that time were read out, with the addition of Sgt. A. J. Suter

> *"of whom they were uncertain… who had been reported missing, and who was a member of the church choir and a true son of the church."*

Little did they all know then that it was to be yet another three months before there was any official confirmation, and then only that his death could now be 'presumed'. The *East Sussex News* for 8th March 1918 carried the following paragraph:-

> *Lewes N.C.O. Presumed to be Dead*
>
> *"Official intimation has this week been received to the effect that Sgt. A. J. Suter of the Royal Fusiliers (son of the late Mr & Mrs G. Suter) who was reported missing on May 3rd last, is now presumed to be dead."*

It was ten years or so before Sgt. Suter was officially commemorated on The Arras Memorial. This imposing edifice commemorates some 35,700 casualties of the British, New Zealand and South African Forces who died between Spring 1916 and 7th August 1918 (excluding Battle of Cambrai in 1917), and have no known grave. It was designed by Sir Edwin Lutyens, architect of Thiepval and other Memorials, and is in the form of a cloistered colonnade. The men's names are carved in stone tablets on the cloister walls, and Sgt. Suter's is in Bay 3. The whole Memorial is situated within the Faubourg d'Amiens Cemetery, near the Citadel in the western part of the town of Arras, two kilometres west of the station.

Arras Memorial.

Thomas Robert COLEMAN   1.19
28th May 1917 aged 18
near Ypres
Pioneer 165725
47th Signals Coy., Royal Engineers

HOME   2 The Course, Southover
BURIED   Bedford House Cemetery, Ypres

Thomas was born at Hampden Park, Eastbourne, then grew up in Lewes. His parents were Thomas R. and Mrs. A. E. Coleman. He was a boy chorister at Southover Church, as was his younger brother after him. The family lived in The Course, a few doors along from his best friend George Osborne Eade (see no. 22). On leaving school, he became a clerk in the Telegraph Office of the London, Brighton & South Coast Railway Co. at Lewes Railway Station.

The Course, Southover: the Coleman home at no.2,
with Tom's friend George Eade's home next door at no.3
(see 1.22 below).

Pioneer Coleman' non-combatant role

He enlisted at Lewes late in 1916, as soon as he had passed his eighteenth birthday. He was one of the new breed of 'Pioneers', who were being used increasingly by the Army as their "work horses" and to relieve the Infantry of some of its non-combatant duties. Pioneers were "organized and intelligent labour… (who) wired, dug and riveted in all weathers and all terrains. On many occasions they had to abandon their working tools to fight off enemy advances…"

Thomas went out to the Front in the early months of 1917. He was attached to the Royal Engineers and was stationed at Hooggraaf, just outside Ypres, with No. 3 Section of the 47th (London) Divisional Signals Co'y. (This was the same Co'y. that Brian Glover had been with before he was 'seconded' to the Royal Flying Corps. a year earlier - see no.1.6). From April 1917, they were engaged in laying buried cables, and also in the use of 'message dogs' and pigeons in transmitting information between trenches, air balloons and motor cycles. It was a wet spring, which made for flooding difficulties, and there were shortages of cable which delayed things. The strength of the Unit at 30th April 1917 was 8 Officers and 264 'Other Ranks'.

Bedford House Cemetery
with the restored Ypres Town in the distance.

Thomas was involved in cable-burying at 'Bedford House', the troops' name for the near-derelict moated Chateau Rosendal at Zillebeke, just outside the Lille Gate in the old Ypres city walls. Its grounds were much broken up by shelling, and the moats and lakes were no longer contained. But for Thomas, straight from the telegraph office at Lewes Station (not to mention the annual flooding of his home in The Course by the Winterbourne Stream), it would have been a job well suited to his skills and experience.

His death and burial

On 28th May, all of a sudden while going about his business, Thomas was killed by a shell which burst outside his dugout. His Commanding Officer must have written almost immediately to the boy's shocked and grieving parents, for parts of his letter were printed in the *Sussex County Herald* on June 16th, as follows:-

> *"Your son had been with us only a very short time, barely one month, but he had already earned the good opinion of those around him. His cheerful spirit and the real interest he took in all his work, would I feel have made him a very valuable member of the Section had he been spared to us."*

In the same issue of the *Herald*, his parents put their own notice in the 'Return Thanks' column:-

> *"Mr & Mrs Coleman and family of The Course desire to thank their many friends for their kind letters of sympathy, which are too numerous to answer."*

A few weeks later, on Aug 11th, the paper quoted some extracts from a letter written by young Thomas' best friend next door, G. W. O. Eade (see no. 1.22), to his own father, having already heard the news of Thomas' death:

> *"Well, Dad, I have been lucky today. I received a parcel and in it was the 'County Herald'. Well, I opened the paper and saw my old pal Tom's photo in the Roll of Honour. I have cut it out and put it in my pocket book in remembrance of my best pal."*

By the end of the war, several small cemeteries had been made in different parts of the Chateau grounds in which Tom Coleman had been based. Four of these have been amalgamated to form the Bedford House CWGC Cemetery, but they retain the original groupings in separate 'Enclosures'. Tom's grave is in the largest of these, Enclosure No. 4, initially used mainly by his own 47th (London) Division. There are nearly 3,500 British and Commonwealth graves, set in beautiful surroundings with views over the grazing sheep in the lush water-meadows, to the restored spires of Ypres.

Tom's grave is no. 20, Row B, Plot II, and it is in Enclosure No. 4.

Shortly after the war, the rest of his family moved to 5, Railway Road, Newhaven. But before they left there was an event at Southover Church that they, and indeed everyone else there in the packed church, must have found extremely moving. It was the Memorial Service in honour of those from the parish who had already fallen. Tom Coleman's name was of course among those 23 read out, and the choir, organ, buglers, and preacher, all played their parts in commemorating their loved ones (see account of the Service, in the *East Sussex News* of 21st December 1917, attached at the end of Part Three on 1917). One of the most poignant contributions to the service must have been that made by Tom's younger brother, following in his footsteps in the choir:-

"In place of the anthem, Master A. J. V. Coleman sang 'O rest in the Lord' from 'Elijah', with much feeling."

Tom Coleman's grave in Enclosure No.4
of Bedford House Cemetery.

Frederick Cecil HILLMAN   1.20
27th June 1917 aged 19
in hospital at Hove
121806 Sergeant
Anti-Aircraft Section, Royal Garrison Artillery

HOME   15 Southover High Street
BURIED   Southover Churchyard

His branch of the Hillman family

Frederick was baptised at Southover on 26th September 1897. He was the younger of two sons born to Edward and Harriet Hillman, who lived by then at 15 Southover High Street. Edward was the local wheelwright, and carried on his business in the courtyard and outbuildings behind the iron gates at his home, between Southover Manor and the old Priory Rectory on the south side of the High Street. Edward had been brought up at the far end of Southover High Street, beyond The Swan, where he and his brother Joseph were sons of the blacksmith, John Hillman. William Alfred, the sub-postmaster at the church end of the High Street, was another brother (or possibly a cousin), so Frederick Cecil would have been first or second cousin to Billy Hillman (who was killed at Loos back in September 1915 - see no.1.06).

Forge Cottage, the old Blacksmith's adjoining The Swan where Fred Hillman's family came from.

His Southover youth

Frederick's older brother, Edward George, was baptised at Southover just eighteen months before him. Their lives continued closely connected, and both joined the local Territorials before war broke out; Fred played the bugle on parades and drills, and was "Trumpeter No. 427". Fred's day-time job was as Assistant Dispenser to Mr. Frank Loud, who was both Surgeon at the newly-opened Lewes Victoria Hospital, and Physician and Vaccinator to parts of the Lewes Union Workhouse and Orphanage (between King Edwards Road and de Montfort Road, where the flats now are). His residence, and possibly Consulting Rooms too, were at Albion House, Albion Street (where Dr Blake's Surgery subsequently was). This Mr. Loud, or a relative, was also an officer in the Territorials, first as Captain then Major in the same 'C' Co'y. as Fred Hillman then joined.

His war with the Artillery - spent mainly in hospitals

Fred and his brother Edward were among the first to leave Lewes for the war with the Royal Garrison Artillery. Edward went as a Gunner/Signaller, and Fred. was attached to an Anti-Aircraft Section. According to the obituary eventually written on him by the Sussex County Herald (30th June 1917), Fred had died of 'consumption'. The article continued:-

> *"(Sgt. Hillman had) not enjoyed good health, and throughout his military career (was) far from strong… (he was) most anxious to serve his country, and has done his best to make himself fit for the Front. While training in Dover last year, his health broke down (Aug. 1916), but he recovered sufficiently to be sent to France, though not to remain for long. He has been in various hospitals but returned home on Sunday a week ago, very ill, and gradually grew worse till he died on Wednesday."*

Sergeant Hillman had been in the Eastern General Hospital, Portland Road, Hove, but according to one of the local papers actually died after a couple of days back home. One of the 'floral tributes' at his funeral was from his 'comrades at The Bungalow' at E.G.H., presumably the fresh-air annexe of the hospital, fashionable then for the treating of T.B. patients. The funeral was held a few days later on 2nd July at Southover Church, led by the Rector, the Rev. Theodore Henry Windle. The *Herald* had announced on 30th June that the funeral would be held at 3 p.m. on Monday 2nd July, "should his brother Signaller Edward Hillman, who has been telegraphed for, arrive in time". But in the event, as they reported a week later, Edward "was unable to be present as he is serving in France".

The paper reported *"a very large congregation… a large number of friends at the graveside… and unusually numerous floral tributes."*

The family mourners it listed after his parents included Fred's uncle Mr A. Hillman; his uncle and aunt Mr & Mrs J. Hillman (who sent a floral tribute from 'Uncle Joe and Aunt Florence'); his aunt Mrs Noel; and his great-aunt Mrs S. Hillman. This latter was probably the Aunt Sarah included in the bouquet from his parents and brother. Other bouquets specifically mentioned were one from his "godparents and chum Harold", and one from Major and Mrs Loud.

The reporter then concluded his unusually full and fulsome article as follows:-

> *"Sorrow is widely expressed throughout the town and wherever the deceased was known, at the early termination of a life so full of promise."*

Mr & Mrs Hillman then used the 'Return Thanks' columns of the *East Sussex News* in their

> *"wish to return sincere thanks for the sympathy extended to them in their recent bereavement."*

Southover High Street looking east towards the church, from near where Fred grew up at no.15. The local policeman and Southover children would no doubt have been part of his childhood. (BC)

Edward James WARES 1.21
3rd August 1917 aged 30
near Ypres
40425 Private
12th Battalion The Middlesex Regiment

HOME 5 St Pancras Place, Southover
COMMEMORATED Menin Gate Memorial to the Missing, Ypres

Lewes childhood

Edward J. Wares was born in 1886 and spent his early childhood up at the top of the town, near Bull Lane, Greene Lane and the West Gate. At the time of the 1891 Census, he and his family were at 1, Western Passage, off Western Terrace. He was four and was the eldest of the three children his young parents then had; Herbert was two, and Lilian was three months. They and their parents had all been born in the parish of Lewes All Saints. Both his mother Louisa and his father Edward G. Wares were 26 at that time, and his father was a bricklayer's labourer.

Milkman and proud young father

When he left school, the young Edward became a 'milk carrier' for Uridge's Dairies in Southover. He would have pushed a handcart or driven a horse and cart with pails of milk on them, pouring out the required amounts into customers' own jugs or bowls. Later on, he and his young wife, Alice Mary (nee Freeman), lived at 2 Priory Cottages, and then moved to 5 St Pancras Pace by the beginning of the war. This was one of the many little streets, now demolished, which were around the old Brewery and St Pancras Gardens. Their eldest, Ivy Louise, was born on 20th June, 1909, and her sister Josephine Alice, three or four years later, being baptised at Southover on 22nd February 1913. This was a private baptism, which could suggest the baby was poorly; she may not in fact have survived long, as she does not re-appear in any records.

Edward had been able to defer going to war until after his wife had given birth again; Edward James, junior, was born on 12th April 1916, and baptised at Southover on 30th April. Little Ivy was by then nearly seven, and was removed from Southover School from 17th March to 3rd May, to go to Tunbridge Wells. This was presumably to stay with relatives there while her mother was imminently expecting the new baby Edward. This must have been a particularly poignant and stressful time for them all, having lost one child and being about to lose father to the Army. Edward the soldier then left home during May 1916, just a month after the baby was born.

Twice wounded, then back home with a 'Blighty'

He joined the Middlesex Regiment, and had a short but eventful war. He did not reach the Front much before the end of September 1916, but within a month was wounded or the first time. It was not serious enough to warrant a 'Blighty' (i.e. return to England for hospital and / or convalescence), and he was back in action after only a short break. Next time he was not so lucky: in March 1917, he was hit by shrapnel in the back of the knee. On Saturday 11th March 1917, the *Sussex County Herald* reported that

> "*... Mrs Wares received a Field Card from her husband on Tuesday, which informed her that he had been wounded in the right thigh. He is now in a hospital in France.*"

This wound then needed hospital treatment in England, and he was sent up to the Military Hospital in Leeds for some weeks. Hopefully, this stay had at least some home leave added on, for he did not return to the Front till June 8th. Perhaps he was even able to be at home for his baby son Edward's first birthday on April 12th. There was never to be another opportunity for him to be with his family.

Third Battle of Ypres

June and July 1917 were months of intense preparation on the Western Front for the Third, and it was hoped final, Battle of Ypres. June had seen much blowing of mines and assaults on craters in a line from Hill 60 and St Eloi in the north, through Wytschaete ('White Sheet' to the troops) and Messines, (including the taking of the Messines Ridge by the New Zealanders), right down to 'Plug Street Wood' again. By the end of July, it was the part of the Front Line to the north and east of Ypres, that was again most under fire.

On July 29th, Private Wares wrote a letter to his wife "stating that they were going into a big battle".

In the early morning of July 31st, the Allied offensive began in bad weather. The greatest advance that day was in the region of Bikschote, where the

Menin Gate Memorial, Ypres

Allies penetrated to a depth of nearly two miles. On August 1st the villages of St Julien, Frezenberg, Pilkem and Westhoek were captured. Sanctuary Wood and Hooge then fell to the Allies after "very severe fighting." There was then a lull for a fortnight, while units re-grouped and retired, and reserves were brought in.

His death and commemoration

Private Wares died on August 3rd, at the very beginning of that lull, or even while that first advance was going on, or from wounds sustained during it. The day he died was the same day as his new young widow received the letter he had written her from the Front on July 29th, while waiting to go forward. This is reminiscent of Mrs Turk's experience back in October 1914 (see no. 1.1). The news of his death and the letter reached the Sussex County Herald for their edition of September 1st, 1917.

The *East Sussex News* a week later carried the family's Death Notice, and Mrs Wares' 'Return Thanks' from her and her family

> *"... to their many kind friends for the kind expressions of sympathy in their sad loss."*

Private Wares' body was never recovered, so he is commemorated on the Menin Gate Memorial to those missing on the Ypres Salient between 1914 and mid-August 1917. Nearly 55,000 names are inscribed there, including the three from Southover, all with no known grave. The names of his missing comrades from the almost legendary 12th Battalion of the Middlesex Regiment, cover three whole Panels (49 - 51) on this Memorial. Edward Wares, having began his life beside the West Gate of Lewes, thus had its ending marked on another old town Gate.

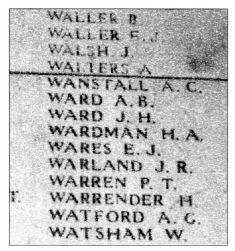

Private E.J. Wares' name inscribed on the Memorial, with some of the other Privates missing from his 12th Battalion of the Middlesex Regiment.

Those he left behind: widow Alice re-marries six years later

His daughter Ivy was just nine when she lost her father. Within three months, this child had another major change and loss to cope with, when on November 16th 1917 she had to leave the familiarity of Southover School and move to Brighton. There is a tantalising lack of background information about this move, and a long gap in local paper entries of any relevance, (though it is highly likely she would have been back in Lewes for the Unveiling and Dedication of Southover's War Memorial on All Saints Day 1921). By the time Ivy re-appears in the records, she is a young girl of 14, and old enough to be a witness at a wedding.

This wedding was at Southover Church on 6th January 1923, and the bride was her own mother, Alice Mary Wares. Alice was a widow of 34, and they had moved round the corner to 16 St Pancras Lane, where the new stepfather, William Alfred Scrase, who was a bachelor of 27, also lived. This was another example of a war widow with young children re-marrying, and where the new bridegroom was several years younger than the bride. This young man William Scrase, would also taking on a step-son, assuming the young Edward James had survived; the boy would by then have been rising seven years old, and no doubt very ready for another Dad in his life.

George William Osborne EADE   1.22
5th August 1917 aged 19
near Ypres
57547 Private
26th Battalion, Royal Fusiliers

HOME   3 The Course, Southover
BURIED   Godewaerswelde British Cemetery
          near Poperinghe, Flanders

Family and youth in Southover

This young lad was the eldest of at least five children of gardener George W. Eade and his wife Anna Maria. He was born in Lewes in 1897 or 1898, and soon had two young brothers in quick succession, Ernest born in 1899 and Frank in 1900. There was then a gap before their two sisters were born, Nora in 1905 and another one early in 1914. The Eade household would have been turned somewhat upside down, by the arrival of the youngest after a nine year gap. It may well be that the new baby was a step-sister, if George's mother had died young, perhaps after the birth of Nora, or possibly even earlier after the birth of Frank. They all lived in The Course, Southover, so would have been flooded out several times in their childhoods, when the Winterbourne Stream burst its banks. There were several different Eade households there and elsewhere in Lewes, and mostly Georges and Williams; there are indications that this lad was known by his third name Osborne, perhaps to distinguish him from his relatives.

Pte. G. W. O. Eade, Royal Fusiliers

When he left school, young Eade went to work at Lewes Station. He worked for three years up to the outbreak of war as a porter at the Goods Yard of the London, Brighton & South Coast Railway. Once he was 18, he joined up in March 1916, having already made himself "a useful member" of the Lewes Men's Voluntary Aid Detachment (V.A.D.) of the Red Cross.

Going off to the war

When George first enlisted, it was with the no. TR 21574, in the 30th Training Reserve Battalion (These TR Battalions were formed of volunteers who, at the time of enlistment, were too young to serve overseas). After his preliminary training at Dover in the spring and summer of 1916, he went off to France with 26th Battalion Royal Fusiliers.

It seems from the snippets of correspondence from and about him, as quoted in the local papers of the time, and his open friendly-faced photo, that he was a particularly cheery and affectionate lad. The obituary on his best friend Tom Coleman makes reference to young Eade (see Coleman, 1.19) living next door to the Colemans in The Course, and his great sense of loss on hearing of Tom's death in May 1917. Perhaps because his (step-) mother's hands would have been so full with a toddler, Private Eade's correspondence was mainly with his father. The *Sussex County Herald* quotes part of the last letter home to his father, written on July 25th from "somewhere in France", as follows:-

> *"Wishing you the best of health, as it leaves me, A1 at present…"*

It then continues as already quoted (under Coleman, 1.19 above), and giving his family the same advance warning about the same big impending action as Private Wares had already written to his wife along the road. In the event, it is highly likely that these two young soldiers, who lived round the corner from each other in 'old Southover', both received their mortal wounds in the same action on the same day, probably 2nd or 3rd August, in the same Ypres sector of the Front, specifically the Battle of St. Julien, Flanders.

The *Sussex County Herald* for Saturday 11th August 1917 entitled their news item about Private Eade:

> *"Southover Lad's Tragic End"*

This article gave the details of his pre-war life and friendships as quoted above, and continued

> *"… had served well in the ranks of the Lewes Branch of the RAMC under Mr W F Ingram* [one of the surgeons at Lewes Victoria Hospital]*, and had joined the Army and gone to France. From him, pleasant letters, hopeful and full of references to friends in Lewes, followed.*

> [After the family's receipt of his last letter] *a telegram from Regimental medical officials at the Front followed, and was succeeded in a few hours by a letter, stating:*

> *"In confirmation of my telegram, I regret to inform you that a report has been received to the effect that 57547 Pte. G. W. Eade of the 26th Royal Fusiliers is dangerously ill from gunshot wounds and fracture of the right leg."*

The *Herald* then continues:

> *"A Sister-in-Charge of the hospital in France to which the soldier was taken, wrote later stating that the limb had to be amputated and that the patient was in a critical condition.*

The same Sister-in-Charge wrote again on 5th August:

'… He passed away quietly at 5 a.m. this morning. He was not suffering a great deal. Everything possible was done for him, but it was hopeless from the beginning.' "

An affectionate message was sent by the dying man to his relatives."

Godewaersvelde and its British Cemetery

The Cemetery where Private Eade is buried is just in Belgium, about 10 miles south-west of Ypres, and halfway between Poperinge in Belgium and Hazebrouck in France. It is one of nearly

200 British War Cemeteries in this rural part of Flanders, in among wheat, beet and hop-fields. His grave is in Plot I, Row C, Grave 21. During the Great War, this was the great hospitalisation area, relatively secure behind the lines, and was dotted with all types of Advanced Dressing Stations, Casualty Clearing Stations, and Field Hospitals. It was well served by light railways, both pre-war from the mining areas to the coast, and newly-constructed to aid troop movements and casualty evacuations.

Pte.Eade's grave in Godewaerswelde Cemetery near Ypres; third from right in front row, with spire of Godewaerswelde Church beyond.

Godewaersvelde particularly was well-placed between forward battle areas, off-duty troops' rest and recreation areas at such small towns as Poperinghe, medical facilities behind the lines, and as an entry point to the railway network for Red Cross ambulance trains back to the Channel ports and 'Blighty'.

It remained throughout the war a haven of care and comfort for the troops, but also as a place-name quite un-pronounceable to the average 'Tommy'. It therefore became known to them as "God Wears Velvet",

Memorial Tablet, Godewaerswelde Cemetery: with line of old narrow gauge railway bringing the wounded out from front line to hospitals in the Godewaerswelde - Vlamertinghe area, or for onward transportation to the Channel ports, or for burial instead (it is now a long distance walkway, with municipal campsites at intervals)

nicely evoking the gentle care of the hospital personnel in the last stages of this life, and also its place on the 'Front Line' between this world and the next.

The main hospital development there was built for the influx of wounded expected from the Battle of Messines in June 1917, and the subsequent Battles of Ypres from July 1917 onwards. The Cemetery was developed partly as one of the inevitable destinations of patients no longer needing hospitalisation, but also as the final resting place of those many who did not survive the added trauma of a rough and cramped journey by ambulance train on top of the severe injuries they sustained in the first place. Between the summer of 1917 and the spring of 1918 alone, over 700 British and Commonwealth soldiers found their last resting place in this Cemetery tucked away in rural Flanders. Another two or three hundred were added since the Armistice, as the CWGC continued to gather in bodies hastily buried in local battle-area graves.

His own grave.

Those he left behind

Back home in Southover, just as arrangements were under way for the unveiling of Southover's own War Memorial, Private G. W. O. Eade's younger brother, Ernest Wilfred, got married at Southover Church on June 13th 1920. He had served abroad himself, and came back to his peaceful job as a gardener, following in his father's footsteps. He married at 21 to a local girl called Kathleen May Rose, who was already 24, and was the daughter of Albert Rose, a postman.

There is an Eade grave in Southover Churchyard with a headstone that names both a Rose Eade and a Louisa Eade. Louisa was the wife of G. W. Eade, and died in January 1915 when in her 44th year. It may therefore be that she was the second wife of George's father, and was the mother of the new baby girl born early in 1914.

Ernest Victor PAYNE   1.23
12th September 1917 aged 26
near Ypres
27708 Gunner
152nd Siege Battery, Royal Garrison Artillery

HOME   5 St Pancras Terrace, Southover
BURIED   Artillery Wood Cemetery, Boesinghe, near Ypres

Ernest Payne is distinguished by being the first Artillery man from Southover to be killed in action in this First War, and by being one of the few on the Southover Memorial who were already in the Army before the outbreak of war. He was also another of those many lost from Southover who was born and brought up in the old St Pancras Gardens area of Southover, that is no longer; Winterbourne floods, Second World War bombs, and rising housing standards, all contributed to the loss and re-development of what must have been a particularly close-knit and old-established 'community within a community'.

Family background

He was born at 5 St Pancras Terrace early in January 1891, and was baptised at Southover Church on 19th March that year. According to the Census of April 1891, he was the youngest of six children born to Edward and Fanny Payne. It is likely that he remained the youngest, as his parents (at 53 and 47 respectively when he was born) could hardly have been expected to have yet more children. His brother Edward George (baptised Southover 3rd August 1884) had been the youngest for six years up to Ernest's birth. Above him in age (with their ages at the 1891 Census in brackets), were their three sisters, Beatrice (8), Caroline (11) who had been baptised as Candice Jane at Southover on 28 December 1879, and Sarah (12). The eldest of them all was another brother, Albert (16), who was working as a "Shepherd's Assistant" but still living at home. He had been born when they lived at Laughton, and Sarah while they were at Hamsey, but the other children were all born after the family's return to Lewes around 1880.

Both parents, Edward and Fanny, had also been born in Lewes. Edward senior, the father of them all, had himself been in the Royal Field Artillery for twenty-one years, retiring with the rank of Sergeant. He then took work, along with so many Southover men of the time, as a gardener. He was still working in 1891, as a painter, but both he and Fanny his wife had died by the time Ernest went off to war.

Home and away with the Artillery

Ernest had followed his father's footsteps into the Artillery. He had in fact joined up with them several years before the war, and was posted with them to Hong Kong. Up till that time, he had worked round the corner from home at Ballards' Brewery (where Boehringer Mannheim now

94

is). He was a great sportsman, and was a well-known player in local football teams. He was unmarried, but his home was still in Southover. He was apparently as widely known in sporting circles in Uckfield as in Lewes; one of his sisters had married a Mr C. G. Turner of Uckfield, and had moved there with him. At the outbreak of war, Ernest's unit was recalled from Hong Kong to England, and was then sent straight to France. He had served virtually the whole war there, or at least on the Western Front in 'France and Flanders', apart from one short spell after being seriously wounded.

Ernest's death and burial

Six weeks before Ernest was killed in action, the Third Battle of Ypres had begun, and had already claimed the lives of two Southover men, Privates Wares and Eade (nos. 21 & 22) from infantry regiments. One of the first engagements of 'Third Ypres' had been the Battle of Pilckem Ridge, fiercely fought to the north of Ypres and across the Yser Canal. The British and French made significant advances on 31st July, including a night crossing of the Canal with the aid of many pontoon bridges. Also in that Battle, there was the Guards Division capture of Artillery Wood, a copse there then was on the east of the Canal, on the north side of the railway from Boesinghe to Thourout. It was the Guards Division who began, after that battle, a front line Cemetery there that was to be taken over by the CWGC and added to after the Armistice, and named Artillery Wood Cemetery. Initially, in 1918, it contained 141 graves, 42 of which were of Royal Artillery men, including now (and probably then as well) that of Gunner Payne.

On 12th September 1917, he was left on guard over the guns during the night. The *Sussex Express* for 19th October 1917, continues the story as follows:-

"LEWES FOOTBALLER KILLED

"…in the morning, he and two other Gunners who had been with him, were found dead in their dug-out, which had been penetrated by a direct hit from a gas shell. In writing to his relatives, his Captain states that death must have been instantaneous, and adds:

'He was a most useful Gunner who always did his work well, and was a good soldier in every way. I am having a cross put over his grave, in memory of him who did his duty to his country right up to the last.'"

The Commonwealth War Graves Commission has now amalgamated over a thousand further graves from smaller battlefield cemeteries all round Boesinghe, so that the present-day Artillery Wood Cemetery contains 1,295 War Graves, largely of U.K. men but some from the

Plaque on Belgian cemetery wall, recording the gratitude of the people of Belgium for the sacrifices made on their land, and giving the land for each cemetery as a memorial in perpetuity.

Dominions, and over five hundred of them un-named. It stands in open farming country, on the northern outskirts of modern Ypres, quite near the new motorway to Bruges. It is bounded on one side by a red brick wall, on the other sides by a low curb and a thorn hedge, and is planted with pollard willows and rambler roses. Gunner Payne's grave is no. I. C. 18.

Gunner Payne is one of the very few single Southover men who outlived both his parents, and left no widow or children behind.

Reginald Harry HORNE   1.24
22nd September 1917 aged 27
near Ypres
TF/240163 Private
5th Bn (Cinque Ports) Royal Sussex Regt, 'D' Coy.

HOME   "Stable Cottage". 24 Southover High Street
BURIED   Vlamertinghe New Military Cemetery, near Ypres

His home and family

Reginald Harry was the youngest of three soldier sons of Harry and Annie Horne of "Stable Cottage", 24 Southover High Street. This remains, with its old stable forecourt and drinking trough, nearly opposite The Swan Inn, between the present Southover Cottage, and the bend in the High Street with the Glover family home at "Brookside" opposite, beside the Juggs Lane. The Horne family seems to have come from St Martins, Suffolk, which is where Reginald was born in 1890. "Stable Cottage" may have started out as the stables to Southover Old House, at 22 Southover High Street, but more probably as the stables for the old Ballards Brewery nearly opposite, where the dray horses would have been quartered.

"Stable Cottage", 24 Southover High Street: site of Ballards' Old Southover Brewery stables for their dray horses, almost opposite where the Brewery was. An old stone drinking trough for the horses remains in this courtyard.

There seem to be no easily accessible records of any of the Horne family being in Lewes up to the outbreak of war, so it may be that they only moved in just before the war.

Reginald's two older brothers also joined up early in the war, and both seem to have survived it. One of them, Corporal A. W. Horne, enlisted with the 2nd Battalion Royal Sussex Regiment; he was then promoted Sergeant, and was awarded the Military Medal for gallant conduct at Pozieres on the Somme on 4th August 1916. He had been wounded during 1915, but had recovered and been back at the Front since February 1916. It was he who had been a friend of Corporal Arthur Head, and wrote a letter of condolence to Arthur's father on hearing of his friend's untimely death at the hands of a sniper on 7th October 1916 (see no. 1.17). The other one, A. V. Horne, was initially a Corporal in the Royal Field Artillery.

His last summer

The War Diary for the 5th Battalion Royal Sussex Regiment shows that in July 1917 they were in and around Vlamertinghe, to the west of Ypres, working on canal bank strengthening. While there, they were subject to gas attacks, and suffered some casualties. On 9th September, Private Horne's 'D' Coy. started working on the construction of shelters in what had been old German lines. Then, on 15th September, 'C' & 'D' Coy.'s camp was bombed by an enemy aeroplane; they suffered the loss of five killed and 14 'other ranks' wounded. A week later, on 22nd September, the same camp was bombed again, and another five were killed, and this time 19 were wounded. One of those killed on that second raid was Private R. H. Horne. The next day the two Coy.s were moved to a different camp just east of Brielen, the other (possibly safer) side of Ypres.

(The Battalion's total casualties in the Ypres area from 6th July to 14th October 1917 were: killed: 2 Officers, 39 'Other Ranks'; wounded, including gassed: 7 Officers, 306 'Other Ranks'.) Then, by the end of November, the Battalion had gone from the Ypres Salient, and were posted to Italy.

His death and burial

Aerial bombardment as a cause of death, either for soldiers in action or for civilians at home, was a sufficiently unusual phenomenon in 1917 for the *Sussex County Herald* to give it a special heading in their news item announcing his death on Saturday 6th October, only three weeks after the event:-

"KILLED BY AEROPLANE BOMB".

The article then quoted from a letter received by Private Horne's parents from Captain E. G. Bramall, who was O/C 'C' Coy. (possibly having to take over the writing of such letters for relatives of men in 'D' Coy. as well, as his opposite number commanding Private Horne's own 'D' Coy. had been a casualty himself of the same bombing raids):-

> ' *"It is my painful duty to have to tell you that your splendid son, Pte. Horne 240165, was killed this morning by a bomb dropped from an aeroplane. I hope it may comfort you a little to know that he died instantaneously and suffered no pain.*
>
> *Your son has been out here all the time without a break, and has always done well. He*

will be very much missed by us all. Please accept my heartfelt sympathy in your terrible trouble." '

The *Herald* continued their obituary as follows:-

"Lewes has, by the death of Pte. Horne, two of whose brothers are also serving in H.M. Forces, lost a man popular among his comrades and fellow-townsmen. When the 'call to arms' came in 1914 (they) responded, and have ever since been abroad."

In the same issue of the Herald, Mr & Mrs Horne had put their own announcement in the 'Acknowledgements' column, referring with thanks to the

"many expressions of sympathy (received), which are too numerous to acknowledge individually."

The original War Cemetery at Vlamertinghe, the nearest to where Reginald Horne was killed, had been filled by the summer of 1917. (This was referred to above in no. 1.15 in describing Henry Williams' burial there in the autumn of 1916; of all the lost men of Southover, it was Henry and Reginald who lived nearest each other). Vlamertinghe New Military Cemetery was therefore established, on the southern edge of the village, to take those who died in the last eighteen months of the war.

Vlamertinghe New Military Cemetery near Ypres, begun in 1917 when the original Vlamertinghe Cemetery in the village was full, after Reginald's neighbour Henry Williams (1.15) was buried there in 1916.

Pte. Horne's own grave in Vlamertinghe New Military Cemetery.

Many of those buried there are from Artillery units, and many were brought there by Field Ambulances from both the many local military hospitals and battle areas in the vicinity. The total number of British and Dominion graves is now 1,813; they are surrounded by a raised grass terrace, and the boundary is planted with willows.

It is today a beautifully peaceful place, and although not any distance from ring roads and the highway to Ypres, is surrounded by farms and meadows of grazing cattle, with a distant view of low hills through the trees. Private Horne's grave is in Plot X, Row G, grave number 7. Below the Cross and the official inscription on his headstone, the family has had added the words:

"PEACE PERFECT PEACE"

James CROUCH
7th October 1917 aged 26
near Ypres
TF/240961 Private
1st/5th Battalion, Royal Sussex Regiment, 'B' Coy.

1.25

HOME   11 St Pancras Gardens, Southover
BURIED   Dozinghem Military Cemetery, near Ypres

His family and life before the war

James Crouch was born in Lewes around 1891. There were several different 'Crouch' families in the town at the time; the only one in Southover just then was a couple who were caretakers somewhere in the parish, and had a daughter Minnie baptised in Southover Church on 27 August 1882. They were Robert and Elizabeth Crouch, and it could have been that it was they also became the parents of James, and that Minnie was his older sister.

Old St.Pancras Gardens, in the 1915.floods (Bob Cairns)

It seems that James was married by the time he was 20 or 21, and lived with his wife Jessie at 11 St Pancras Gardens. This was another of those lost addresses (now demolished) in that close-knit part of old Southover between the old Brewery and the Winterbourne stream. James was then, or had earlier been,

ST. PANCRAS GARDENS.
6 St. Pancras Lane. No Thoroughfare
(Left from St. Pancras Lane)
1 Holder, Mrs.
2 Holder, G. W.
3 Holder, John. jun.
4 French, Mrs.
5 Pollard, Horace
6 Pollard, James
7 Tucknott, A. A. E.
8 Dyer, Miss
9 Baker, James
10 Norman, Thomas

(Left returning)
Errey, Joseph
Rawlings, William
Lower, Charles
11 Mitchell, William A.
11aTester, H.
11bColeman, Thomas R.
11cStephens, James
12 Haffenden, William
13 Payne, Edward
14 Williams, John
15 Wren, George F.
16 Bassett, Henry
17 Payne, Albert

ST. PANCRAS LANE.
55 High St. Southover, to Rotten Row
(Left from High Street)
3 Cheal, Leopold
4 Isted, Mark
St. Pancras Place—
1 Thorpe, A.
2 Errey, Mrs.
3 Stevens, Frank
4 Brown, Charles
5 Larkins, William
6 Wooderson, Frederick
Richardson, George, general shop
(Here is St. Pancras Gardens)

6 Mepham, Mrs.
7 Reed, Mrs.
9 Harris, H.
St. Pancras Terrace—
8 Larkin, John
7 Pelham, William
6 Larkin, John, junior
5 Mockford, John
4 Clayton, Frederick
3 Richardson, George
2 Packham, W.
1 Prodger, F.

(Right from High Street)
1 West, T. C.
2 Richardson, E.
(Here follow Cleve Terrace and The Course)
St. Pancras Villas—
3 Holland, Mrs.
2 Smith, Albert
1 Mitchell, Charles
(Here is Grange Road)

ST. PANCRAS PLACE.
(See St. Pancras Lane)

ST. PANCRAS TERRACE.
(See St. Pancras Lane)

Street Directory for the whole St.Pancras Gardens area, showing how the streets led off each other.

working as a cowman for Mr F.J. Cornwell of Barcombe. By the time the war broke out in 1914, James and Jessie had at least one of their two children. Their son Leslie was born around 1912, and their daughter Iris followed in 1914 or 1915.

Either way, it must have been a hard decision for James then to enlist as he did, in Lewes in 1915, leaving these two little ones as well as his young wife behind, coping single-handed. He joined the same Battalion of the Royal Sussex that lost so many of its Lewes men in that early disaster, the Battle of Aubers Ridge on 9th May 1915; but he may not have been sent to France early enough in 1915 to have seen action with them then.

His death and burial

James Crouch's unit had been engaged in that first week of October 1917, in much the same work as Private Reginald Horne's was in the previous month (1.24). Both were in the supposedly relatively 'safe' parts behind the lines to the north of Ypres, on and around the west bank of the same canal, and on *"forward roads and tracks"*. On 28th September, a week before he was mortally wounded, the Battalion War Diary records that his 'B' Co.y was *"working on the St. Julien - Triangle Farm road"*, and that it had *"very few reinforcements during the month (despite) having heavy casualties. Co'y.s in temporary rest were being trained in drill and musketry"*.

Private Crouch died on 7th October in a French/Belgian Military Hospital, two days after being struck by a shell while working with the Pioneers. He was taken to hospital on 5th October with *"severe wounds in the arms and legs."*

Little more is known of this soldier, except what can be gleaned from the warmth of the letters of condolence to his widow , as reproduced below.

Barely six weeks after his death, the Sussex County Herald was able to quote extensively, on 27th November 1917, from these unusually warm and glowing letters his widow had already received, firstly from one of James' comrades in the same 'B' Coy. of the battalion, Pte. T. Cornford:-

> ... *"I was very sorry to hear of his death, as he was a good chum to me. I was with him the night he got wounded, and he took his pain like a soldier and a man. He was one of the true British boys, willing to do anything for anyone. All his pals feel his loss very much, and they extend their sympathy to you and your children in your sad loss..."*

The CQM Sergeant H. Roberts of Pte. Crouch's own 'B' Co.y, then wrote as from the Regiment:-

> ... *"The sad news came as a great shock to us, as none of us had the slightest idea that your husband was badly injured.*
>
> *He was so extremely popular amongst the men of the Co'y., and I can assure you that we shall miss him for (much) more than one reason. He was such a cheerful man, and such a hard worker. We had both joined the Co'y. the same day, he coming from leave and I from hospital."*

Finally, extracts of a letter from (? Sister) A. V. Jackson, writing for the hospital staff, were also quoted:

… "He was admitted here on 5th October suffering from severe wounds. (I now write) with deep regret to inform you that, in spite of every care and attention, he died on 7th October… Although the wounds were most severe, the patient did not suffer much pain. He was buried at the Cemetery here."

Dozinghem Military Cemetery is a few kilometres south of Westvleteren village and 8 km. from the renowned 'rest and recreation' town of Poperinghe, fondly known to the troops as "Pop". It is 12 km. to the west of Ypres, and near to the French border, and is on the light railway linking the two. There were many Casualty Clearing Stations and military hospitals in the immediate area, particularly the new ones set up in the early summer of 1917 in anticipation of massive casualties from the British offensive in July, at the start of the Third Battle of Ypres. To quote from the CWGC Cemetery leaflet,

" Westvleteren was outside the Front held by British troops in Belgium during the war, and the Cemetery is its one historical link with the British forces. In July 1917… groups of Casualty Clearing Stations were placed in readiness at three positions, called by the troops "Mending'em", "Dosing'em", and "Bandage'em"."

There are now over 3,100 British and Commonwealth graves in this Cemetery, reached along a woodland track between the village of Krombeke and Poperinghe itself, off the Leeuwerikstraat. The reference for Private Crouch's grave there is Plot VII, Row I, Grave 1.

Private Crouch's grown children

A little sequel can now be added about the Southover weddings of both the Crouch 'children' between the wars. It was Iris who married first, when she was a "spinster of 19", on 27th January 1934. Her new husband was a bachelor of 22 at the time, called Richard William James Tucknott, and he was a labourer who lived very nearby at 22 St Pancras Gardens. Her mother Jessie, and her brother Leslie, were the two official witnesses on the Marriage Register. Up to the wedding, the young bride had lived with them both at 34 St. Pancras Lane.

Leslie himself waited four more years to get married, when he was a bachelor of 26 and working as a bricklayer. His bride was Agnes Jane Weller, a spinster of 22 from further along in the old St Pancras Gardens. Her father was Alfred Weller, a prison warder at Lewes Prison.

The date of Leslie's wedding was 6th August 1938, just at the height of the 'Munich Crisis'. The bombings of the Spanish Civil War had been lived through, and 'The Situation' even in England was developing apace, even to the extent of gas masks becoming available in anticipation. Those children of those who had fallen in the 'War to end all Wars', were to re-experience in only a year's time at the start of yet another World War, what they had already lived through in their infancy first time round, and what their father and so many countless thousands like him, had died to prevent ever happening again.

George PACKHAM   1.26
22nd October 1917 aged 36
near Ypres
121001 Driver
'B' Battery, Royal Horse Artillery

HOME   8 St Pancras Terrace, Southover
BURIED   Solferino Farm Cemetery, Brielen, near Ypres

Family background

George Packham, and his younger sister Kate and brother Alfred James, were all born and brought up in Lewes. Their mother Margaret was also from Lewes, but their father James came from Newick, though there were several other Packham families living in Lewes. At the time of the 1891 Census, George and his immediate family (apart from the as yet unborn Alfred), were all living at Mill Cottage on the western edge of the borough. The cottage was somewhere between Rotten Row and Winterbourne Lane, possibly where buildings in the grounds of County Hall and St Anne's Special School now are. The parents were in their late thirties, George was ten, and Kate five. James, the father, was in work as a 'roadman': whether travelling on them, building them, or collecting taxes on them is not clear. Alfred James was then born during 1893, and baptised at Southover Church on 27th August that year. At that time, their father was recorded as 'Labourer, of Southover'.

From Boer War to Great War

George joined up with the Royal Horse Artillery in the last years of the century, while still in his teens. He served for eight or nine years as a Regular Soldier with them, including throughout the South African Campaign. Once those Boer Wars were over in the early years of this century, he returned to England and left the Army. He moved over towards Eastbourne, and started working at what was then known as the East Sussex County Asylum at Hellingly.

On the outbreak of this next war in 1914, he volunteered and re-joined his old Royal Horse Artillery, enlisting at Eastbourne. He remained single, but was still regarded as a Southover man by virtue of his childhood address, and now by the rest of his family living at 8 St Pancras Terrace (if not him as well when on leave). By the time of his death, a little over three years later, he had given twelve years Army service, and had become the Leading Driver of a gun carriage team. He thus went to war riding the leading horse driving the team, as now seen only at the Royal Tournament and state funerals.

Driver Packham's 'B' Battery in the Third Battle of Ypres

His 'B' Battery was assigned an important role in bringing the Third Battle of Ypres to as 'successful' a conclusion as possible before the onset of the fourth winter of the war. During

102

October 1917, the last month of Driver Packham's life, the British Front was extended some seven miles from Poelkapelle to Broodseinde, with their right flank on the slope of the Passchendaele Ridge. That Ridge was not taken completely, nor Ypres fully relieved, until 6th November after "the bloodiest battle in history".

It was in the build-up to that final battle of 1917, that yet another battle for Houthulst Forest at the northernmost point of the Ypres Salient, had to be fought, though without complete success for nearly another year. Napoleon had described this Forest as the 'key to the Low Countries'. In this Allied advance that Driver Packham was involved in during the Third Battle of Ypres in October 1917, only the southern extremities of it were reached. The whole region was subjected to gas attacks, and there was very fierce fighting with heavy casualties on both sides.

Driver Packham's death and burial

Driver Packham himself became one of those casualties on 22nd October, and news of his death reached the local papers by November 10th. A letter to his parents from his Commanding Officer, Captain C. J. P. Ball, R.H.A., giving details of his death was quoted on that day:-

> "...he was coming up into action on the Steenbeck during the Battle for Houthulst Forest. A 5.9" H.E. Shell scored a direct hit on the team, killing the deceased and another Driver instantaneously, and severely wounding two Drivers and a Sergeant. Seven horses were killed... Driver Packham was a first-class Driver in every respect; he was the real type of the horse artilleryman, and is a great loss to the battery.
>
> Please accept my sincerest sympathies, and those of all his comrades, with you in your great bereavement."

George was one of a hundred of his fellow Artillerymen to be buried in a small Cemetery at Brielen, a few kilometres north-west of Ypres, called Solferino Farm Cemetery. It was only begun during October 1917, and only has 295 War Graves all together, nearly all British. It is long and thin in shape, and is surrounded by flat agricultural land. George's grave is in Plot I, Row C, grave no. 4.

So passed another of the 'old Army'.

Soon after the loss of their eldest in this way, his parents moved out from Southover to Rodmell when the new Council Houses were built; perhaps James had retired as he would have been well over sixty by then.

Southover War Memorial
showing George Packham's name.

Wilfred Gordon ANSON   1.27
22nd October 1917 aged 27
near Ypres
265915 Private
14th Battalion, Gloucestershire Regiment

HOME   Southover Rectory, Rotten Row
COMMEMORATED   Tyne Cot Memorial to the Missing,
                         Passchendaele

Pte. Anson was the third of the three Southover soldiers to die in as many weeks in the northern and eastern outskirts of Ypres in October 1917. The fierce fighting in that Third Battle of Ypres, and in the Fourth Ypres nine months later, particularly the battle for Houthulst Forest in both, was of the greatest strategic importance in safeguarding Allied control of the channel ports, including Dunkirk. Had Houthulst Forest not been held, it is likely that both Ypres and the channel ports would have fallen. The course of our history could then have been very different.

Family background

Wilfred Anson came from *"a somewhat long military ancestry"*, and seems to have been the only son of his parents, The Rev. Harcourt Suft Anson and his wife Edith (nee Busk). He was born on 14th September 1890 at Little Over Vicarage, Derby, where his father was the Vicar. They all then moved south when Wilfred was a child, and his father became Vicar of Westmeston, near Ditchling. Wilfred's childhood was thus spent in a country vicarage, possibly somewhat secluded, but with village and 'big house' life on the doorstep, and surrounded by Sussex Downland. He probably grew up knowing something of both Lewes to the east and Brighton to the west, but mostly would have known Ditchling, just a few miles to the west, as he went to school at Eastfield House there.

When Wilfred was sixteen, his parents moved to Lewes, and his father became Rector of Southover in March 1907. The Rectory was still at Southover Old Rectory in Rotten Row (where County Hall and St Anne's Special School now are). While still at home, the young Wilfred was a keen bell-ringer at Southover Church, and as the Sussex County Herald wrote on 10th November 1917, he *"took a great pleasure in the work."*

He then completed his education at Brighton Technical College. By the time war broke out in 1914, his parents had moved to Salisbury, and he to Bristol. His father must have had some position in the Salisbury diocese or cathedral, and his parents moved to a house called "The Gables" in The Close there. Wilfred himself was working, in some apprentice/pupil capacity, at the Bristol Aeroplane Works. He was still unmarried, and his parents remained his next of kin throughout the war.

Pte. Anson's war

He enlisted in Bristol on 3rd October 1914 into The Gloucestershire Regiment. He was with the 1st/6th Battalion initially, then the 14th. His original Army number was 3315, though that was possibly while with a Territorial regiment before the war. He embarked for France with The Gloucesters on 31st March 1915. He was wounded in May 1916, and possibly again early in 1917. His late Colonel had, at any rate, occasion to write to Rev. Anson in April 1917, and made mention of his own *"high praise for his (Wilfred's) unassuming heroism."*

Tyne Cot Memorial to the Missing, near Ypres: the Cross of Sacrifice.

Pte. Anson's death came just six months later on 22nd October, the same day that Driver Packham was killed in the same Houthulst Forest (no. 1.26), and a fortnight after Pte. Crouch (1.25) was killed further over to the north-west of Ypres near Brielen. It came, according to the Sussex County Herald on 10th November 1917, *"during a gallant advance made by the Gloucesters"* in the Forest.

But for the Anson family there was never to be the comfort of knowing that his body had been found and given a decent burial. Wilfred's body never was found, so they were left to imagine the horrors of his annihilation by shellfire or mud. Those who perished in the Ypres Salient earlier in the war and similarly without a known grave, were recorded by name on the Menin Gate at Ypres, but after 15th August 1917 up to the Armistice, the Tyne Cot Memorial to the Missing was used.

As the CWGC describes it,

> *"this Memorial represents the most desperate offensive fighting of the British Armies in Belgium."*

It is set in an agricultural area surrounded by widely scattered and now rebuilt farms and villages, with distant views to the restored spires of Ypres, some five or six miles away to the south west. It was designed by Sir Herbert Baker, and forms the north-eastern boundary of

Some of the Memorial panels round the semi-circular wall at Tyne Cot.

the Tyne Cot Cemetery. It is so named because of the names given by the decimated Northumberland Fusiliers who fought there, (along with the 2nd Australian Division), to the three remaining German blockhouses now incorporated into the Cemetery, on the now grassy slope leading up towards Passchendaele.

Pte. Anson's name inscribed on Panel 72 at Tyne Cot, with the other lost Privates of his 14th Gloucesters.

Wilfred Anson's name is engraved on one of the Portland Stone panels (nos. 72/75) placed on the semi-circular flint wall that stands fourteen feet high, and is five hundred feet long. Wilfred's Gloucestershire Regiment has some 642 names on those two panels. They are only a fraction of the total of nearly 35,000 British and Commonwealth names at Tyne Cot, and of nearly 55,000 on the Menin Gate in Ypres itself. At Tyne Cot there are, in addition, the graves of nearly 12,000 soldiers of the Empire.

Trenches in the regenerating Sanctuary Wood in the Ypres Salient.

Frederick JEFFERY   1.28
30th November 1917 aged 38
near Arras
27432 Private
9th Battalion, Royal Fusiliers

HOME   c/o Gables Cottage, 55 Southover High Street
COMMEMORATED   Cambrai Memorial, France

Pte. Jeffery's family

Fred. Jeffery remains less well documented than many of the Southover men, and there seems to have been no home address within Southover for him. He remained unmarried, and his next of kin during the war was his father Mr. A. Jeffery, at that time of "Tainters", Pilt Down, near Uckfield. This house today is a substantial and beautifully restored half-timbered house, secluded in woodland adjoining the Piltdown Golf Course; but by the end of the second world war, if not long before, it had apparently become a very run-down group of tenement cottages occupied by gypsies and tinkers and their animals.

The Jeffery family originally came from Framfield, the other side of Uckfield from Piltdown, and it may be that Fred's home was still there. He had a brother, Archibald J. Jeffery, who by 1915 lived at 19 Friars Walk, Lewes, with his wife and family. Before the war, Archibald and family had been living in Crowborough; their son, George (Fred's nephew) had been born there on 13 August 1908. This lad George had started school in Crowborough, then transferred into Southover School on 31 May 1915 at the age of six. A year later, on 19 May 1916, he was moved again, into Malling School, though not necessarily as part of a whole family move. We only know that by the time the details of the fallen were being collected up by the Town Council for their School Hill War Memorial in 1920, Archibald Jeffery's family was living at "Gables Cottage", Southover.

Fred the Gardener

This move of schools to Malling corresponded roughly with Fred. Jeffery joining up in March 1916. He had worked as a gardener for many years, mainly in Malling for Mr. R. H. Powell of Malling House. Later he moved to work for Mr. R. Parker of Southover, probably Mr. Reginald Parker at 56 Southover High Street, whose house was in a row of several shops and some larger houses, between Potters Lane and St. James's Street. There may have been a big enough garden at no. 56 to warrant a gardener, or Fred. was maybe by then working in the house, or even the shop. Either way, he certainly kept up gardening as a hobby, and was renowned as a member of Lewes & District Horticultural Society.

107

Pte. Jeffery's short war

Already well into his mid-thirties, he joined up with the Royal Fusiliers in March 1916, very much among the older ones to do so. By the time he had received some training and crossed the Channel, there were only eighteen months of his life left. The whole area around Arras and Vimy Ridge was devastatingly heavily fought over throughout 1917 and 1918, with massive loss of life on both sides. During the autumn of 1917, Allied forces were advancing eastwards ever closer towards Cambrai. The actual Battle of Cambrai started on 20 November 1917; there was much severe fighting, with gas and tanks being used on both sides. By the end of November, the British divisions had taken 11,000 prisoners and 140 guns. It was on that last day of November that Pte. Jeffery was killed, though some early reports gave 25 November as the date. The place was broadly given as "near Arras".

People in Southover did not hear the news of his death until just after Christmas, and were unaware of it when they held their Memorial Service in church on Sunday evening, 16 December 1917. His name was not among those read out, or inscribed on the Roll of Honour at that time. Then on Saturday 28 December, the Sussex County Herald carried the briefest of news items, under the heading:

'A GARDENER KILLED'.

It seems to have taken another whole year for any further details to emerge. On Friday 29 November 1918, the *East Sussex News* carried this announcement in its "In Memoriam" column:

'JEFFERY

In loving memory of dear Fred… who was killed in France on 30 November 1917, while in the act of carrying a wounded officer to a place of safety.

"He truly gave his life for another". E.M.'

We are left intrigued as to who this 'E.M.' might have been, how he or she had obtained this information, and perhaps even why such gallant action did not lead to a posthumous medal award.

At least he did have one admirer, even if anonymous, to honour his memory, and to record the event.

The Cambrai Memorial to the Missing, Louverval

Pte. Jeffery is commemorated with some 270 of his comrades in the Royal Fusiliers (City of London Regiment) on Panels 3 and 4 of the Cambrai Memorial. This is in a corner of the Louverval Military Cemetery, near the rebuilt village of Louverval, on the long straight road between Bapaume and Cambrai, some 24 kms. south-east of Arras, and 16 kms. south-west of Cambrai. The names of the dead are carved on a semi-circular wall behind a colonnade, and at the entrance the following inscription appears in English and in French:-

"To the Glory of God and to the enduring memory of 7,048 Officers and men of the forces of the British Empire who fell at the Battle of Cambrai between the 20th November and the 3rd December 1917, whose names are here recorded, but to whom the fortune of War denied the known and honoured burial given to their comrades in death."

Officers and men from some eight main regiments are represented, with the London Regiment taking the greatest number of losses (587). Pte. Jeffery's Royal Fusiliers lost the next highest number, 270.

There were several other regiments whose losses were numerically much smaller, right down to the five who were lost to the 4th South African Infantry Regiment. These officers and men fell, for the most part, in the "soldiers' battles" at Bourlon, Fontaine Notre-Dame, Gouzeaucourt and Villers-Guislain, in the few square miles that were won or lost after the second day of the attack. Those many who were killed on the same day as Pte. Jeffery, 30th November, fell on the first day of the German counter-attacks, following the Allied tank victories of 20th and 21st November on the Hindenburg Line, and the capture of Bourlon Wood on 28th.

It should be added that these 7,000 names on the Memorial to the Missing represent only a small part of the total Allied losses in the same operations over the same few weeks; 20,000 more of their comrades were found, and lie in named graves in many other cemeteries in the same area.

Cambrai Memorial.
(CWGC)

Southover Church interior as at 1906

HONOURING LEWES HEROES.

MEMORIAL SERVICE AT SOUTHOVER CHURCH.

On Sunday evening a memorial service for the officers and men of Southover, Lewes, who have fallen in the war, was held at Southover Church. Lewes has approximately one-fifth of its population serving with H.M. Forces, and is bearing its share of the losses and anxieties of the war in the true spirit. The crowded congregation, despite the very unfavourable weather, bore testimony to the public appreciation of the service. The pillars and windows of the church were draped with the flags of the Allies, and the Roll of Honour at the west end of the church, surrounded by wreaths of laurel, was also draped with the National Colours. Among the congregation were many who have lost relatives in the war. The Lewes Company of the Sussex Volunteer Regiment held a special parade for the purpose of attending the service, and a strong muster assembled under Lieut. E. A. Glover, Second-Lieutenant G. Montagu Harris and Second-Lieutenant T. J. Farncombe. The men of the Military Agricultural Company and members of the Royal Defence Corps also atended. The Mayor (Councillor A. E. Rugg) was present, and other members of the Lewes Town Council attending were Councillor Martin, Councillor Taylor and Councillor Verral.

Prior to the commencement of the service the Organist (Mr. F. S. White) played "The death of Asa" (Greig) and "Solemn March" (Walford Davies). The service, which consisted of a shortened evensong, conducted by the Rev. A. S. Dendy (curate) and the Rev. E. Griffiths (who is helping at Southover during the absence of the Rector owing to illness), opened with the hymn, "Abide with me." In place of the anthem Master A. J. V. Coleman sang, "O rest in the Lord," from *Elijah*, with much feeling, and the hymn, "Peace, perfect peace" was also sung.

The sermon was preached by the Rev. A. S. Dendy, whose text was St. John viii., 51. He reminded those present that they were subjects of the King and subjects also of the King of Kings—the Almighty, eternal, all-loving and all-wise Father. Soldiers of the King called to fight their earthly enemies were also soldiers of the Heavenly King called upon to fight the spiritual enemies—the powers of darkness. They were citizens of Lewes, no mean city; and citizens also of the heavenly city, whose foundation stone was Christ Himself. They were assembled in God's House of Prayer that evening to remember and to honour the gallant heroes of Sussex who right manfully played their part and offered their bodies in the present colossal conflict. He would read out their names as they appeared on

the Roll of Honour in that church, which was kept with such loving kindness by Mrs. Stewart-Jones. They were Capt. T. A. Stewart-Jones, Capt. B. H. Glover, 2nd-Lieut. Brian Glover (who was awarded the Distinguished Conduct Medal and the Medaille Militaire), Sergt. F. C. Hillman, Acting-Sergt. R. E. Sandals, Corpl. A. H. Head, Corpl. J. Moore, Lance-Corpl. H. F. Neville, Gnr. E. V. Payne, Pioneer T. R. Coleman, Privates F. D. Turk, A. J. Blagrove, W. N. Hillman, R. J. E. Holland, G. Fellows, W. T. Martin, H. D. Williams, A. Harding, G. W. O. Eade, E. J. Wares, R. H. Horne, J. Crouch and W. G. Anson (the son of a former Rector of Southover). Another man of whom they were uncertain was Sergt. A. J. Suter, who had been reported missing and who was a member of the church choir and a true son of the church. Pte. W. N. Hillman was also a member of the choir. He had the privilege of preparing a few of these men for confirmation and he knew many of them. These men had sacrificed themselves in the noble cause of truth and righteousness and for the brotherhood and sisterhood of humanity. "Soldiers who have done this grand deed," continued the preacher, "if you can hear, in the Name of God, we salute you, we honour you, we thank you." Theirs, he added, was the sacrifice laid upon the altar of love and duty, and it was only this that redeemed the fierce clashing of legions of warriors from being a mere spectacle of brutal force. It was said that the blood of the martyrs was the seed of the church, and might they not say that the blood of these men and of the wounded heroes, too (for they must not forget them), was the seed of their homes and of the nation's existence? For these were the things that were at stake—their national life and social life and the common every-day life they lived were at stake in this great crisis. Their sons offered themselves in this great cause and had laid down their lives for it. They were not dead. Their bodies were dead; but they lived in God's kingdom. It was a comforting thought to know that in the face of great sorrow and in the face of death to know that they were separated from their loved ones only for a while, and that one day they would join them in their Heavenly Father's Kingdom.

So greet thou well thy dead across the homeless sea,
And be thou comforted because they died for thee;
Far off they served, but now their deed is done,
For evermore their life and thine is one.

At the close of the sermon Mr. White played very impressively Chopin's "Funeral March." Following this Corpl. Pender and Bugler Carter, of the Lewes Company, Sussex Yeomanry Cadets, standing before the Roll of Honour, sounded "The Last Post," and after the singing of the hymn, "For all the saints who from their labours rest," they sounded "Reveille." The concluding organ voluntary was "Marche Solennelle" (Mailly).

The offertory was on behalf of the British Red Cross Society.

Report of 21st December 1917 on Memorial Service for the then fallen

PART FOUR

1918

The War to End All Wars

The fact that 18 of Southover's 46 First War losses were killed in this last year of the war, more than twice as many as in each of the first two years, helps to show how desperate was the 'fight to the finish'. The last nine to die in fact all gave their lives in the last six weeks of the war, though one lingered on in hospital to the following spring. As in 1917, the Artillery lost four Southover men; the Cavalry and the Royal Flying Corps. each lost one man. The Royal Navy lost one, and one was from the R.N. Division. Only two of those lost in 1918 were from the Royal Sussex Regiment, in direct contrast to losses in the earlier years.

Still the majority was killed in action, though by the last months some eight died in hospital from wounds or disease. From the summer of 1918 onwards, the papers reflected the widespread optimism of ultimate victory; it must have been particularly hard for those families whose loved ones were still to fall right at the very end of the war. India and Palestine were by now added to the more usual Western Front places of death and burial for Southover's men; war even for Southover was becoming more global. Again, three of Southover's lost men were over 35 when they were killed, and two were under 20. Two young babies and two older children were left fatherless in this year alone.

Home address		Name		Number in book
1	St.James' Street	Francis George	GREEN	29
20 and/or 48	Priory Street	Frederick Arthur	THOMPSON	30
	Address unknown	William Walter	COMPTON	31
11A	St.Pancras Gardens	Charles Henry	FRENCH	32
20	Eastport Lane	George Walter	MOORE	33
28	Lansdown Place	Joseph George	NEVILLE	34
	Canning St.,Brighton	Alfred Alexander	DEAN	35
5	Grange Road	Charles Walter	HALL	36
40D	Southover High Street	Edward George	STEADMAN	37
15	Priory Street	Augustus Stanley	TURK	38
3	St.Pancras Terrace	Alec	RICHARDSON	39
	Address unknown	Harry Spencer	WEST	40
40B	Southover High Street	Frederick	POLLARD	41
2	St.Pancras Gdns.	George William	HOLDER	42
40E	Southover High Street	Alfred	COLE	43
32	Grange Road	Sydney James	SELBY	44
3	St.James' Street	George	PUTLAND	45
53	Potters Lane	Frank Harold	MARTIN	46

111

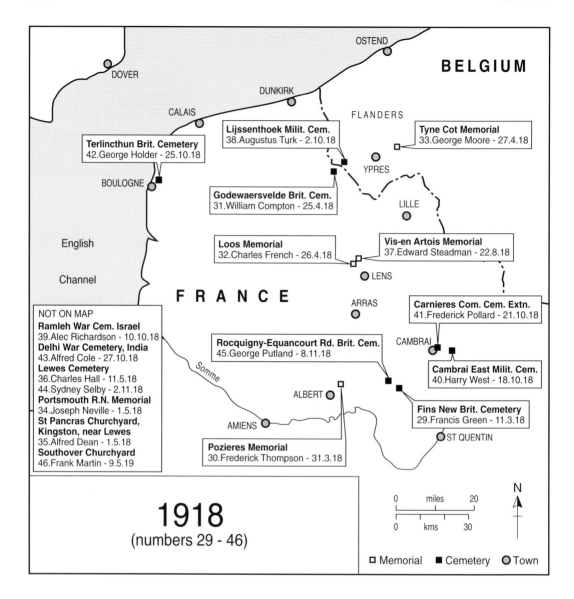

1918
(numbers 29 - 46)

Map labels:

OSTEND

BELGIUM

DOVER

DUNKIRK

FLANDERS

CALAIS

Lijssenthoek Milit. Cem.
38.Augustus Turk - 2.10.18

Tyne Cot Memorial
33.George Moore - 27.4.18

Terlincthun Brit. Cemetery
42.George Holder - 25.10.18

YPRES

BOULOGNE

Godewaersvelde Brit. Cem.
31.William Compton - 25.4.18

LILLE

English

Loos Memorial
32.Charles French - 26.4.18

Vis-en Artois Memorial
37.Edward Steadman - 22.8.18

Channel

F R A N C E

LENS

ARRAS

NOT ON MAP
Ramleh War Cem. Israel
39.Alec Richardson - 10.10.18
Delhi War Cemetery, India
43.Alfred Cole - 27.10.18
Lewes Cemetery
36.Charles Hall - 11.5.18
44.Sydney Selby - 2.11.18
Portsmouth R.N. Memorial
34.Joseph Neville - 1.5.18
**St Pancras Churchyard,
Kingston, near Lewes**
35.Alfred Dean - 1.5.18
Southover Churchyard
46.Frank Martin - 9.5.19

Carnieres Com. Cem. Extn.
41.Frederick Pollard - 21.10.18

CAMBRAI

Rocquigny-Equancourt Rd. Brit. Cem.
45.George Putland - 8.11.18

Cambrai East Milit. Cem.
40.Harry West - 18.10.18

Somme

ALBERT

Fins New Brit. Cemetery
29.Francis Green - 11.3.18

AMIENS

ST QUENTIN

Pozieres Memorial
30.Frederick Thompson - 31.3.18

0   miles   20
0   kms   30

N

□ Memorial   ■ Cemetery   ● Town

Some local newspaper items from 1918

Jan 4th

Southover Slate Club, which has its headquarters at the King's Head, has just completed its 19th year. This last year, its members contributed a total of £121.15s.10d. Of this, £19.13s.4d. was dispersed to 10 members for 236 days sick pay. A further £2.4s.0d. was raised from a levy on the death of a member's wife. 86 members then received £1.1s.3d. each.

A Badminton Match was held in the Corn Exchange between the staff and patients of School Hill House Hospital… The patients won, but the ladies were in excellent form.

Jan 11th

Evacuated child dies after accident in Priory Street: A four year old child, newly arrived at 30 Priory Street, Southover, from London (because of air raids), ran across the road to the milkman and was hit by a taxi, which was being driven by a woman. The child was taken to Victoria Hospital, where it was found to have a fractured skull, and died four days later.

Jan 18th

Butchers to close: all Lewes butchers shops are now to close for two days every week, because of the great scarcity of meat.

Snow: much work in clearing deep snow at Lewes all week. A snow plough was early on the scene, and soon followed by German prisoners with shovels, under an armed guard of Defence Corps. and Sussex Volunteers.

Friendly Games Evening: Southover Social Club beat St Anne's at billiards, but St Anne's won at snooker and cribbage.

Apr 2nd

Potatoes: last year Sussex produced 26,200 tons, but consumed 58,900 tons. The county will need to make every effort to reduce the deficit of 32,300 tons.

Cost of newspaper: the cost of the *Sussex Daily News* is being raised from 1d. to 1½d.

June 21st

Great Fire at Lewes: a great fire has raged all night at The Bear Hotel in Cliffe High Street. The building was 300 years old, and many neighbouring properties were also destroyed…

Oct 29th

Influenza epidemic: the first of the funerals has now been held in Lewes…

Nov 8th

Army Allowances:

- childless wife unable to work… 6s. 6d. p.w.;
- allowance towards commitments entered into by husband before enlistment, up to 12s.0d. p.w. (e.g. rent, insurance premiums, H.P.);
- children over 14 in school or apprenticeship: allowance can be paid to bring Separation Allowance up to amount payable for children under 4;
- Illness grants now payable for wife and children;
- Maternity grants of up to £2 now payable when wife has not insured herself under the National Health Insurance Act;
- Funeral grants now payable, up to £5 per adult and £2.10s. per child.

Nov 12th

Armistice Day in Lewes: Armistice was finally signed at 5p.m. yesterday… much merrymaking in the streets of Lewes…

wounded soldiers with flags waving from their crutches… policeman being carried shoulder-high…

Mayor appeared on Town Hall balcony…

Nov 13th

Red Cross Ambulance Trains:

- Another trainload of wounded men arrived at Brighton Station at 2a.m. yesterday. There were 23 Officers and 52 men on stretchers… it was the first such train to arrive to street-lights… (after years of lighting regulations)
- today's convoy was met by 16 Motor Ambulances driven, admirably, by young ladies, and the

clever and charming girls of the Night Convoy Workers' Canteen… all run by the St John Ambulance Brigade.

- The first Ambulance Train to arrive in Brighton was on Setember 1st 1914… no ambulances for transfers then, till much later; 50 private motor cars were lent by residents for the first convoy;
- Only one Military Hospital could receive these early convoys, the 2nd Eastern General in Dyke Road (using the buildings of the recently opened Brighton & Sussex Grammar School);
- Now there are many more, including the Dome, the Royal Pavilion, many of the largest schools, and other public institutions;
- The Sussex V.A.D. have now had the sad honour of handling 30,000 cases from 1916 - 1918;
- There were 92 Red Cross Ambulance Trains into Brighton in 1917, and 75 so far in 1918.

Munitions Workers have now been put down to half-time work only. Their pay is to be made up to the following levels: 30/- p.w. for men of 18 and over, 25/- p.w. for women; 15/- p.w. for boys under 18, 12/6d. for girls under 18.

Nov 15th

Southover Church Bells rang out a joyful peal once more. Scarcely had the official news (of the Armistice) arrived, ere the belfry was occupied by ringers past and present (11 names), all intent on pealing forth the news… The tower was again visited in the evening, when more ringing took place. In addition to the above-named, two former ringers who were home on leave from France after 14 months' absence, also helped.

Nov 18th

P.O.W.s are returning in great numbers, and many in pitiful states. 800 have been landed at Dover, and 1200 at Hull… in addition, many have been seen by War Correspondents marching back across France and Belgium…

Nov 21st

Lewes Carnival was held last night (after 4 years with no Bonfire)… The Band of the 14th Hussars led the procession to the Bonfire… the special Torchlight Procession included buglers, VAD Nurses, and new banners paid for by public subscription:

> *"Lewes Honours her Brave Sons - Neuve Chappelle, Festubert, Somme, Peronne, Ypres, Italy, and other engagements."*

Nov 22nd

Thanksgiving Services: Rarely, if ever, have the local places of worship held larger congregations than last Sunday (17th). Services of Thanksgiving for the signing of the Armistice and the termination of hostilities were held… In the Parish Churches, a special form of service was used…

Farewell to Reverend A. S. Dendy. After 5 years as curate of Southover, Rev. Dendy is moving to the parish of St.Saviour's, Tonbridge. At a farewell ceremony, he was presented with a cheque for 50 guineas and a fountain pen, and with a handbag for Mrs. Dendy.

Francis George (Frank) GREEN   1.29
11th March 1918 aged 36
Hindenburg Line, near Peronne
SD/4776 Private
13th Battalion Royal Sussex Regiment

HOME   1 St James' Street, Southover
BURIED   Fins New British Cemetery, Sorel-le-Grand

Family background

Frank Green was born and brought up in Southover, and for some years around his birth in 1882 his family lived at 8 Southover High Street. This was before the Hillman family moved there and took on Shaw's Stores and the Post Office (see 1.06). When the 1891 Census was held, the return for that address showed the young Frank as a boy of nine, a scholar, and the fifth of six children born to their parents Henry Stephen Green and his wife Mary. Frank was the first of the family to have been born in Lewes, and the family seem to have moved about a bit earlier on, possibly with the military.

*8 Southover High Street
Frank Green's birthplace and childhood home.*

To Southover via Sheffield, Co. Kildare, and Chichester

His father Henry had been born at Thornham, Norfolk in 1840 or thereabouts; his wife Mary was ten years younger, and came from Bishop's Waltham, Hants. Their eldest child (of those still at home for the 1891 Census) was Ernest; he was then 18 and working as a printer's apprentice in Lewes, but had been born way up in Sheffield. The family seems then to have moved to Ireland while he was a baby, as their next child was born in Co. Kildare, Ireland; she was a girl called Phoebe, who by 1891 was 16 and a dressmaker's apprentice in Lewes. Very soon after she was born in Ireland, the growing family moved to Sussex and the next two children, Albert and Maud, were both born in Chichester. By 1891, Albert was 15 and also a printer's apprentice, and Maud at 13 was still at school. Then came the two youngest, both born in Lewes; Frank was nine and Victor was four, both shown as 'scholars'.

115

Father's military past

In that 1891 Census, their father Henry's age was given as fifty, and his employment as "Serjeant Instructor of Volunteer Corps." At that time, the East Sussex Artillery Militia had a Depot and Drill Ground above the Kingston road, where 'Saxonbury' now is, and behind "Brookside" where the Glover family lived (see 1.09 & 1.12); the Drill Hall later moved to Watergate Lane. There was also the Drill Hall in Ham Lane used by the Territorials, the Lewes Troop of the Sussex Yeomanry, and the 'D' C'oy. of the 5th Battalion Royal Sussex Regiment. Wherever Sgt. Green's work was based, he would have been well known to almost all these "Men of Southover", as the same generation as his son Frank; he would no doubt have been a significant figure in their early training in Lewes.

Frank's marriage and hospital work in Lewes

By the time Frank went to war, his elderly parents had moved into 1 St. James' Street with their youngest son Victor, then in his late teens. Frank was possibly married by then, and may well have been living there too with his wife Harriet. He was working up to the war as Caretaker at the Lewes Infectious Diseases Hospital (in Wallands Park, near where the St Mary's Social Centre now is), so he and Harriet may have been living up there in some 'tied flat' at or near the hospital. There are no baptism details of any children in Southover.

1 St James' Street
Frank Green's parents' wartime home.

Private Frank Green's war

Piecing together what little is recorded about his war service, it seems Frank joined up in 1915 or 1916 having enlisted in London, and then or later joined the 13th Royal Sussex. By the autumn of 1916, if not earlier, he was back from France having been wounded seriously enough to warrant a 'Blighty' (hospital treatment back in a UK hospital). Throughout November 1916, he was hospitalised in Cardiff, recovering from his wounds. It may be that his marriage to Harriet did not in fact happen till that home leave, or even a later one in 1917.

Frank's father's death then his own

A major Green family event happened in Southover in the middle of the war, November 1916: the death and funeral of his father. Frank could not be there as he was still in hospital in Cardiff, but Harriet was not there either, nor is there any mention of Frank having even been married by then. His father, by then with the rank of Sergeant-Major, was 78 when he died in the first week of November 1916. The *East Sussex News* for Friday 17 November 1916, described the old man as having had 21 years' service with the Royal Sussex Regiment, and then 16 years as

Instructor to the Lewes Rifle Volunteers. The funeral in Southover Churchyard on Saturday 11th November 1916 was conducted by the Curate, the Rev. A. S. Dendy. (That date had not of course yet become associated with the nation's remembrance).

Frank's newly widowed mother was there, with her eldest son Ernest, and her youngest son Victor who was there with his wife. One of the daughters (a Mrs Langridge) was there, either Phoebe or Maud, with two adult Langridge grandchildren, Miss K. Langridge and Bombardier Alfred Langridge of the Royal Field Artillery.

Frank Green returned to the Western Front sometime after his father's death, with less than eighteen months left of his own life. He was at the time of his death engaged in the fierce resistance to the advances made by the Germans in their 'Spring Offensive', their desperate last-ditch stand of March 1918. Many of the villages between Cambrai and Peronne, particularly those on the Hindenburg Line, were repeatedly fought over and changed hands many times, with appalling loss of life on both sides. He lies buried in the Fins New British Cemetery at Sorel-le-Grand, in the Département of the Somme on the road from Fins to Heudecourt.

His grave is in Plot IV, Row D, Grave 4. There are now eight plots, and these include graves brought in after the Armistice from little local Cemeteries in the area, and they include nearly 300 graves of German soldiers. At the time of Private Green's death on 11th March 1918, there were just the first 590 burials from July 1917 to March 1918. The Cemetery now has a total of 1,193 graves in over 4,500 square metres. It is surrounded by a brick wall on three sides, and is on the eastern slope of a long valley by which the railway comes from Etricourt.

Next-of-kin remaining

By the time Lewes and Southover were getting their War Memorial details sorted in 1920, both Private Green's parents had died, but he was still shown as having two next-of-kin, his brother and his widow. His local 'informant' to the organising Committees was his younger brother Victor, still living at 1 St. James' St., but his widow Mrs. Harriet L. Green had left Lewes. Her address by 1920 was in Sea Lane, Ferring, Worthing, but whether that was her making a fresh start, or returning to the comfort of whence she came, history does not yet relate.

P.S.

Later on after the war, there were some Green marriages in Southover. Two children of Richard Stephen Green of 49 Southover High Street (recorded as a 'railway signalman, deceased') married at a double wedding on April 19th 1920. They were his son, Frank Clyde Green, a railway guard, and his daughter Kate Bertha Green. Another daughter, of the same address, was married on 28th March 1921. The connection between all these marriages was that the witness to all of them on the Green side was Victor George Green, younger brother of Frank. The deceased Richard Stephen Green may well therefore have been either a still younger brother, born since the 1891 Census, or perhaps an uncle or other relative already living in Southover before Frank's branch of the family moved to Lewes from Chichester. So the weddings were very probably those of Frank's cousins.

Frederick Arthur THOMPSON   1.30
31st March 1918 aged 26
Somme
33891 Private
8th Battalion, East Surrey Regiment

HOME   48 Priory Street, Southover
COMMEMORATED   Pozieres Memorial, France

Family and work in Lewes

Frederick Thompson was born in Lewes in 1891 or 1892 to Mr and Mrs Albert Thompson. They also had at least one other son, and he too gave his life during the war, in November 1917, just six months before Frederick. Their mother was by then widowed and was living at 23 Lancaster Street, Lewes (behind the Police Station, where the Scout Hut was built after the World War II bombs had damaged so many houses in that part of town). As her other son is not commemorated on the Southover Memorial with Frederick, it seems likely that they both grew up in St John sub Castro parish at their mother's address in Lancaster Street, rather than in Southover. (Frederick is probably named on the Southover Memorial by virtue of his marriage to a Southover girl and his wartime address at her Priory Street home, and the baptism of their baby at Southover Church - see below).

Frederick's first job was in the Cliffe, with Messrs. Curtis & Co. They were Saddlers, and had their shop at 24 Cliffe High Street, between Elphick's and St. Thomas a Becket Church. He was then employed by Mr G. Holder, one of the carriers running wagons between Lewes and Brighton, and was with them until the war started.

Frederick Thompson's War

He enlisted in Chichester, but when or with which regiment is not known. It may well be that he initially joined one of the Royal Sussex battalions, and was then transferred into the East Surreys later on in the war after being wounded and sent back to 'Blighty' for treatment.

The Western Front was ominously quiet through the winter of 1917/18. By February 1918, it had become clear that the German Army was massing itself for a major new 'Spring Offensive' between Arras and the old killing grounds of the Somme. This was the most critical time of the whole war, when despite the great influx of over a quarter of a million American soldiers in support of our hard-pressed and worn-out troops, and the greater use of tanks in tank-to- tank combat, the line between defeat and victory was very thin indeed. Enormous losses were expected on all sides, and it is likely that troops in the units earmarked for front line action in meeting this assault, and who were owed home leave, would have been allowed what for many of them would turn out to be their last visit to their homes and families.

Fatherless Baby

Pte. Thompson must have been one of these men, for nine months later his wife gave birth to their only son. This birth must have been one of many occurring in such poignant situations, for the father had been killed when back with his unit just over seven months earlier. Southover Church's baptism register for 29th December 1918, already six weeks after the Armistice, reads as follows:-

> *"Alec Henry Arthur Thompson, born 9th November 1918, at 48 Priory Street; parents:*
> *Edith Thompson, and Fredk. Arthur Thompson, soldier (deceased)."*

The whole of March and April 1918 was a period of great crisis for the whole British Army, and particularly for its Fifth Army (which included the 8th East Surreys), whose sector of the Front proved impossible to hold. There were forty Divisions attacking it over the unusually dry Somme valley marshlands. By 31st March the Fifth army had on paper at least ceased to be; its remaining troops were transferred into the Fourth Army, which was in reserve. The total British Army casualties for these 'First Battles of the Somme, 1918', between 21st March and 5th April alone, were in excess of 180,000 killed, wounded or captured, but have never been officially published.

Although the date of Pte. Thompson's death was at just about the deepest trough of despair and carnage of the whole of the war, the place where he died was in fact a relatively quiet little village on the south side of the Somme, not being fought over at the time. As the East Surreys' Hon. Archivist writes:

> *"It would appear that he was killed at Marcelcave, a small village near Cachy. No attack*
> *was taking place at the time, and I would think he was the victim of stray shell fire."*

It was 5th May 1918 before the local papers carried their brief reports of his 'death on the Western Front'. His wife would have been only just three months pregnant when she heard that her baby was to be fatherless.

Pozieres Memorial

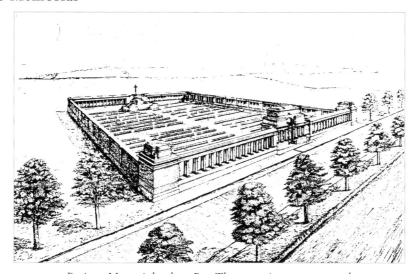

Pozieres Memorial, where Pte. Thompson is commemorated.

As Pte. Thompson's body was never found (or if it was his grave was later destroyed in the further heavy fighting that covered the same area) his name was included with those commemorated on the stone tablets around the wall of this British Cemetery at Pozieres. There are 14,644 of these names, and 12,741 of them fell just in those sixteen days of the second half of March, 1918. The names are grouped with those from their own regiments, and there are five regiments who each lost over 470 men that fortnight. Pte. Thompson's name is with some 175 of his comrades from the East Surrey Regiment, on Panels 44 and 45. The Cemetery is on the north-west side of the long straight road from Albert to Bapaume, about 7 kms. from Albert and just a mile or two from Thiepval.

The process of recording all the relevant names in this area, was a particularly long and arduous one. It was not complete until 1930, by which time young Alec Thompson would have been a lad of 12. By that time, too, his widowed mother had re-married (at Southover Church) and had become Mrs Edith Lower. She had also moved on re-marrying, to another little house in St John Street, no. 49. This was right behind the Police Station, and also just a few doors along from her late husband's mother at no. 23.

Priory Street, early 1900s

William Walter COMPTON   1.31
25th April 1918 aged 26
near Ypres
Second Lieutenant
Royal Field Artillery

HOME   ?29 Oriental Place, Brighton
BURIED   Godewaerswelde British Cemetery, Flanders

Family and cricket before the war

William Walter was born in Southampton in 1892, the eldest son of his parents Richard Spencer and his wife Edith Compton. There were several Compton families in Southampton and the Isle of Wight in the turn-of-the-century years, and more than one of the cousins he would have grown up with down there, also gave his life in the Great War. It has not been possible to identify any Southover connection or home address for this young officer, apart from his active playing membership of the Lewes Priory Cricket Club. His parents seem to have moved to Brighton before or during the war, and were living at 29 Oriental Place, Brighton, when William first went to France. Later on, his father became proprietor of the Crown Hotel, Ryde, on the Isle of Wight.

Working 'in timber' in Lewes

William certainly worked in Lewes, and up to the outbreak of war was employed by Messrs. Chatfield & Son Ltd. at 183 High Street (between the Rainbow Tavern and the Law Courts, which were then the old County Hall), a few doors along from the Suter family, (1.18). Messrs. Chatfield's were timber merchants, and must have been a firm of some substance, being one of the early Limited Companies in Lewes, and the first subscriber to a telephone line, "Tele. no. 1" as listed in the Street Directory. William's job there apparently involved some riding out to country districts on the firm's motor bicycle.

Officer Training with the Artillery

As with some others of his wider family, he joined up with the Artillery, and at some point was transferred within the Royal Field Artillery to some training unit for Cadet Officers. The *East Sussex News* reported his War Commission thus, on 12th October 1917 (though he had actually received it on 26th August 1917):-

"COMMISSION FOR LEWES CRICKETER.

Mr. W.W. Compton of Lewes, and a member of the Lewes Priory Cricket Club, has been gazetted Second Lieutenant in the Royal Field Artillery, from a Cadet Officers' Unit."

121

Death and burial in Flanders

Barely eight months later he was dead. April 1918 saw the beginning of the German offensive in Flanders, when our lines to the south of Ypres were broken, due to the loss of many lives and much previously held ground. Many units had to withdraw to relative safety behind the lines, and it seems to have been in so doing that William Compton was killed.

He was one of the few to have had a military funeral near both the time and place he fell; his was at Godewaerswelde, on the railway link between Ypres and Hazebrouck, surrounded by the new encampments of Casualty Clearing Stations and Field hospitals. William Compton had the perhaps rare honour in death, that his funeral was attended by both the Major in command of his Artillery battery, and no less a figurehead than the General in command of his whole Division, who would have been well-placed to

Cross of Sacrifice, Godewaerswelde Cemetery; with Mont des Cats in distance, with hospital for those with self-inflicted wounds hoping to be sent home. (no connection with 2nd Lt. Compton).

get there from the Divisional H.Q. at Bailleul, just over the border in France. It could of course have been that he was brought to one of the hospital units around Godewaerswelde, and died of his wounds there.

William Compton is one of many Artillerymen who were laid to rest in Godewaerswelde British Cemetery, between Hazebrouck and Poperinghe. His is among a total of 968 War Graves, all set in cultivated and pastureland in this now-peaceful part of Flanders. (For more detail on the Cemetery itself, please also see 1.22 on Pte. Eade). Photographs show the Cemetery as it is today, overlooked now as it was then by the Mont des Cats, a remote and wooded hillside on which deserters and other miscreants were on occasion taken out and "shot at dawn."

They also show the rebuilt Godewaerswelde Church spire in the distance, near where the famous "Remy Sidings" were, for loading and unloading all manner of casualties at all stages between battle, 'Blighty', and burial.

Much of that sad little railway line has now been dismantled, to form a long-distance footpath and cycle track, with public camp-sites where stations and sidings, and so much suffering, were.

2nd. Lieut. Compton's grave is in Plot I, Row R, grave no. 21.

Below the official inscription on his headstone, the family have put the following:-

THY WILL BE DONE.

Dearly loved and so sadly missed.

It was just a month after he was killed that the *East Sussex News* reported it on 24th May 1918:-

"2nd Lt. W.W. Compton Killed in Action:

His many friends in Lewes will regret to hear… The deceased… was particularly well-known in the country districts around Lewes as, in pursuance of his duties (with Chatfields), he travelled about a great deal on his motor cycle.

He was a good cricketer, and had played for the Lewes Priory and other local clubs."

Afterwards, the Major commanding his Battery wrote to William's father:-

"… He was absolutely one of the family, and his loss leaves a big gap with us. During his time with us, he had done exceptionally well, especially during the last hard month when his example and cheerfulness did us all a world of good. By his death, the Army has lost a gentleman and a gallant Officer."

*2nd Lt. Compton's grave (nearest) with Memorial Stone beyond,
and Godewaerswelde Church in distance, far left.*

123

Charles Henry FRENCH   1.32
26th April 1918 aged 20
near Bethune
41049 Private
1st/4th Battalion Kings Own Royal Lancashire Regiment

HOME   17 St Pancras Gardens
COMMEMORATED   Loos Memorial, France

Charles French is another of the lost Southover men whose childhood and wartime home has been lost to the developers. He was born and brought up at 17, St. Pancras Gardens, between Ballards Brewery and the Winterbourne Stream, in what was a small and close-knit 'community within a community'. He was baptised at Southover Church on 26th February 1899. His parents were Henry, a labourer, and his wife Hannah, and it seems that Charles Henry was the eldest of their three children. William James French came next and was baptised at Southover Church on 26th August 1900, and then there was Elizabeth Rose who was baptised on 26th February 1905, also at Southover Church.

They moved between various addresses in St. Pancras Gardens and Spring Gardens over the years before the war. There were several other 'French' families in Lewes and Southover, and with confusingly similar names and details.

Private French's war in France

Charles would have been only sixteen at the outbreak of war, and it seems he may have enlisted in Lewes for 'home service' with the 8th Bn. Royal Sussex Regt. initially. Once he got to France, probably during 1915, he would have been allocated to an Infantry Training Unit, and drafted from there to his 4th Battalion of the Kings Own. Very little is known about the course of the war for Private French on the Western Front, or for the family he left behind in Southover.

He was killed in action with the 4th Bn on 26th April 1918, at a time of particularly desperate fighting on all sides. His Battalion alone lost 42 Officers and 785 'Other Rank' throughout the war, and they saw action at Festubert, and on the Somme, around Ypres, Cambrai and Givenchy, and then the final advance in the summer of 1918. In the few weeks up to Charles' death, his Bn. was in the area round the La Bassee canal, and *were accommodated comfortably in billets at Marles-les-Mines" in the colliery district near Bethune. The days around the middle of April were fully occupied with a succession of bathing rotas, parades, fatigue parties for road clearing, until they had to undertake "embussing" to move to the Vaudricourt area. They arrived there early in the morning of 23rd April and *owing to sunny weather, the day was comfortably spent in the woods."*

The 26th April itself was a day full of intense action for the 1st/4th Bn; there was a combination of *"rushing enemy positions", "heavy hand-to-hand fighting", "withdrawal under cover of machine gun fire", "gaining touch with the 2nd/5th Lancashire Fusiliers".* By mid-afternoon the War Diaries of the 1st/4th Battalion record that:

> *"The King's Own reached their objectives after fierce fighting during which 40 prisoners were taken".* Later in the evening, they were *"surrounded on three sides and were forced to give some ground. After bitter fighting we accomplished a successful withdrawal to our former lines, inflicting heavy losses on the enemy."*

> *By 8p.m. the withdrawal was complete, and congratulations were received from Corps, Division, and Brigade Commanders on fine fighting."*

quoted from the Battalion war diaries with the permission of the K.O. Lancs Regimental Museum, Lancaster.

Sadly, after the intensity of that day's fighting, and with much more to come all summer, Pte. French's body was never recovered. He is therefore commemorated on the renowned Loos Memorial, about 5 miles to the south-east of Bethune, with several of the earlier Southover casualties from 1915.

The memorial has 172 names from the Kings Own Royal Lancs. Regiment, on Panels no. 19 and 20. They are but a small fraction of the total of 20,583 men who are honoured there. Only about 1,785 of those are in graves; the rest have "no known grave".

First War trenches preserved in Sanctuary Wood,
Ypres Salient.

George Walter MOORE   1.33
27th April 1918 aged 31
near Ypres
G/15796 Private
11th Battalion, Royal Sussex Regiment

HOME   20 Eastport Lane, Southover
COMMEMORATED   Tyne Cot Memorial to the Missing,
                  near Passchendaele

The Moore family

Pte. Moore was the second of five sons and one daughter born to Harry and Mary Anne (Polly) Moore. By the time of the 1891 Census, they were living at 20 Eastport Lane with George Walter's older brother Charles (who was six), and George himself was four. They were both already at Southover School. Their maternal aunt, Emily Hughes, was 17 and was a domestic servant living with them, though perhaps working for some other family nearby. Their father Harry was at that time working as a porter to a tallow chandler.

His older brother Charles was to join the Royal Garrison Artillery and serve in France. His next younger brother, Jesse, had emigrated to Canada before the war and had then returned to fight with the Canadian forces in September 1915, only to be killed in action at Loos a month later. [for full details on Jesse, and on the family background, see entry no. 1.08 above]. The youngest, Fred, was still only 20 in 1918, and had by then been to France twice with the Royal Fusiliers, won the Military Medal, been wounded twice and gassed once, and then posted to Ireland.

Very little is known about George's life or his death, even to the extent that some of the Moore family researchers had not known of his existence. Perhaps he had a colourful past which nobody wanted talked about. His parents were given as his next-of-kin, so we can assume he was unmarried. He was a gardener at Southover Grange, and therefore presumably employed by the Stewart-Jones family (who had lost the father of their young children back in May 1915), long before the Council took it over. He was also a bell-ringer at Southover Church, and had been able to get back up into the tower during a spell of home leave in December 1917.

George Moore's war

It seems that George Walter did not join up until about 1916, when he was 29. He joined the 11th Bn. of the Royal Sussex Regiment, one of its new service battalions. He just happened to be home on leave in Southover when the news came through of the momentous liberation of Jerusalem from centuries of Turkish rule. This was when Allied forces under General Allenby re-entering the city on 11th December 1917. It was doubtless felt as a great thrill and honour by George Walter and all the other Southover Ringers who climbed up the tower to ring a special peal in celebration of that great liberation.

He would presumably have been 'back at the Front' well in time for the last Christmas of the

Tyne Cot Memorial to the Missing with Cross of Sacrifice and some Panels

war, but hardly knowing it was also to be the last Christmas of his life. His death came within four months, in the face of the last great 'Spring Offensive' of the German Army who were determined to break through Ypres to the sea. He was killed in action on 27th April 1918, playing his part in stemming that tide.

Throughout April 1918, the British Army was engaged in the 'Battle of the Lys' to stem the tide of nearly the last great German advance. These desperately fought-over battlefields of the Ypres Salient were to continue being pushed backwards and forwards right up to the Armistice in November.

The Moore's heard nothing of their son's death for over a month, until confirmation finally came through at the very end of May. The *East Sussex News* then gave much of the above detail on Friday 31st May, under the heading "Patriotic Family's Second Bereavement". The *Sussex Daily News* of 3rd June 1918 also carried it briefly, under the heading "Two Sons Killed: Lewes".

His body never was found, and he is one of the countless thousands with 'no known grave'. Panels 86-88 of the Tyne Cot Memorial to the Missing, near Ypres, commemorate him and his 312 comrades from the Royal Sussex Regiment who fell in the Ypres Salient after June 1917. (see 1.27 on Pte. Anson for more about this Memorial).

And finally, the words of the Commonwealth War Graves Commission's own booklet about the Tyne Cot Memorial, written in 1927, seem to leave us with a fitting epitaph for both George Walter Moore and Wilfred Anson:

"The Armistice was followed by three years of active search for the unburied dead... Neither then nor since did the battle fields give up all their dead; bodies are even now being found, and will be found for some years to come. But the men who are named (here) are secure of their position among those who challenged the tide of war and would not go back. They fell beyond the limits of organisation, in places where courage alone held good. No man knows of their graves to this day."

G.W. Moore's name inscribed with other Privates of the 11th Royal Sussex on Panels 86 - 88

Joseph George NEVILLE   1.34
1st May 1918 aged 20
North Sea
23561 Signalman, Royal Navy
H.M.M.S. Blackmorevale

HOME   28 Lansdown Place
COMMEMORATED   Royal Naval Memorial, Portsmouth

Joseph Neville was the younger son of Henry William and Jane Neville. He was born in Nunhead, London S.E., and grew up mainly in Woking. His father worked for the Gas Board there, and was later transferred to Bognor and later still to Lewes. Joseph joined the Navy as a Boy Cadet in 1912, after a year or two working in the Stationmaster's Office at Woking. He then spent much of his first few years in the Navy out in the Dardanelles. His older brother Henry was killed in September 1916 (1.16).

These two brothers are among the few named on the Memorial who did not grow up in Southover; it is doubtful whether either of them visited Lewes at all, except on the occasional home leave.

Joseph's sister's memories

Joseph's only surviving relative, his younger sister Mildred, was in October 1995 in her 99th year and in a Lewes nursing home. She did not remember ever hearing any details of his service in the Navy. But she clearly remembered his last home leave, just six months before the end of the war. She remembers their shock and horror on hearing that just two days after returning to his ship, it had struck a mine and gone down in the North Sea.

The parents and their three girls had moved to Lewes from Bognor soon after the outbreak of war, once both the boys had joined up. Mildred remembers her father continuing with his Gas Board job in Bognor initially, commuting by train from Lewes. Their home at 28, Lansdown Place was at least very convenient for the station. Mildred was about 12 when she left school, and remembers her first job being at Baxters the printers before moving to a Department Store in Brighton. During the 1920's, her father died tragically in a fall down the stairs at home, and the funeral was at All Saints Church. Some time later, mother and daughters started going to Southover Church, a link that continued for Mildred into the 1990's, though many of her intervening years were spent in Brighton where her mother died.

Joseph's loss at sea

The ship on which Joseph went down on 1st May 1918 was a minesweeper, the "Blackmorevale". She was one of twenty in the new 'Hunt Class', the world's first Fleet Minesweepers. She was built at Ardrossan on the west coast of Scotland, and was launched there

128

in March 1917. She was not completed until July 1917, so had seen less than a year's service when she struck a mine and went down off Montrose. She had a ship's complement of 71 Officers and men, and had served with the 2nd and 3rd Minesweeping Flotilla based in Scotland.

On 10th May, the *East Sussex News* gave this brief report:

"TWO SONS KILLED IN THE WAR

Mr & Mrs H.W. Neville have received official intimation that the vessel on which their younger son, Signalman Joseph Neville, was serving has been lost, and that he was not among the survivors who had been landed.

He was 20 years of age and had been in the Royal Navy about five years…

The elder son, Lance/Cpl. H.F. Neville of the Royal Sussex Regiment, was killed in action in September 1916 at the age of 21."

In the years following the Armistice, much thought was given to how the CWGC could best honour the dead of the Navy in the Great War, the vast majority of whom could inevitably have no grave on land. The Admiralty decided that the three manning ports (Chatham, Plymouth and Portsmouth) should each have "an identical memorial of unmistakable naval form: an obelisk which would serve as a landmark for ship-ping."

Royal Navy Memorial, Portsmouth

The form chosen for them all was a stone tower supported by four corner buttresses, and topped by four ships' prows and representations of the four winds, all supporting a copper globe at the very top. All round the base are bronze panels with the names of the sailors com-memorated, cast on them. In the case of Portsmouth, these number 9,666. (Signalman Neville's name is on Panel 29).

On the sides of the tower are further bronze panels bearing the names of the principal naval engagements fought in the war, and the following inscription:-

"IN HONOUR OF THE NAVY AND TO THE ABIDING MEMORY OF THOSE RANKS AND RATINGS OF THIS PORT WHO LAID DOWN THEIR LIVES IN THE DEFENCE OF THE EMPIRE AND HAVE NO OTHER GRAVE THAN THE SEA."

Alfred Alexander DEAN   1.35
1st May 1918 aged 37
in hospital at Littlehampton
38554 2nd Air Mechanic
Royal Flying Corps

HOME   Canning Street, Brighton
              then 10 Grange Road, Southover
BURIED   St Pancras Churchyard, Kingston near Lewes

His family

Alfred Dean was born in London to George and Amelia Dean. They had another son, Archibald, as well. Archibald survived his brother, but both the parents had already died by 1918. Nothing further is known about the family at all, or whether Alfred himself had ever lived in Southover.

Alfred had not joined the Royal Flying Corps until the summer of 1916, shortly before it became known as the R.A.F. At that time he was married and living with his wife, Mary Elizabeth (nee Back), in Canning Street, Brighton. They apparently had no children born to them, but had adopted a daughter. Alfred's wife had come from Lewes, and it seems that after his death she moved back to live with her parents and sister, Lucy Back, at 10 Grange Road.

Air Balloon accident and its aftermath

While Alfred Dean was serving with his unit in France during 1917, he was involved in the launching and servicing of air balloons. These were widely used at the time mainly for aerial reconnaissance and photography behind enemy lines. There was then an accident during a launch Alfred was involved with seems to have led directly to his death, though many months or even a year later. He had been

> *"carried off his feet by a balloon which got away before everything was ready. He hung on until exhausted, and then fell a considerable distance, causing injuries to his spine which led to his death."*

Following this accident, he had been in hospital in France for a short period, before being transferred to a hospital in London (possibly St George's). He had several different operations and orthopaedic treatments, and complications set in. He was then transferred from London to the Duke of Norfolk's Nursing Home in Littlehampton, presumably when it was realised that nothing further could be done for him.

The funeral at St Pancras Churchyard, Kingston

The *Sussex Daily News* for Tuesday 7th May 1918, carried a detailed report of this "Brighton Air Mechanic's Funeral at Kingston" the previous day. The funeral is described as having been

Alfred Dean's war Grave in the peace of a Sussex churchyard, at Kingston near Lewes.

"semi-military", with members of the Royal Sussex Regiment walking beside the hearse and, at the close of the service, firing three volleys over the grave, while a bugler sounded the Last Post. The article continues: *"The interment at Kingston was according to the wishes of the deceased"*, and goes on to list the mourners, who included Alfred's brother Archibald.

The "floral tributes" are also listed: these were wreaths from his widow; one from his fellow-patients at the Nursing Home, and one from the nurses there; one from his parents- and sister-in-law, the Backs in Lewes; and finally "a spray from his adopted daughter".

His CWGC grave is in a peaceful corner of the graveyard, immediately outside the east wall of the church. The words "Till Jesus Comes" are inscribed at the base of the headstone, under the official inscription and R.A.F. badge.

Those he left behind

All that is known about the rest of the family after the war is that his widow later re-married, to a Mr Anscomber of Somerset Street, Kemp Town. He was a carpenter and joiner, the son of a baker, and was a "bachelor, of full age". They married at Southover Church on 4th September 1920, then set up home at 26A, de Montfort Estate, Lewes.

His grave alone, with family inscription "Till Jesus Comes"

Charles Walter HALL   *1.36*
11th May 1918 aged 32
at home
Saddler-Sergeant
Royal Naval Division

HOME   5 Grange Road, Southover
BURIED   Lewes Cemetery

Neighbours

This unfortunate man died within a week of the burial at Kingston of Aircraftman Alfred Dean (1.35), and lived five doors along Grange Road from Alfred's in-laws, the Backs, at no. 10. Their families would doubtless have known each other, and would have had quite a lot in common, and hopefully could have been of mutual support. Both men died after many months of illness, in hospital and at home, following injuries sustained at the Front, despite not having apparently had any sort of combatant role there.

Gassed

Charles Hall had an even shorter war than most of the Southover fallen. He did not get to France until April 1916, and then by the end of that year had been invalided out and returned to England, gassed.

He had first joined the R.N. Division (which served in some surprisingly inland settings) in November 1915.

Saddles and music

He then became a Saddler-Sergeant with the R.N. Division. This was presumably because of his pre-war experience while working with Messrs. Curtis & Co., Saddlers, at 24 Cliffe High Street. He would have been well-versed in the ways of horses and their equipment. He would probably also have been known to Fred Thompson (1.30), who also worked at Curtis's before the war. His main interests outside work had been as a member of both Southover Church Choir, and of the Lewes Town Band.

Two Weddings and a Funeral

It seems that Charles' mother had died before the war, and that his father Charles James Hall had by then re-married. He apparently had one brother and three sisters, all of whom were at his funeral in Lewes Cemetery. This was taken by the curate, the Rev. S. Dendy, as the Rector was still away on some sort of a 'rest cure'.

The *East Sussex News* for Friday 17th May 1918 lists the principal mourners at the funeral two days previously, as follows: father, Mr. C. J. Hall, and step-mother Mrs Hall; brother, Mr. A. Hall; sisters, the Misses Lily, Edith and Ethel Hall; brother-in-law and step-sister, Mr. & Mrs. A. Harris.

All three of his sisters had married at Southover Church, within the next six years after Charles' death.

Southover Church, where Charles Hall sang in the choir.

George Edward STEADMAN   1.37
22nd August 1918 aged 18
at Bray-sur-Somme
718241 Private
1st/23rd Battalion London Regiment (East Surreys)

HOME   40D Southover High Street (became 3 Priory Place)
COMMEMORATED   Vis-en-Artois Memorial to the Missing

The Steadman family

This young soldier came from a long line of inter-connected Lewes families, some spelt 'Steadman' as he was, and others as 'Stedman'. He was the youngest of four sons and a daughter born to John Farncombe Steadman and his wife Sarah Ann, around the time they moved down from St.Anne's parish to Southover in the last years of the old century. George Edward was baptised at Southover on 31st December 1899, when his father was an "oilman of Southover".

The other children were also all baptised at Southover, as follows:-
John Farncombe on 26th June 1887, when father was "Grocer/Porter, of St. Anne's" (junior - known as 'Jack')
Amy Jane on 25th Aug. 1889, when father was "whitesmith of St.Anne's".

William James on 30th Sep. 1894, when father was a "Mailman".

Charles Henry on 30th May 1897, when father was a "labourer of Southover".

George's father was a bellringer at Southover, who later on had the misfortune to die while in the belfry some time in the early 1930's, and is buried in the churchyard. All George's brothers joined up before he was old enough to do so, and it seems they all returned at least alive. His brother Bill was five years older than George, and had been with the 5th Royal Sussex at Aubers Ridge in May 1915. He was reported missing on the "Glorious 9th", and his photograph was in the local paper at the time.

George's short and desperate months in the Army

George was conscripted in to the Army as soon as he was 18, in the autumn of 1917. He joined the 1st Battalion, 23rd London Regiment; this was a Territorial Regiment affiliated to the Regular Army's East Surrey Regiment. This formed part of 142 Infantry Brigade of the 47th Division (Territorial Force). By the time George reached the Western Front in the spring or early summer of 1918, the war was culminating in a crescendo of the fiercest and most desperate and damaging fighting yet known.

It was a particularly hot summer, and the tide began to turn for the Allies with the start of the Battle of Amiens on 8th August. Amiens, the capital of Picardy, was on the Seine and on all routes between the Channel ports and the battlefields, and therefore of very great strategic importance. It was the entry point for most battle and medical supplies, and provisions in general. It was also a major centre for many army hospitals and Casualty Clearing Stations, from where so many thousands of casualties began their final return across the Channel.

The headlines in the *Sussex Daily News* on Friday 23rd August, which proved to be the day after George had been killed near Bray on the Somme, read:

> *"BIG DAY FOR ALLIES. BRILLIANT PROGRESS BY BOTH BRITISH AND FRENCH.*
>
> *Albert Re-taken: Haul of over 5000 prisoners by British in 2 days."*

George's short war had been lived among heat and dust, sweat and thirst, blood and poppies, and on a surge of triumph in the papers that probably felt very different on the chalky dust of the hills around the Somme. Then after the weekend, the same paper reported on Monday 26th August that:

> *"Bray and Thiepval were taken on Saturday, on the old Somme battlefields. In three days' fighting since 21st August, over 14,000 prisoners and a large number of guns have been taken. There are signs of collapse of the German Army, with large numbers of desertions."*

Bray was an old town, built on the steep northern banks of the Somme, and was finally re-taken by the Australians in a moonlight attack on the night of 24th/25th August.

A few days before that, the German Higher Command had apparently admitted to its Emperor in private that their victory was no longer possible.

Killed in action

It was to take about a fortnight for the news of George's death to reach his family in Southover. It must have been particularly difficult for them to absorb the news, coming as it did at a time of such national rejoicing over the successful advances, and the beginnings of seeing the war as all but over. On Thursday 12th September, the *Sussex Daily News* was reviewing the 'month since the tide turned' on the Western Front, and reported that our armies had taken 75,000 prisoners and 750 guns in that time.

The next day, Friday 13th, the *East Sussex News'* Deaths Column carried the family's sad announcement that George had been killed in action. A week later, they put in a further announcement:

> *"Mr and Mrs Steadman and family wish to return their most sincere thanks to all those who have so kindly sympathised with them in the sad bereavement they have sustained in the loss of their dear son. 3 Priory Place, Southover."*

His Memorial at Vis-en-Artois

Such was the ferocity of the fighting in those hot August days, that George's body was never found.

After the war, he was commemorated with nearly 10,000 others on the stone panels of the Vis-en-Artois Memorial to the Missing. They were all soldiers of the United Kingdom and South Africa who fell in Picardy and Artois in the 'Advance to Victory' after 8th August 1918. His name is on Panel 10. This Memorial is west of Haucourt on the north side of the Arras to Cambrai road. It has been built at the back of the British Cemetery there, where George's fellow-

Vis-en-Artois Memorial to the Missing, Picardy.
(*CWGC*)

135

Southoverian Brian Glover (see 1.09.) was re-buried after the war, having been killed in air combat above Vis-en-Artois in March 1916.

The next generation

Although both George's parents were still alive at the end of the war, it seems that by the time details were being collected up in Lewes for the town's and Southover's own War Memorial around 1920, his next of kin was given as Mrs. W. J. Steadman. She was his aunt by marriage, wife of his Uncle Bill, and it is their descendants who today run the Lewes Bathroom Centre.

Today's Bill Steadman (nephew of George) is now in his seventies, and still living in Lewes. He has now retired as a plumber, and has passed the business on to his son Andrew. He can remember his Uncle Bill dying in the belfry when he himself was a lad of eight or nine, and

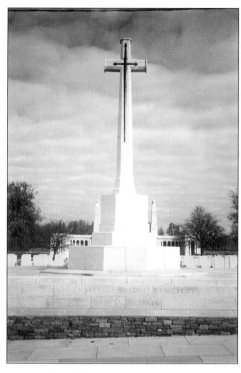

Cross of Sacrifice at Vis-en-Artois Cemetery, in which the Memorial is, with Memorial Panels beyond

he remembers hearing that his cousin George was "blown to smithereens" in the war. Some of the other details in this biography are new to the family, who have become interested to uncover more. A nephew was able to include a battlefield and Memorial visit while on a holiday visit to France last autumn (1997), and has provided the adjoining photograph.

Private Steadman's great-nephew Robin visiting the Memorial, beside his great-uncle's name on Panel 10.

Augustus Stanley TURK   1.38
2nd October 1918 aged 23
in Flanders
20065 Lance-Corporal
'C' Coy. 23rd Battalion, The Middlesex Regiment

HOME   15 Priory Street, Southover
BURIED   Lijssenthoek Military Cemetery, Ypres - Poperinghe

His pre-war youth in Lewes

Augustus was born in 1895, the youngest of three sons born to Spencer and Mary Ann Turk. At that time the family lived in Kingston near Lewes, and they were still there two years later when their youngest child, Mona Irene, was born there in 1897. Augustus's next eldest brother, Dennis Frank, had also been born in Kingston in 1893, shortly after the family had moved out there from Garden Street, Southover.

Dennis and Augustus were to become another pair of Southover brothers who both gave their lives in the Great War, Dennis in fact being the first of all the Southover men to do so. Augustus was one of the last, in that there were only another five weeks of the war to run when he was killed. But there were still another eight Southover men to die after him. (see 1.01 for the rest of the Turk family background).

Sometime during their childhoods, the family moved back to Southover, and lived at 15 Priory Street thereafter. Horses seem to have played as much of a part in Augustus's early life as they did for his older brother Dennis, who had gone into a Cavalry regiment. Augustus worked first for Mr. R. W. E. Morse at Rise Farm, Southover, on the way across the brooks from Kingston, and of course almost all farm work at that time was powered by horses. He then had a short while working in the Winterbourne area for Mr. Tom Fitton, who was one of the many racehorse trainers in stables all around Lewes at that time.

15 Priory Street
the Turk family's home from Augustus' childhood.

His war with The Middlesex Regiment

Augustus enlisted in April 1916, when he was 20 and when his older brother Frank had already been dead over eighteen months. He joined The Middlesex Regiment, one which had earned its title to fame as "The Die Hards" way back in the Peninsular Wars. They continued their illustrious military record right up to and throughout the First World War; from Boer War to Great War they expanded from 4 to 43 battalions, and had 19 of those serving on the Western Front in 1914 - 1918. They were by then the third largest regiment in the British Army, but sadly lost over 12,000 officers and men in that war. (The Middlesex Regiment as such exists no longer, but since 1966 has been amalgamated with the other old county regiments of Sussex, Surrey and Kent, to form the new Queen's Regiment).

By August 1916, the new Private Turk was serving with his battalion in France. He then had a spell on the Italian Front with them, before returning to France with them in March 1918, ready for the great forthcoming offensives on the Western Front. He must have been showing enough promise in all this, to be promoted from Private to Lance-Corporal. No sooner had this happened, than he became a casualty.

He was severely wounded, and also gassed at the same time, somewhere in the Franco-Belgian border country near Ypres. Augustus was one of those to benefit from the new army Casualty Clearing Stations and hospitals that had been set up behind the lines at Poperinghe since 1917, as possibly the Army's worst casualty predictions were realised in 1918.

His death and burial

He died of his wounds in one of those hospitals there, on 2nd October 1918, (though how long that was after he had received them is not known). His parents were informed within a week or so, and passed the details above to the *East Sussex News*, which printed them on Friday 11th October 1918. They also quoted from a letter the parents had just received from an Army Chaplain:

> *"It will be a comfort to you to remember that your son was a brave boy, and that he did his duty."*

It was in the Lijssenthoek Military Cemetery that he was buried, with over 10,700 others who fell in that frontier area or who died in its hospitals, as he did, from their wounds. This is the next largest Cemetery on the Ypres Salient, second only to the Tyne Cot Cemetery. It is set in particularly beautiful gardens, and outside its walls are the CWGC Nurseries, where plants are propagated for use in all the cemeteries of the region. It is about 8 miles west of Ypres, off the new Poperinghe Ring Road, towards the French border.

Extraordinarily, it is less than a dozen miles from the country churchyard at Neuve Eglise where his brother Dennis was buried four years earlier, at the very beginning of the same war. Augustus was not fighting on horseback as his brother was, but he had travelled part way round western Europe to get to almost the same place.

Alec RICHARDSON
1.39
10th October 1918 aged 31
in Palestine
87820 Private/Driver
53rd Battalion, Machine Gun Corps

HOME   3 St Pancras Terrace, Southover
BURIED   Ramleh War Cemetery, Israel

The Richardson families of Southover

There were many different Richardson families in Lewes around the turn of the century, particularly in Southover, which has made for difficulties in researching where Alec fitted in, until I was able to meet with his nephew Tony and niece Jean who both still live in Lewes. Through them and the Southover Parish Registers, and records held at the County Record Office, the following picture emerges.

Young Alec was born in 1888, and baptised at Southover on 24 June that midsummer. At that time, he was the youngest of five children born to George and Matilda Richardson of 3 St Pancras Terrace. This was another of those addresses between the Winterbourne stream and the old Brewery, that had been part of 'old Southover' before it was demolished after the Second World War to make way for the flats and shop in the new St. Pancras Gardens. Their father George was Lewes born and bred, and was a bricklayer by trade, but by the time Alec was born worked on the railway. Their mother had come from Seaford originally, but Alec and all his brothers and sisters were born and brought up at the same address in Southover throughout.

Three more brothers and sisters were to follow, up to the turn of the century, Walter, Minnie and Nell. The four older ones were Kate , George, Annie and Frank. The eldest son George was some ten years older than Alec, and worked as a drayman for the Brewery up to the outbreak of war. He was married by then, and lived with his wife Mary Elizabeth and their two young children, George Edward and Lilian Mary, at 5 St Pancras Lane, just round the corner from his parents, and his children's Uncle Alec.

Three of the Richardson brothers:
from L to R,
Alec (Machine Gun Corps);
Frank (R.E.), sitting;
Walter, MM (RAMC).

The wartime exploits of all these Richardson brothers

achieve a mention in the local papers. Like the Moore's of Eastport Lane, who also had several sons in the forces together, they were considered very 'patriotic families'. These four Richardson 'boys' do all seem to have had particular interests and skills in driving, and in the supplies and transport side of Army life. The *Sussex County Herald* for Saturday 17th July 1917 carries the following article:-

"FOUR SONS ON SERVICE: ONE WINS MEDAL.

Mr. George Richardson of St. Pancras Terrace, a well-known resident of Southover, has all his four sons serving the King, one of whom has been wounded while in France.

He is Private Walter* Richardson, R.A.M.C., but the wound though serious is not a dangerous one. "I was wounded", says Pte. Richardson in a letter to his parents, "in action by shrapnel to the chest on 23rd May. I have won the M.M. for 'rescuing wounded comrades under very heavy shell-fire'.

Mr. Richardson's other three sons are Driver George Richardson of the Army Service Corps; Driver Frank Richardson of the R.E., who went very soon after war broke out, and Private Alec Richardson, with the Machine Gun Corps."

* (the name given in the paper was actually William rather than Walter, but the family agree this must have been a misprint as it was their father Walter who won the MM).

Alec and the Machine Gun Corps.

This Corps. that Alec joined, grew out of the Army Service Corps and was later to become the Royal Tank Corps; later still it was incorporated into the Royal Corps of Transport.

When Alec first joined up, he was in the Army Service Corps with the number T4/275827. At the outbreak of war this Corps was fully operational as the Army's supply organisation; by 1915, it had expanded from 6,500 to 326,000 all ranks, with their number of Motor Transport vehicles increased from 100 to 120,000. In 1913, the Corps had fed 164,000 men and 27,000 animals daily; by 1918 it was feeding 5,400,000 men and 898,000 animals daily.

A large number of ASC drivers were then transferred to the 'Heavy Branch' of the MGC, later to become the Royal Tank Corps. Heavy and siege artillery tractors were also driven by ASC drivers. There were also close links with the Royal Engineers and their specialist railway transportation section, in France and world-wide; they were both laying new lines, maintaining older ones, and operating both locomotives and waggons. Alec and his brothers George and Frank could have been serving in any of these units

Even just the Machine Gun Corps part of this whole organisation was very large, with many of its different units serving in Egypt and Palestine towards the end of the war. The likelihood is that Alec, with his ASC background, was then transferred from the ASC itself to a motorised element of the MGC as a Driver; this was probably a Light Armoured Motor Battery, and/or a Light Car Patrol, as there were many of these active there in the Middle East at the time.

The Palestine Campaign

The Egyptian Expeditionary Force (EEF) under General Allenby had been fighting its way northwards towards Jerusalem through the autumn of 1917, around the famous Balfour Declaration of early November. This gave British support to the establishment in Palestine of a Jewish homeland, but in co-existence with the local Arab and Muslim populations, and was also strategically linked to the whole Suez question and keeping Britain's links with her substantially Muslim Empire out east. The EEF, with Driver Alec Richardson, won victories in this cause at Beersheeba on 31st October and in the desert around many other Palestinian towns, such as Gaza and Hebron. This then moved up to the final capitulation of Jerusalem to General Allenby on 11th December 1917. The sacrifice of some 17,000 Allied lives in those Egyptian and Syrian campaigns was part of the price paid for the eventual restoration of Israel as a nation some thirty years further on, and for keeping the Suez Canal in the meantime.

In the meantime, much relief work had to be undertaken among the starving and poverty-stricken populations of Jerusalem and other erstwhile Arab towns. Driver Alec Richardson's unit would have been heavily involved in this, and in the maintenance of the British military administration of the region, throughout 1918. The EEF, including his unit, also had further fighting to undergo even as late in the war as October 1918, to ensure Allied control of the whole of what would become Israel. The fighting at this time was very mobile, mainly involving cavalry and armoured cars, and it was just then that Driver Richardson was killed, with barely a month left of the Great War.

Alec Richardson's death, and burial at Ramleh

Since so many First War army records were lost to Blitz and fire damage during the Second War, not much more can be ascertained about the circumstances of Driver Alec's death. However, as the photograph shows, more is known about where he was buried once it was all over for him.

He was buried at the Ramleh War Cemetery, in the environs of old Jaffa and Lydda, and on a present-day bus route from Jerusalem to Tel Aviv. I was in fact able to make this fascinating bus trip during a recent 'Shoresh Tour' of Israel. But despite a most helpful Arab taxi driver for the last few miles, and after abortive visits to several other Jewish, Arab, and even Crusader burial ground in the vicinity, I was only able to visit the War Cemetery as a whole, sadly not to identify Alec Richardson's own grave in particular. I now know that his grave is no. 58 in Plot Z there,

Ramleh Cemetery, near Tel Aviv, Israel.

141

but there had most unfortunately been some communication slip-up between me and the CWGC about its exact location in that Cemetery.

There are over 3,500 graves there, from both local military hospitals and the surrounding battlefields. Well over one third of them are UK soldiers, and the three other largest groups represented are the Egyptian Labour Corps. and Camel Transport Corps, the Turkish Army, and the Indian Army. It is approached by a long avenue of eucalyptus trees, and the various national plots are surrounded by hedges of rosemary, acacia trees and other shrubs. It remains a haven of peace and beauty, even though the surroundings outside have been encroached on by urban sprawl and new ring roads out to Tel Aviv airport. The view of the distant desert hills to the east across the Jordan is still there between the trees, and on the Stone of Commemoration inside the main gates, are the words:

"I WILL LIFT UP MINE EYES UNTO THE HILLS"

Those he left behind

After Alec's eldest brother George returned from the war, he ran the sweetshop on the corner of the then St Pancras Gardens.

The youngest, Walter, who won the Military Medal and was hospitalised in France during the war, returned home to the St. Pancras area and became a painter and decorator. In 1926 he married Winifred Halsey at Southover, an ex-Army Nurse (Queen Mary's Army Ambulance Corps) he had met in France. Walter worked in a munitions factory in Norwich between the wars; sadly, he contracted T.B. and died at the age of 49.

However, he and Winifred had three children who live on in Lewes today, two sons Kenneth Alec and Anthony George (both named after their father's brothers), and a daughter Jean. They were all born in the old St. Pancras Gardens (and Kenneth Alec still lives in the present St. Pancras Gardens), and they have lived in Lewes all their lives. Tony still has his Uncle Alec's war medals and lives in De Montfort Road, and Jean lives in Western Road. Both have been most helpful in the background information for this biography, and have a wealth of memories about many of those Southover men of their own generation who died in the Second War.

Harry Spencer WEST   1.40
18th October 1918
near Cambrai
374393 Gunner
224th Siege Battery, Royal Garrison Artillery

HOME   ? Brighton
BURIED   Cambrai East Military Cemetery, France

Gunner West is the 'Southover' casualty about whom least is known. The Royal Artillery records list him as having been born in Brighton, and having enlisted there. As there is no date of birth given, we do not know how old he was when he died. It seems he had a brother Edward, but there is no indication of any connections with Southover in childhood, in family background, or in later employment, to account for his inclusion on the Memorial. Nor does there seem to be any local paper obituary article.

The date he died of his wounds, 18th October 1918, was only three weeks before the Armistice. It was also just nine days after the British and Canadian armies finally recaptured the major garrison town of Cambrai, which had been four years in enemy hands. It was a town of great strategic importance, lying as it does on the canalised River Scheldt, and at the intersection of two main railway lines, one from Calais to Basle, and one from Paris to Douai. It is also the seat of an Archbishopric, and has for centuries been a city of great importance in the history of France and the Low Countries.

One of the last big battles of the war

This recapturing was the last of the Battles of Cambrai, and victory was not finally assured until 9th October. This was the culmination of the Allies breaking through the notorious Hindenburg Line, but sadly the historic old town was very severely damaged in the process of the German retreat, as they were ordered to mine it and fire it as the Canadians and British advanced on it. The main square was still burning two days after the fight. This victory was then enshrined in the subsequent re-naming of the town's main square as 'La Place du 9 Octobre'.

During October and November 1918, there were no fewer than four Casualty Clearing Stations posted there. It would have been to one of those that Gunner West was taken, presumably at some time around 9th October. The Cambrai East Military Cemetery where so many of the battle casualties were buried, including Gunner West, had been started during the four years of German occupation. After the capture of the city, British troops added four further Plots for their newly fallen comrades; three more British Plots were added after the Armistice by bringing in those who fell in the surrounding area. Gunner West's grave is in Plot 1 of these new Plots, Row 1, Grave 13, among the 483 British graves.

Frederick POLLARD, MM + Bar, DCM   1.41
21st October 1918 aged 30
near Cambrai
42580 Corporal
6th Battery, 40th Brigade, Royal Field Artillery

HOME   5 Priory Place, Southover High Street
BURIED Carnieres Communal Cemetery Extension
near Cambrai

Family background:

Frederick Pollard was born on 8th February 1887. He was the third son of Henry Ephraim Pollard, a machine printer, and Mary Ann (nee Tulley) his wife, who had come from Brighton. They lived at 11 Eastport Lane, Southover, between St. Barnabas Church which was then on the corner with Garden Street, and with the Bell Inn two doors along the other way. The Pollard side of the family, and several other branches of it, had been in Lewes over several generations. (They were not, however, directly related to the other Pollards on the two Southover War Memorials; further family tree details are available). Henry Ephraim and Mary Ann had two other sons, Arthur and Albert, before Frederick was born. Then after him came the two sisters, Edith Mary and Mabel.

His childhood and youth

Frederick himself was baptised (privately) in Southover Church on 22 October 1892, when he was already five. He was just the same age as young George Walter Moore, who lived a few doors along at 20 Eastport Lane; they would have played and worked and worshipped together, and went through Southover School together, with Frederick also being a choirboy at Southover Church. (Frederick was in fact to outlive George by just six months, and they were to fall in battle not many miles apart, in the very last months of the war - for George Moore's life, see 1.33).

After leaving school, Frederick became a signalman on the South Eastern & Chatham Railway, at Eridge on the line between Uckfield and Crowborough. After some time there, he joined up (probably at the previous 'call to arms' for the South African Campaign), and served as a regular soldier for six years. He then went back to work as a signalman, while continuing in the Army Reserve. As soon as war was declared in August 1914, when he was 26, he immediately re-joined the Colours.

The war years 1914 - 1917

His army career from that point is well documented by the Royal Artillery, with whom he served throughout. The "Army Commemoration Book of the Royal Artillery" gives the following summary of his war service, from Mons to the Somme in the first two years, and then on to

Ypres in the third:-

"He proceeded to France with the 40th Brigade Royal Field Artillery in August 1914, and served with the Brigade Headquarters at Le Cateau, and all ensuing actions. At the beginning of 1916 he was posted to the 6th Battery R.F.A. as a telephonist.

During the attack on Serre by the 3rd Division in November, he volunteered to act as signaller attached to the Forward Observing Officer of his battery. The attack failed, most of the attacking infantry were casualties, and fearing a counter-attack by the Germans, all available men had to man the front line. Pollard immediately took up a rifle and helped to rally the remnants of the infantry, remaining fighting with them until reinforcements arrived.

For this he was awarded the Military Medal."

This commendation was recorded in the *Sussex County Herald* on 30 December 1916, as follows (but presumably before the actual award of the Medal)

"Lewes Man Commended:

The latest of Lewes' sons to achieve distinction on the battlefield is Gunner Pollard, R.F.A., who has been commended for good conduct on the field."

The Army Commemoration Book of the Royal Artillery then continues the story.:-

"During the Ypres offensive in October 1917, Pollard was awarded a Bar to his Military Medal for continuous gallant conduct at the battery position during heavy days of shelling."

Wartime Wedding

Very shortly after this, Frederick was able to get home on leave, and had an important date to keep.

On 20th October 1917, he married his childhood sweetheart, Alice Emily Cheesman, at Southover Church. He was 29 and she was 26, and they had known each other for years having grown up in old Southover together. In the years up to the wedding, while Frederick was away at the Front, Alice had been living at 'Longbank', The Wallands; this was the home of Mrs. Richardson, the widow of a previous Rector of Southover for whom she worked.

Her father George Cheesman, had been a soldier but had died by then; her mother lived on at 5 Priory Place off Southover High Street. She and several others from both Cheesman and Pollard families were

Corporal Pollard on his wedding day while on leave at Southover, 20th October 1917, with his new bride Alice Cheeseman.

Family group after the wedding, at the back of Priory Place
L. to R. standing: bride's sister Lily; ? ; groom's sister Flo; groom's brother Arthur;
bride's sister Edie; bride's sister Ann; groom's sister Mabel.
L. to R. seated: Grandma Cheeseman, bride's mother; bride and groom; 'Uncle' Taylor (best man);
front standing: cousin Molly, daughter of bride's sister Lily.

able to get to the wedding, despite wartime limitations. The best man had to be 'Uncle Taylor' from a cottage in The Cockshut although he was no relation, as apparently Fred's brother Arthur who it would otherwise have been, was not felt to be sufficiently able to hold his drink at the same time as performing the necessary duties. They had a group photograph of them all taken, as well as the one of the bride and groom, in front of the wall at 5 Priory Place. There was a family gathering there after the wedding , and it was there with Alice's mother that the young couple made their home. Had he survived, they would have moved back to the Signalman's House at Eridge Station after the war.

But Frederick may hardly have had any more home leave after the actual wedding day. The young couple were to have just one wedding anniversary, and that not together, before the Battle of Cambrai was to claim Frederick as another of its Southover casualties, the very day after his and Alice's first and only anniversary.

However, one very 'happy event' did follow that October wedding, and without it virtually none of this biography could have been written. Their daughter Edith was born on 10th July 1918, and was baptised in Southover Church a few weeks later. The photograph of the baby Edie with her mother and grandmother, was all that Frederick was ever to see of his daughter; it was found on him when he died a few months later.

1918: the last year of the war

The Royal Artillery's Commemoration Book continues the story of Frederick's army career:-

"At the beginning of 1918 he was promoted to Corporal Signaller, and placed in charge of the battery of telephonists. Time and again during the great offensive operations which started in August 1918, Pollard volunteered to accompany the Forward Observing Officers, but his services were so valuable in the battery position that he was not allowed to leave it… However, he was allowed to go at last on September 2nd, when the 3rd Division attacked Moreail and Lagnicourt.

Their daughter Edie's christening at Southover, August 1918 with her mother and grandmother.

Quite early in the attack the F.O.O.s were mortally wounded. Corpl. Pollard carried Lieut. Lambert to the nearest advanced aid post, and then returned and established an observation station, where he took charge and kept Brigade Headquarters accurately informed of every development in the attack, giving all map references correctly and sending back information of the utmost value. He carried on by himself until joined by the relieving Officer.

For his work on this occasion he was awarded the Distinguished Conduct Medal."

The Commemoration Book then moves on to describe details of his last action and death, in the aftermath of the fall of Cambrai to the Allies on the 9th October. His death was to come less than three weeks before the Armistice, and contrary to the Artillery's own obituary quoted below, was in fact on 21st October 1918

"On October 22nd 1918, he was mortally wounded near Solesmes while laying a telephone wire to a new Forward Observing Station under heavy fire.

Pollard was a fine type of those soldiers of the old Army who, having passed to the Reserve, when the call came, at once and without question and without demur, instantly threw up everything and poured back in their thousands to form the original Expeditionary Force.

In a tight place he could be relied on absolutely to keep his head and to do the right thing, and in all his actions he exemplified the three great soldierly virtues of courage, endurance, and self sacrifice."

His young widow was thus left with her three month old daughter just a year and a day after their one and only wedding anniversary. She put the notice in the Deaths column of the local paper, with this verse from herself and Fred's sisters and brother:-

"Hard it is to part with those
We hold on earth so dear;
The heart no greater trial knows,
No sorrow more severe."

She had to wait several weeks before she received any further details of how he died. She then did receive several letters from her late husband's commanding officers, and these may in some small measure have been some comfort to her.

Capt. N. Carbutt, who was commanding the 6th Battery when Fred was hit, wrote on 26 October 1918, and these are excerpts from his letter:-

"… He was one of the most cheerful, bravest, and best workers this battery has known.

He was beloved by all who knew him, and his lack of fear has many a time set a wonderful example to others. At the time he was hit, he was on the way to the Observation Post with me, laying out telephone wire. Even though mortally wounded, he ordered his fellow signaller to go on with the work.

I attended to him myself and he was taken to hospital at once, where he died the same evening…"

Alice heard next from Major Edsall Munt, who wrote from his home in North London while on leave on 3rd November 1918. She must have been very pleased to receive this letter, and I quote it in full:-

"Dear Mrs Pollard,

I have just heard from Captain Carbutt, who is commanding the 6th Battery while I am on leave, of the sad news of your husband's death in action, and hasten to offer you my sincerest sympathies in your great loss.

Corporal Pollard was one of the finest soldiers and bravest men I have ever known, and his loss is almost irreparable both to me personally and to the Battery as a whole. He seemed to have a charmed life, and we all thought he was destined to get through alright.

He has several times spoken to me of you and of your baby, and was longing for the end of the war, to get back to you both.

One thing is certain, that no man ever did his duty more thoroughly and more bravely than he, and you can be sure that he died the death he would have chosen. When you have got used to the idea, you will I know be proud to have made the sacrifice so many other brave Englishwomen have made.

No. *81*
(If replying please
quote above No.)

ARMY FORM B. 104–82.

R. H. & R. F. A. Record Office,

Woolwich

6th November, 1918

Madam,

It is my painful duty to inform you that a report has been received from the War Office notifying the death of:—

(No.) *42580.* (Rank) *Corporal.*

(Name) *Frederick Pollard.*

(Regiment) *C/40 Bde. Royal Field Artillery*

which occurred *in France,*

on the *21st October 1918.*

The report is to the effect that he *died of Wounds, received in action*

By His Majesty's command I am to forward the enclosed message of sympathy from Their Gracious Majesties the King and Queen. I am at the same time to express the regret of the Army Council at the soldier's death in his Country's service.

I am to add that any information that may be received as to the soldier's burial will be communicated to you in due course. A separate leaflet dealing more fully with this subject is enclosed.

I am,

Madam,

Your obedient Servant,

W. Y. Cuthbert

Capt..
l, Officer in charge of Records.

Mrs A. E. Pollard.

18640. Wt. 5529/M 2529. 150w. 7/17. R. & L., Ltd. Forms B 104—82/2.

P.T.O.

Royal Artillery's Notification of Corporal Pollard's death.

When I return to France I will make sure that his personal kit is
passed on to you,

With sincerest sympathy, Believe me . . "etc.

Shortly after receiving this letter, Alice Pollard would have received the Army's official notification, dated 6th November, of his death barely a fortnight earlier. (also reproduced by kind permission)

She would no doubt have been thankful that she received the Major's personal letter first.

She must then have written to Major Munt on his return from leave asking for some more information, for there is a reply from him dated 12th December 1918:-

"My dear Mrs Pollard,

I received your letter a day or two ago, and have been making
enquiries.

Your husband was laying a telephone line from the Battery to
the Observation Post near the village of St. Python, not far from
Solesmes. A shell burst quite near, and a large splinter hit him in
the side, penetrating the stomach. I am told that he at once ordered
the signaller with him to leave him and get on with the line.

Captain Carbutt was about 100 yards in front, and one of
the Signallers fetched him back. They bandaged your husband's
wound, and sent for a stretcher on which he was taken straight to
the Dressing Station. He was hit about 4 o'clock in the afternoon.
As soon as was taken to the Dressing Station, the R.A.M.C. took
charge of him, and sent him to the Casualty Clearing Station where
he died about 11pm. I don't think he suffered much pain.

He was buried at Carnieres, near Cambrai, on October 23rd
(sic.) the day after he was hit. I am afraid I can't tell you what his
last words were, as he had been taken right away in a motor
ambulance. He was partly unconscious most of the time; the only
thing he said was that his side ached a bit.

His personal kit was sent to the Base, and will arrive in time,
but I am afraid they are rather slow about it, as they take very full
precautions to see that everything goes to the right place.

I am afraid this is not very full information, but during a big
battle everything goes so quickly that in the interests of the wounded
one can only send them back as quickly as possible."

Those he left behind

Edie Pollard, Alice and Fred's daughter, who has of course been my major source of all this information about the father she never met, has provided all the photographs, including that of his grave in the Carnieres Cemetery. She was particularly pleased to go on a visit there with friends in 1993, while on holiday in France. It was a very special moment for his daughter to be able to put her arms round his gravestone, "the nearest I ever got to my father". The grave is in fact in the Carnieres Communal Cemetery Extension, which was not originally a War Graves cemetery, but has now been taken over by the CWGC. It is Grave No. 7, in Plot I, Row D. Below the official inscription on his headstone, the family have had added the words:

"Until we meet again"

Edie has also of course carefully kept all his war medals. (see photograph below)

Alice and baby Edie stayed on after the First War with Alice's mother at 5 Priory Place. This was later re-named as 40B, Southover High Street; it was part of a tucked away little enclave approximately behind 55 Southover High Street. Edie then went through Southover Primary and Central Schools, but she was not able to take up the place at the County Grammar that she won at 11+ because her mother could not have afforded the cost of the books. She remembers being chosen, as the daughter of one of the Fallen, to the lay the wreath one year at the Southover War Memorial. She and her mother regularly put bunches of flowers there throughout her childhood. She has happy memories of seaside holidays throughout her childhood, staying with her 'Pollard' aunts Edie and Mabel, who had moved to Bognor and Portsmouth respectively, with her cousin Percy.

In addition to the awards already referred to, he had the "Mons Star" that was given to all those who served with the B.E.F. between 5th August and 22nd November 1914. There were also the general Service medals, and the disc made from gun metal, and inscribed with his name followed by: "He died for Freedom and Honour".

EDWARD REEVES

Cpl. Pollard's Medals with his daughter Edie holding his photograph:
Medals from L. to R.:- 1. His War Disc, made from gun metal for all the fallen, inscribed with his name and "He died for Freedom and Honour"
2. Distinguished Conduct Medal, inscribed.
3. 1914 - 1918 Medal.
4. Military Medal for Bravery in the Field and Bar.
5. Mons Star, 5 Aug - 22 Nov. 1914.
6. "The Great War for Civilization".

The next generation in the next War

In the six years between her leaving school and
going away to serve with the W.A.A.F, Edie
worked for the Revd. and Mrs. Matthews at the
old Southover Rectory up to and after the
outbreak of the Second War. She particularly
remembers the last part of that time, when she
was looking after twins who were evacuees from
London. While there, she began her war service as
a Firewatcher. She remembers dark nights posted
at the top of Southover Church Tower, particularly the night that many footsteps could be heard
crunching up The Cockshut from the river valley.
Edie and her colleague were trying to convince
themselves this was not the beginnings of the long
awaited enemy invasion up the Ouse from
Newhaven, when a flock of sheep emerged from
The Cockshut into Southover High Street ! Soon
after that, Edie joined the WAAF and served four
years with them, much of it as Cook in the
Officers' Mess at RAF Downham Market in
Norfolk.

*Cpl. Pollard's grave at Carnieres Communal
Cemetery Extension*

That little row that had contained Edie's
childhood home in Priory Place, had also been
home to several of the other families who lost son
or husband from Southover. When it was demolished in 1941 Edie and her mother, along with
several of the others, were re-housed in Landport. Edie kept up her Southover Church links
throughout her years in Landport, but it was not till after her mother's death in 1981 that she
returned to live in Southover, and moved into one of the then new St. Pancras Gardens flats.
She remains widely known and loved throughout Southover, and I am greatly indebted to her
for a very great deal of help with this book, both text and photographs.

George William HOLDER   1.42
25th October 1918 aged 30
Hardeloo Hospital, Boulogne
121810 Private/Gunner
'J' Anti-Aircraft Section, Royal Garrison Artillery

HOME   2 St Pancras Gardens, Southover
BURIED   Terlincthun British Cemetery, Boulogne

Family background

George Holder was another of the Southover servicemen who came from a Lewes family with many different branches and large numbers of children, mainly in Southover. In his case, the great majority of them all seem to have been called George or William, which has made the searching somewhat convoluted. He himself was born in Southover, probably at Spring Gardens (beside the Winterbourne Stream, where the St Pancras Flats now are). His mother was Lucy Holder of Southover, who is shown in some records as having been on 'Parish Relief', and in others as having been "supported by relatives". In yet others, she is also shown as the wife of John Holder, who worked on the railways. It seems that her parents, also called John and Lucy Holder just for good measure, also lived in Spring Gardens. It is not clear where George William was brought up, but it may well have been in the four rooms at 1 Spring Gardens, where his Holder grandparents lived. At the April 1891 Census, they certainly had their 4 year old grandson William Holder living with them, as well as three of their own children (Frederick - 26; Olive - 12; Rose Ellen - 10).

St.Pancras Gardens (where Gunner Holder spent much of his life) in the 1915 floods; no.2 is presumably the first house on either the right or the left.

Southover youth

In the years up to the war, George himself was employed by the Corporation as an assistant at the Pumping Station. This was probably part of the waterworks near where the Stanley Turner Sports Ground now is. Sometime around 1910, it seems that he married a girl called Agnes Baker, when they were both in their early twenties (though not in Southover, which has no entry for it in their Marriage Registers). By May 1912 they had had a son, yet another William George Holder, who was baptised at Southover on 30th June 1912. This child went to Southover

School from November 1917 till March 1922, when he moved on to Central School.

War in France

George then enlisted in Lewes, at the very beginning of the war, when his toddler son was barely two. He became Gunner Holder of the R.G.A., and was later on attached to an Anti-Aircraft battery.

While he was away at the beginning of June 1917, a well-known old lady of Lewes died at the age of 81. She was Lucy Holder of Spring Gardens, Southover. She was almost certainly the grandmother who had probably brought him up, but there is no indication that he was able to get back for the funeral.

He was next due to be sent home in mid-October 1918, on convalescence or for further treatment. He was in Hardelot Hospital, on the southern outskirts of Boulogne, being treated either for wounds received or for disease of some sort. This was an area with a heavy concentration of Base hospitals, and other General, 'Stationary' and Convalescent hospitals, on the way down to the famous tented Army hospitals round Etaples. Troops would have been brought there from any part of the Western Front by long Red Cross hospital trains, for major surgery or onward transfer to specialist hospitals back home.

A sudden setback in Gunner Holder's condition prevented his embarkation, and he died in hospital there just across the Channel from home, on 25th October 1918. Another three weeks and he would have served the whole war through, and seen his 31st birthday. As it was, his widow made contact with the *East Sussex News*, and was able to let them have details from a letter she had received from the Matron of Hardelot Hospital. The ESN had an article about it on Friday 1st November:-

"DEATH OF A CORPORATION EMPLOYEE IN FRANCE"

"… He was to have been sent to England last Saturday morning, but a few hours before the time fixed for him to start, he had a severe attack of haemorrhage from the lung which proved fatal. The Matron, writing to Mrs. Holder, says:

'Please accept my deep sympathy, and my assurance that everything possible was done for him. While in hospital, your husband was always a brave and good patient.'"

Terlincthun British Cemetery, Boulogne

By those last few months of the war, it had become clear to the medical and army authorities in Boulogne that insufficient space remained in the local French cemeteries for the expected numbers of burials from the many local hospitals. Thus, from mid-June 1918, a new British War Cemetery was established at Terlincthun, near Wimille, on the northern outskirts of Boulogne. This was just a few miles inland, near where the first British rest-camps of August 1914 had been. It lies among hills and in view of the sea, and with a view of the Napoleon Column in the hills away from the sea.

There are over 3,500 war graves from the first World War there in sixteen plots. Almost all of these men died, as did Gunner Holder, in the Base Hospitals at Boulogne and Wimereux.

Gunner Holder's grave is in Plot VI, Row D, number 31. The remaining plots continued to be used until July 1920, while the local hospitals were emptied of those who died before they could be transferred back home.

Those he left behind

Just over a year after George Holder died, his widow Agnes re-married. She was still at the same 2 St. Pancras Gardens address, and was 27 by then. The wedding was at Southover Church on 20th December 1919, and the bridegroom was a near neighbour, Leonard Morris, of 6 St. Pancras Terrace.

He was some years younger than Agnes, being a bachelor of 22, and was a "labourer" as was his father Thomas before him.

The two witnesses who signed the Register in church, were Rose Ellen Rusbridge of Lewes, described as sister-in-law of the bride; and Henry Williams, grocer, of 36 Southover High Street. It was he who had lost his elder son at Ypres back in September 1916 (see no. 1.15), and ran the grocer's shop just round the corner in the High Street. Rose Ellen (nee Holder) was one of the children who grew up with the deceased George William at Spring Gardens. She was six years older than him, and may have been his half-sister, or quite possibly his aunt.

Gunner Holder's son, the young William George, was still at Southover School at the time of his mother's re-marriage and taking a step-father on board. A year later, in November 1921, there would be more memories of his own lost father at the Unveiling of the Southover War Memorial. Six months later, at Easter 1922, the young lad had yet another change when it was time to leave the small familiar Southover School and move on to the larger Central School in Southover Road.

The base of the Memorial outside Southover Church

Alfred COLE   1.43
27th October 1918 aged 29
in hospital at Delhi
6124 Corporal
14th King's Hussars

HOME   6 Prory Place, 40E Southover High Street
BURIED   Delhi War Cemetery, India

The Cole family in Southover

When Alfred was born in 1889, his parents Alfred and Elizabeth Hephzibah Cole lived in four rooms at 52 Priory Street, Southover. His father was a bricklayer's labourer at the time, but later on became a bricklayer, as were some of his wider family nearby.

His mother came from East Hoathly, as did her nine year old daughter, Georgina Hunnisett, (apparently from his mother's previous marriage), who was also living with them in Priory Street. Georgina's seven year old brother Charles was there too, and had been born after their mother arrived in Lewes. Priory Street and Garden Street had several other Cole families living in them at that time, so the young Alfred would have had plenty of young cousins to play with. His cousin Robert H. A. Cole was just the same age, and lived round the corner at 13 Garden Street, with parents Thomas and Elizabeth, and grandparents George and Eliza Cole opposite at no. 16.

He was himself baptised at Southover Church on 30th June 1889. By the time he was seven, he also had his own younger brother John (baptised Southover 26 July 1891), and sister Elizabeth who was baptised at Southover on 26th April 1896. His brother John was to become a Gunner with the Sussex Royal Garrison Artillery, and served at Dover in the early months of the war.

Alfred Cole's war

Alfred was 16 in 1902, and it seems he enlisted at Chichester as soon as he could after that. He was initially with the Highland Light Infantry, but then transferred to the Cavalry. He went off to foreign parts with the Hussars, and had certainly arrived in India with them by 1908, if not several years earlier. He would have lived through the 'grande finale' of the British Raj, and the beginning of the end of the British Empire. He had in fact been due for home leave just when the war started in 1914, but he was in the event never to get home again.

British troops from their bases in India, the 14th Hussars among them, were drawn into this global war over many months on the Mesopotamian Front (what is now Iraq and Iran). There were constant battles with heat and flies, thirst and disease, and sick horses to be treated, all among the deserts and mountains of the Middle East. Less often there were Turks holding out in Arab villages, observation balloons to be retrieved, canals to be kept open, sieges to be relieved - though the Hussars were not in time to prevent the disastrous surrender at Kut in December 1915 - but they were involved in the taking of Baghdad in May 1917.

His letter from Meerut to the *East Sussex News*

On 19th February 1915 the *East Sussex News* published the following letter it had recently received from him. It seems remarkably positive and patriotic considering his length of time away, the distance, and the recent dashing of his hopes of already long-overdue home leave - but still eager for the fray on the Western Front, as the poem printed below shows.

Corporal Cole's letter appears under the title "A Message from India", as follows:-

> *"I have been a constant reader of your paper for some considerable time. Having been in India nearly seven years I nearly forget what Lewes is like, but having the 'East Sussex News' sent to me I see a great deal of what is going on, and I am pleased to see Lewes is not behind in this great war. As everyone knows, we need more men, and if you think it worth while publishing these few verses I shall be very pleased, and it may lead a few of my old school chums to the ranks to keep up the good name of Lewes. I say to them:*
>
> *"Don't stay away because you cannot ride. We have horses that can talk, so call at the Drill Hall and tell the colour-sergeant you wish to join the pride of the British Army and go to the Front with us."*
>
> *At present there are three Lewes men serving in the 14th (King's) Hussars. Who'll be the next?"*

The *East Sussex News* then printed the verses Corporal Cole had sent them from Meerut:-

> "Boys, don't lose heart, we'll soon take part
> In crushing the Prussian joints;
> The reason's clear, they keep us here --
> Lord Kitchener's watching points.
>
> It would not pay to send away
> The flower of British cavalry;
> We keep the best until the last
> To pay them for their devilry.
>
> When Uhlan* host are making boast
> That none can face their lances,
> Lord Kitchener brings the 14th King's
> To put them into trances.
>
> We don't care figs for Uhlan pigs,
> With our leader Colonel Stephens;
> We'll make them barge when we get "Charge!"
> We'll give them dashing Uhlans.
>
> So flog spare kit, and keep quite fit,
> We'll soon be going to France;
> And when we start we'll make them smart,
> And dance the deathly dance."

* elite Prussian cavalry regiment

157

His illness and death in India

As it was, neither Corporal Cole nor any of the 14th King's Hussars were to get anywhere near the Western Front throughout the war. Corporal Cole had in fact sustained a leg wound in the course of all these forays into distinctly inhospitable country, and it was serious enough for him to have to go back to Base Hospital at Meerut for treatment. Meerut, in Uttar Pradesh, just to the north of Delhi, had been an army base for the British Raj in India long before the Indian Mutiny, and came more into prominence at that time. Corporal Cole was then also found to be suffering from rheumatic fever, which "disabled him from further fighting", as the *East Sussex News* put it, after "he had seen a good deal of active service on the Mesopotamian Front".

Ironically in all that heat, he then succumbed to what must have been a world-wide influenza epidemic by that time, particularly virulent among the exhausted and run down peoples and armies of Western Europe after four years of war. In his case, it 'went to his chest' and he died of pneumonia on 27th October 1918, just a fortnight before the Armistice.

He died in the Delhi 'Station Hospital', and is buried at the Delhi War Cemetery. This is about 10 or 11 kilometres out from the centre of New Delhi, on the eastern outskirts of the Delhi Cantonment. His grave reference no. is 8. B. 24. The Cemetery has an imposing entrance of Grey Dholpur Stone, and is still maintained by the Commonwealth War Graves Commission.

The base of the Memorial outside Southover Church

Sydney James SELBY   1.44
2nd November 1918 aged 19
in hospital at Dover
97723 Lance-Corporal
5th Battalion Royal Fusiliers

HOME   32 Grange Road (formerly of 12 Garden Street)
BURIED Lewes Cemetery

Two contrasting deaths

It is one of those strange quirks of war that two young Southover men who had lived round the corner from each other, this Sydney Selby and his forerunner in this book, Alfred Cole, should die within days of each other, and both right at the end of the war and in very similar circumstances, yet at opposite sides of the globe, and having had enormously differing experiences of the war.

They both died in hospital of pneumonia following influenza, but for one that was in Delhi and for the other in Dover just six days later.

They had both enlisted immediately they were 18, possibly earlier for Alfred Cole, and spent the rest of their lives on war service, though for one that was over ten years and for the other it was under eighteen months.

They were both in the Army, and served in a war largely associated with the Western Front, yet neither of them ever set foot in France.

They both achieved promotion by their own merit and hard work, yet for both of them illness prevented further advancement.

They both served in regiments other than their county's own, yet for one there were many years of dramatic and 'glamorous' soldiering in far-flung foreign parts, while for the other there was little more than a year of hard slog and study, all within the south-east of England.

Neither of them had married or left any dependants, 'just' sorrowing parents and wider families, in one case Southover through-and-through, and in the other relative newcomers to the parish.

The Selby family

They seem to have come from Worthing, in that that is where Sydney was born in January 1899. His parents were Thomas Henry and Elizabeth Selby, who lived at different times before and during the war years in both Garden Street and Grange Road. There is no record of Sydney having had any brothers or sisters, or of his schooling, or of where he might have worked until he was 18.

159

Sydney's short war

As soon as he turned 18 in January 1917, he went to Brighton to enlist. He joined the 5th Battalion of the Royal Fusiliers, with the number 136004 while in a Training Regiment, and was sent to Bury St. Edmunds in Suffolk for his training. He must have shown some promise, as he then took an additional examination in Signalling, which he passed "very successfully". On the strength of that, he was promoted some time in 1918, from Private to Lance Corporal. He was then transferred to Dover where he became Instructor in Signalling, all without having set foot in a battlefield.

During that autumn, he fell foul of the influenza epidemic that was gathering strength across the country, and as we have seen across the world too. He was admitted to the Castlemount Military Hospital in Dover. Despite careful Army nursing, pneumonia set in (antibiotics for chest infections were not in use until well into the Second World War), and the young Lance Corporal died on 2nd November, still two months off his twentieth birthday.

His body was sent back to Lewes, and he was buried with full military honours in the town Cemetery there on 6th November. His grave, with the standard CWGC headstone, is in the upper part of the Cemetery (ref. no. I.HH.42). At the bottom of the headstone, his parents have had these words put:-

*" Until the day breaks and the shadows
flee away."*

The *East Sussex News* carried a brief report on his death in their issue on 15th November. In it, they were able to quote from a letter written to the young man's mother by the Chaplain of his Company

"It will be a little comfort to you to know that he was the best NCO I had. I could trust him, and he was always cheerful in his manner. He was liked very much by all his comrades. It was a great shock to me when I heard the sad news."

Lance-Cpl. Selby's grave in Lewes Cemetery.

George PUTLAND   1.45
8th November 1918 aged 36
in hospital in France
M/204482 Corporal
Royal Army Service Corps

HOME   3 St James' Street, Southover
BURIED Rocquigny-Equancourt Road British Cemetery,
        Manancourt, Somme.

George Putland was born in 1882, so was one of the older men from Southover to give his life away at the Front. He was also another of those to fall prey to pneumonia rather than shellfire, and in his case just three days before the Armistice. He was the only son of John Barnett Putland, a Surveyor, and Lucy Tod Putland. His father died young, while George and his two young sisters had hardly started school. Even by the time of the 1891 Census, they were a fatherless trio living with their widowed mother alone, in the same house at the top of St James Street that was to be his home throughout his life. His mother Lucy was at that time 32, and was "supported by friends". The eldest child was Margaret Mary who was nine, and had been baptised across the road at Southover Church on 31st July 1881. George came next, and was already eight at the time of the Census, and the youngest Ellen was six.

The Putlands were another Lewes family with many branches in the area, particularly Southover. This particular branch of the Putlands had, it seems, set up quite a little enclave of Putlands opposite the church. George grew up with his elderly grandparents, George (his namesake, and another Surveyor like his own late father) and Anna, living just round the corner at 60 Southover High Street; they had come from Newhaven and

St. James' Street, with a corner of the old Southover School.

Denton, and had his maiden Aunt Anna also living with them. George also had some rather younger cousins living a couple of doors further down at 57 Southover High Street; Adelaide who was four years younger, and Francis who was not born till after the Census when George was already 8. Their father , George's Uncle William, was the younger brother of George's late father, and was a Merchant's Clerk, and was married to Margaret Mary, who was very close at least in age and home address to George's widowed mother Lucy.

Sometime before the war, George's mother had met and married a Railway Inspector by the name of Edwin Rann. He had a daughter, Kate, by a previous marriage, who was a couple of years younger than George. No other details have come to light about his war service, or his pre-war occupation.

George's war

George joined the Army Service Corps, with a different number (892318) initially from the one he ended up with. It seems he became a Driver of one of the bone-shaking troop transport trucks, so often seen in films of the time struggling in the mud of the Western Front. He was attached to G.H.Q. Troops' Mechanical Transport Coy., and presumably by that last week of the war there was a lot of re-deploying of troops and supplies to be done, and at some speed before the onset of winter would have made what roads and tracks were left, even less passable.

When he went down with the flu and had to be hospitalised as it turned into pneumonia, it seems likely that he was in an army hospital at Ytres in the northern part of the Département of the Somme. The 48th Casualty Clearing Station was posted there in 1917, and both it and the 18th C.C.S. used the "Old English Cemetery" nearby for their burials again in October and November 1918, after some months when it was behind the German lines. The nearest village to this Cemetery was Manancourt, and by the time Driver Putland was buried there, the Cemetery was re-named as the "Rocquigny/Equancourt Road British Cemetery". It lies near Etricourt on the road between Rocquigny and Equancourt, about seven miles to the south-east of Bapaume, and a little further to the north of Peronne. It stands on high ground, overlooking the valley of the Tortille and the Canal du Nord. It is planted with mountain ash and other trees, and contains over 1,800 War Graves, nearly all British.

Those he left behind

It may well be that George's mother Lucy did not survive the war, as she is not mentioned as his next-of-kin on his CWGC Casualty Details form. No family details are given at all on that, but when the Lewes Town and Southover Memorials were being prepared, only Edwin Rann as his step-father is given. Then in December 1919, when Edwin's daughter Kate was 32, and just a year after George's death, Kate was married at Southover Church to Ralph Mills, a carpenter from Arundel.

Frank Harold MARTIN
9th April 1919 aged 19
in hospital at Norwich
81748 Private
The Queen's (Royal West Surrey) Regiment

1.46

HOME   53 Potters Lane, Southover
BURIED Southover Churchyard

(see also 1.14, his older brother, who died 27th August 1916 in hospital in France)

Frank was born in the last year or so of the 19th century, when his parents Thomas and Ruth Martin were still living in The Cliffe. His older brother William Thomas had also been born there two years earlier. Sadly, these boys were very quickly to lose their mother. Midwifery services not being what they are now, it is probable that she died at or very shortly after giving birth to the new baby Frank. However, by Christmas 1901, their father Thomas had re-married as a widower and they moved to 55 Priory Street.

They married on Boxing Day 1901 at Southover Church. Thomas at 37 continued in his plate-laying job on the railways, and was no doubt much relieved that his two little boys now had a step-mother. She was a lady of 46, and had not previously been married. Her name was Mary Anne Tulley, a name connected indirectly with Fred Pollard's family and others from Eastport Lane. After some years in Priory Street, they all moved along to Potters Lane, and lived at no. 53 there. It is not entirely clear whether that house is still there and re-named, or whether it was demolished to make way for the garages behind the old houses fronting on to Southover High Street, between them and the 'between the wars' terraced housing coming up from The Course.

Nor is it at all clear when and where Frank enlisted, or even whether he ever served in France or on some other Front, or indeed any at all. Given that he was only 19 when he died, he could only have had a year or two of overseas service at the most. Or it may be that he died of long-term disease, rather then from wounds received in action. All we do know is that he died in "Norwich Hospital" some five months after the official end of the war, and that he has a CWGC headstone on his grave in Southover Churchyard. The assumption therefore has to be that he eventually died of severe wounds or the after-effects of gas, which could not have been appropriately treated had he been transferred to a non-military hospital nearer his home.

Frank Martin's grave in Southover Churchyard.

A tranquil corner of Southover Churchyard.

PART FIVE

SOUTHOVER BETWEEN THE WARS

Southover in each of the wars was pretty much a 'microcosm' of the nation, mirroring fairly closely what was going on in each war world-wide and in the life of the nation as a whole. It was the same in the 1920's and 1930's, and in this brief linking page between the wars, I can only highlight some of the main trends. Robert Elliston's book admirably describes some of these trends and developments for the whole town in his 1995 book on the Second World War "Lewes at War".

AFTERMATH OF THE FIRST WAR IN LEWES

Casualties: Fatalities as compared to survivors

The scale of the death, injury and destruction of the First War was outside human experience until then. In one respect, though, Lewes exceeded even that enormity, as the town's fatal casualties were proportionately far above the national average. Nationally, the fatal casualty figure for the Armed Forces was between 4% and 5%, but for Lewes men the figure rose dramatically to over 10%. The population for Lewes as a whole in the Census of 1911 was 10,972, including 1,447 for Southover and a further 10 in 'Southover without'. This suggests that Southover's 46 men lost might have been an even higher proportion of those who went off to the war from the parish.(p.156 of Robert Elliston's book as above expands on this).

This "Men of Southover" book is only about those men who did not return, therefore those who did return but with appalling war damage and injuries, yet survived, are hardly mentioned. George Fellows (1.13), Alfred Dean(1.35), Charles Hall (1.36), and Frank Martin (1.46) are exceptions from the First War. They all died from their injuries within the course of the war, so are named on the Memorial and therefore included in this book.

United Lewes Service and Peace Celebrations at Dripping Pan, 17th July 1919 (Bob Cairns)

In the Second War part of the book, the major reference to the long-term aftermath includes Douglas Redman's brother, not named on the Southover Memorial, who was hospitalised until his death in 1950. But in the years between the wars, concerns mounted for the ongoing needs of the war wounded. The number of Southover's Second War fatal casualties (22) was, as a proportion of its First War numbers, roughly in line with the national figure of somewhere between a third and a half.

Numbers buried as compared to numbers never found: In the Second War it was only the five Naval men who had 'no known grave' out of the 22 on the Memorial, whereas in the First War nearly half the Southover men who died were never found.

Ladies Race at Lewes Peace Celebrations, as above.
(Bob Cairns)

Numbers killed in action as compared to deaths from disease or wounds: In the First War, fourteen of Southover's 46 men died of wounds or disease, whereas in the Second War only five of the 22 were not killed in action.

Memorials

Parish: Southover's own War Memorial for the 46 who paid the 'supreme sacrifice' in the First War was unveiled and dedicated on All Saints' Day, 1st November 1921. Much of the preparation involved, and the keeping of the Roll of Honour updated through the war years, was done by the mother and widow of Captain T. A. Stewart-Jones (1.04), and the Chairman of Southover's War Memorial Committee was Councillor Mr. E. Glover who had lost two of his sons (1.09 & 1.12).

The former Rector, Rev. H. Anson whose son Wilfred was also one of Southover's fallen (1.27), was invited to come back from Salisbury to give the address at the Unveiling and Dedication ceremony. The photograph on page vii in this book shows the floral tributes put there at the time, and it was the custom on Remembrance Sunday for many years for the children of these lost men to take it in turns to lay the wreath from the parish.

Town and County: The Memorial for Lewes town at the top of School Hill was unveiled nearly a year later on 6th September 1922. Its 236 names include the majority of the Southover men, and the records kept at the County Record Office of the details provided by the families at the time gave me a very useful starting point for my researches.

Chichester Cathedral contains the Memorial panels to the men of the Royal Sussex Regiment, with all the battle honours for each Battalion. There is also in the Cathedral a Book of Remembrance for all the Sussex men lost with the Royal Navy.

Nation: Throughout the 1920's many national Memorials were commissioned for each of the different Services, and nationally at the Cenotaph in Whitehall (see biographies on the Neville brothers, Henry (1.16) & Joseph (1.34) for a little more on the Unveiling of the Cenotaph).

The Royal Navy Memorial at Portsmouth includes the names of all the Southover naval men lost "with no grave but the sea" in both the wars. The Merchant Navy Memorial at Tower Hill was added to after 1945 and now includes the one Southover cadet, Bruce Tindale (2.09), from the Second War.

World-wide: The Commonwealth War Graves Commission came into being in 1921, following on from the Imperial War Graves Commission. As has been referred to in each man's biography, every fallen Service-man has an identical headstone in whichever Cemetery across the world they now lie. These are the same, regardless of rank, and each has its own regimental crest and space for family additions if wished. Sometimes these headstones are in local parish or

Lewes Town Memorial on School Hill

municipal cemeteries, such as Lewes Town and Kingston and Southover Churchyards, for those who died in this country, but the great majority are in the CWGC's own Cemeteries in France, Belgium, Netherlands, Italy, the Middle East, and India and the Far East. Those many men who remained 'missing' at the end of the First War are each commemorated individually by name and fighting unit on the appropriate Memorial for the area and year in which they fell. Those are in France (Le Touret, Loos, Vis-en-Artois, Pozieres, Arras, Cambrai, and Thiepval), and Belgium (Tyne Cot, Ypres - Menin Gate), as have been referred to.

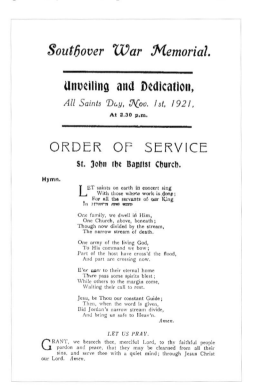

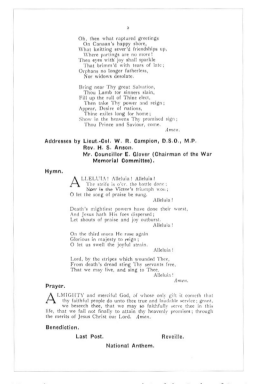

Unveiling and Dedication of Southover War Memorial, 1st November 1921, pages 1 and 5 of the Order of Service.

SOME OF THE TRENDS IN THE 1920'S AND 1930S

1. The Disarmament/Rearmament tension

This was building up nationwide in the years between the wars, and Southover was no exception. As Colin Brent has suggested in his Introduction to Southover before the First War, the patriotic military and Anglican 'front' was very strong in Lewes in those closing years of Empire. As has been shown, the Downs round Lewes as the county town were covered every summer since the Boer War if not earlier, by tented Training Camps for various Territorial Units, particularly the local ones. Volunteers had come forward in their thousands, only to die in disproportionate numbers in that war.

But after the First War, the rise of the pacifist and conscientious objector groups became more noticeable, in Southover as much as anywhere if not more so. The Tribunals which had been such a feature of the First War years, re-convened and heard many cases of appeals against call-up.

2. The post-war generation

The Parish Registers for the immediate post-war months show the baptisms of many babies where the father's occupation is entered as "Soldier (deceased)". It is many of these babies whose own marriages are recorded in later Parish Registers, and whose names then appear on the Memorial to those lost in the Second War. Through the 1920's, many of the young brides in the Marriage Registers are recorded as being widows. It is noticeable that the great majority of them were marrying bachelors who were some years younger than themselves.

3. Social mobility at home, and women at work

Housing: As in other towns all over the country, Lewes and even Southover began to lose their old centres of pre-war population, even between the wars. Many closely packed streets and the tight-knit communities that lived in them were lost then and immediately after the Second War. These old centres were demolished in the name of development and 'slum clearance'. The homes of many of the Southover men from the First War thus disappeared, as the new St. Pancras Gardens area took shape in the 1960s. There were then also the effects of the various Second War bombs dropped on Lewes, which accelerated the move outwards to the outlying estates. The new areas that these old families were re-housed to between the wars included the Winterbourne Estate, the Nevill, and Landport. All these are fully represented in the home addresses of Southover's Second War casualties.

Families and friends: This outward movement obviously greatly affected whole families and friendship networks. People who had grown up together, and the families who had survived the First War together, were now separated. Such was the post-war devastation and hardship for some families, that whole families were broken up. The seeds of decades of hurt and division were thus sown in many families, and children were sometimes brought up knowing only one half of their families. Women were increasingly, from the First War onwards, going out to work as part of the War Effort initially and then later for financial necessity and social needs. In Southover, the main working areas for these women after the First War were farms and nurseries, shops and offices, and even the breweries and iron foundries of Lewes. (Marjorie nee Fellows' picture of her work-mates at the Lewes Iron Foundry in 1942 illustrates this). Once the Second War came, there was a major move into the women's Services and Auxiliaries, locally on the Home Front and nationwide.

4. World-wide mobility of war

In the First War almost all the Southover fatalities served in the Army and on the Western Front. Only one in that war was in the Navy and two in the early RAF. Of the 46 only two died outside Europe, one in the Middle East and one in India. Five of the European deaths were in this country.

But in the Second War, these proportions were reversed: 12 of the 22 were buried outside Europe, and only half of them (11 out of the 22) were in the Army. The remainder were divided between the five in the Navy/Merchant Navy/Fleet Auxiliary, who were all lost in the first three years of the War; and the six RAF men who were lost, all in the last two years of the War.

In each war, one of Southover's fallen was a Canadian returning to the aid of the 'mother country', with their own country's Forces.

The Commission was established by Royal Charter in 1917. Its duties are to mark and maintain the graves of the members of the forces of the Commonwealth who were killed in the two World Wars, to build memorials to those who have no known grave and to keep records and registers, including, after the Second World War, a record of the Civilian War Dead.

The work was founded upon principles which have remained unaltered: that each of the dead should be commemorated individually by name on headstone or memorial; that the headstones and memorials should be permanent; that the headstones should be uniform and that there should be no distinction made on account of military or civil rank, race or creed.

1,700,000 men and women of the Commonwealth forces died in the two World Wars. Over 900,000 are commemorated on headstones over their identified graves and the remainder, who have no known grave, are commemorated on memorials. There are war graves in 140 different countries: mostly in the Commission's 2,500 war cemeteries and plots, but there are also war graves in many civil cemeteries and churchyards throughout the world. To maintain this vast commitment the Commission employs a staff of 1,300, mostly gardeners and craftsmen, and has offices in a number of countries.

At the top of each headstone is engraved the national emblem or the service or regimental badge, followed by the rank, name, unit, date of death, age and the appropriate religious emblem, and at the foot, in many cases, an inscription chosen by the relatives. Where climate permits the headstones stand in narrow borders, where polyantha roses and small perennials grow, in a setting of lawn, trees and shrubs.

In some cemeteries, notably on the Gallipoli peninsula, in Macedonia, the Far East and the Pacific, stone or bronze plaques on low pedestals are used for climatic reasons instead of headstones.

Two monuments are common to the war cemeteries: the Cross of Sacrifice set upon an octagonal base bearing a bronze sword upon its shaft; and, in the larger cemeteries, the Stone of Remembrance, inscribed with the words from the Book of Ecclesiasticus: Their Name Liveth For Evermore. Large cemeteries have pavilions or entrance buildings, where visitors can rest or consult the register. Cemetery and memorial registers published by the Commission are housed in register boxes on site.

The men and women who were cremated or have no known grave or who perished at sea are commemorated on memorials ranging from small tablets bearing a few names to great monuments bearing many thousands.

The cost of the work is shared by the partner governments – United Kingdom, Canada, Australia, India, New Zealand and South Africa – in the proportion of the numbers of their graves, whilst other Commonwealth countries contribute by bearing the cost of maintenance in their own lands.

Commonwealth War Graves Commission leaflet, summarising its work since the First War

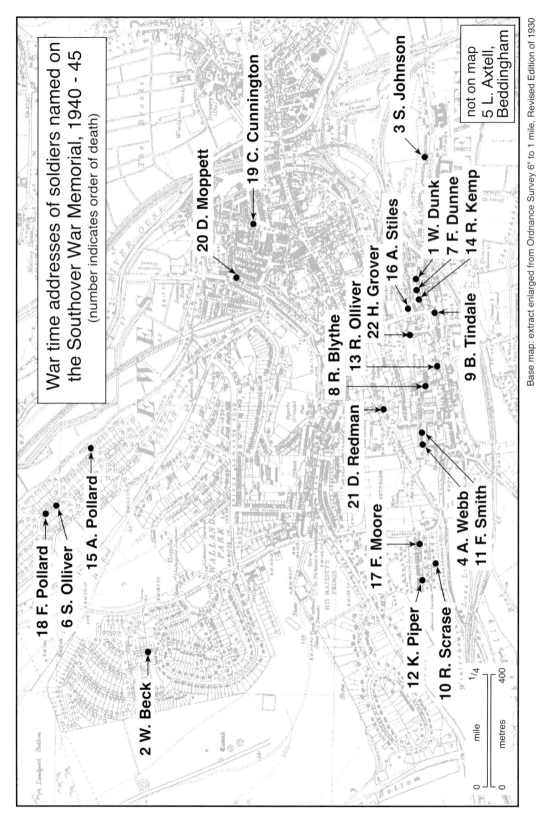

War time addresses of soldiers named on the Southover War Memorial, 1940 - 45
(number indicates order of death)

20 D. Moppett

19 C. Cunnington

3 S. Johnson

not on map
5 L. Axtell, Beddingham

16 A. Stiles

1 W. Dunk

7 F. Dunne

14 R. Kemp

22 H. Grover

8 R. Blythe

13 R. Olliver

9 B. Tindale

21 D. Redman

18 F. Pollard

6 S. Olliver

15 A. Pollard

2 W. Beck

17 F. Moore

4 A. Webb

11 F. Smith

12 K. Piper

10 R. Scrase

1/4 mile

400 metres

Base map: extract enlarged from Ordnance Survey 6" to 1 mile, Revised Edition of 1930

170

Men lost in the Second War

HOME ADDRESSES

Number	Street	First name	Surname	Number in book
14	The Course	Leonard George	AXTELL	5
Eastport Ho.,23	Eastport Lane	Alfred Jas.Wade	STILES	16
5	Manor Terrace, Potters Lane	Ronald Charles	BLYTHE	8
3	Priory Crescent	Bruce Frederick	TINDALE	9
6	Priory Place	Ronald	OLLIVER	13
23 then 45	Priory Street	Frederick Francis	DUNNE	7
45	Priory Street	Robert William	KEMP	14
51	Priory Street	Walter William	DUNK	1
12	Mountfield Road	Stanley Frederick	JOHNSON	3
14	St.James' Street	Harold Russell	GROVER	22
3	St.Pancras Gardens	Frederick Jasper	SMITH	11
5	St.Pancras Gardens	Albert Edward	WEBB	4
21	Dale Road, Winterbourne	Kenneth Arthur	PIPER	12
23	Dale Road, Winterbourne	Frederick Martin	MOORE	17
22	Valley Road, Winterbourne	Raymond Clifford	SCRASE	10
2	Windover Crescent, Nevill	Walter Raymond	BECK	2
11	Horsfield Road, Landport	Frederick Arthur	POLLARD	18
24	Horsfield Road, Landport	Stanley Gordon	OLLIVER	6
18	Landport Road, Landport	Albert Edward	POLLARD	15
	Abinger Place, Lewes	Dennis George	MOPPETT	20
3	South Place, St. John Street.	Cedric Augustus	CUNNINGTON	19
"Greenbank"	Rotten Row	Douglas George	REDMAN	21

Men lost in the Second War

IN ALPHABETICAL ORDER WITH WARTIME HOME ADDRESSES

Name		Home address (Southover, unless specified)	Number in book
AXTELL	Leonard George	14 The Course, Southover	5
BECK	Walter Raymond	2 Windover Crescent, Nevill	2
BLYTHE	Ronald Charles	5 Manor Terrace, Potters Lane, Southover	8
CUNNINGTON	Cedric Augustus	3 South Place Flats, St.John's St.,Lewes	19
DUNK	Walter William	51 Priory Street, Southover	1
DUNNE	Frederick Francis	23 then 45 Priory Street, Southover	7
GROVER	Harold Russell	14 St James' Street, Southover	22
JOHNSON	Stanley Frederick	12 Mountfield Road, Southover	3
KEMP	Robert William	45 Priory Street, Southover	14
MOORE	Frederick Martin	23 Dale Road, Winterbourne	17
MOPPETT	Dennis George	Abinger Place, Lewes	20
OLLIVER	Ronald	6 Priory Place, Southover	13
OLLIVER	Stanley Gordon	24 Horsfield Road, Landport	6
PIPER	Kenneth Arthur	21 Dale Road, Winterbourne	12
POLLARD	Albert Edward	18 Landport Road, Lewes	15
POLLARD	Frederick Arthur	11 Horsfield Road, Landport	18
REDMAN	Douglas George	"Green Bank", Rotten Row, Lewes	21
SCRASE	Raymond Clifford	22 Valley Road, Winterbourne	10
SMITH	Frederick Jasper	3 St. Pancras Gardens, Southover	11
STILES	Alfred James	Eastport La.,28 Southover High St. & Rutland	35
TINDALE	Bruce Frederick	3 Priory Crescent, Southover	18
WEBB	Albert Edward	5 St. Pancras Gardens	25

IN ORDER OF DEATH AND WITH SERVICE DETAILS

No.	Rank	Name	Unit	Date of death	Place of death	Age
01	Boy 1st Cl.	Walter William DUNK, R.N.	HMS Royal Oak	14 Oct.39	Scapa Flow	17
02	AS/Gnr.	Walter Raymond BECK,RNVR	SS Britannia	7 Apr.41	S.Atlantic	23
03	Ldg.Writer	Stanley Fredk. JOHNSON,RN.	HMS Hood	24 May 41	Denmark Straits	23
04	Guardsman	Albert Edward WEBB	3rd Coldstream Gds	17 Jun 41	Libya	25
05	Ldg.Stkr.	Leonard George AXTELL,RN	HMS Fleur de Lys	14 Oct 41	W. of Gibralter	25
06	Driver	Stanley Gordon OLLIVER	R.A.Service Corps.	21 Oct.41	Aldershot(hosp)	35
07	L/Cpl	Frederick Francis DUNN(E)	R.Armoured Corps.	15 Nov.42	Middle East	36
08	F.0/Navigr.	Ronald Chas. BLYTHE	RAFVR,49 Sqdn.	17 Jun 43	North Sea	20
09	Cadet	Bruce Fredk.TINDALE,RFA	MV Empire Stanley	17 Aug.43	off East Africa	18
10	Ldg.A'cftman	Raymond Clifford SCRASE	RAF Regt.	18 Sep.43	Assam,India	23
11	Sgt.Nav/Bombr	Fredk. Jasper SMITH	RAFVR, 100 Sqdn.	17 Nov.43	Middle East	28
12	Driver	Kenneth Arthur PIPER	R.A.Ordnance Corp	18 Nov.43	Birmingham (hosp)	19
13	Private	Ronald OLLIVER	Q.O.Roy.W.Kent Reg	9 Jan.44	Burma	19
14	Flt.Sgt/Eng.	Robert William KEMP	RAFVR 626 Sqdn.	22 May 44	over Belgium	22
15	Rifleman	Albert Edward POLLARD	2nd Q's W'minsters	1 Aug 44	Normandy	27
16	Sgt.	Alfred Jas.Wade STILES	R.Armoured Corps.	14 Aug 44	Normandy	35
17	Sapper	Frederick Martin MOORE	270 Fd.Coy.,R.E.	2 Oct.44	Italy	27
18	Private	Frederick Arthur POLLARD	K.Shropshire Lt.Inf.	17 Oct 44	N.W.Europe	32
19	Corporal	Cedric August. CUNNINGTON	279 Fd.Coy.,R.E.	3 Dec.44	N.W.Europe	26
20	Ldg.A'cftman	Dennis George MOPPETT	RAFVR	6 Jan.45	Moena Is.,Java	24
21	Corporal	Douglas George REDMAN	RAF	3 Apr.45	Italy	24
22	Bombardier	Harold Russell GROVER	6th Fd.Regt.,RCA	19 Apr 45	N.W.Europe	22

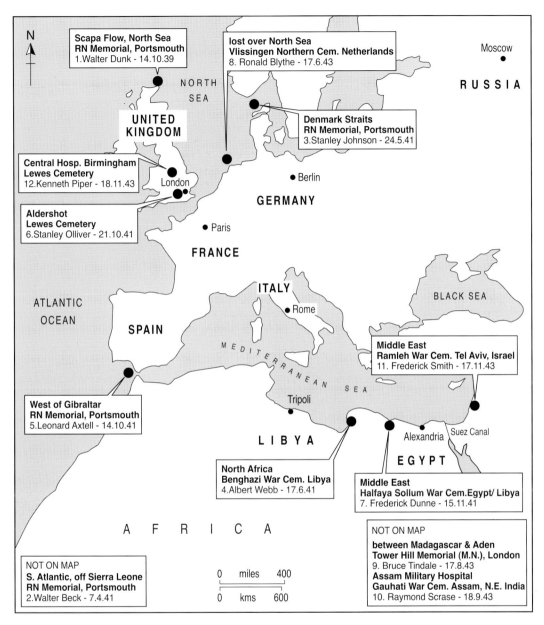

Scapa Flow, North Sea
RN Memorial, Portsmouth
1.Walter Dunk - 14.10.39

lost over North Sea
Vlissingen Northern Cem. Netherlands
8. Ronald Blythe - 17.6.43

Denmark Straits
RN Memorial, Portsmouth
3.Stanley Johnson - 24.5.41

Central Hosp. Birmingham
Lewes Cemetery
12.Kenneth Piper - 18.11.43

Aldershot
Lewes Cemetery
6.Stanley Olliver - 21.10.41

West of Gibraltar
RN Memorial, Portsmouth
5.Leonard Axtell - 14.10.41

Middle East
Ramleh War Cem. Tel Aviv, Israel
11. Frederick Smith - 17.11.43

North Africa
Benghazi War Cem. Libya
4.Albert Webb - 17.6.41

Middle East
Halfaya Sollum War Cem.Egypt/ Libya
7. Frederick Dunne - 15.11.41

NOT ON MAP
between Madagascar & Aden
Tower Hill Memorial (M.N.), London
9. Bruce Tindale - 17.8.43
Assam Military Hospital
Gauhati War Cem. Assam, N.E. India
10. Raymond Scrase - 18.9.43

NOT ON MAP
S. Atlantic, off Sierra Leone
RN Memorial, Portsmouth
2.Walter Beck - 7.4.41

0   miles   400
0   kms   600

Place of death and cemetery/memorial of Southover men killed 1939-43 (nos 1 - 12)
(number before name refers to order of death)

Walter William DUNK, RN   2.01
14th October 1939 aged 17
at Scapa Flow, North Sea
P/JX 157915, Boy (1st Class)
HMS Royal Oak

HOME   51 Priory Street, Southover
COMMEMORATED   Royal Naval Memorial, Portsmouth

LEWES'S FIRST LOSS OF THE WAR:
BOY SAILOR GOES DOWN WITH 'ROYAL OAK'.

Those were the headlines as news of the first disaster of the Second World War reached Lewes.

Lewes childhood in a naval family

'Boy Dunk', as the papers described him, was Lewes born and bred. At the time of his death, he was the only child of his parents, Mr & Mrs F G Dunk, who lived at 51 Priory Street, Southover. A younger brother Patrick was not born until six months after Walter's death. The parents were Frederick George Dunk and his wife Josephine Jane nee Lally, who had married at Southover Church on March 5th 1921. His father was at that time living at 42 Priory Street

P.81 Class April 1938: Naval Training School, HMS St Vincent, Portsmouth;
Boy Dunk is in 2nd row down, 4th from left.

174

and working as a crane driver. The young Walter was then born on 9th January 1922, and baptised within a month at Southover Church.

By the time of Walter's death, his father was working in Brighton in the Southern Railway Engineering Department at that time. But the Dunks were very much a naval family; three of the boy's uncles were also in the Navy in 1939, and a fourth had served in the First World War, when he was lost with HMS Cressy.

Young Walter went to St Pancras School, then to the Central School with Edie Pollard and other Southover people who still remember him there. He also became a keen footballer, playing for the Lewes Wednesday Club, and was also a member of the YMCA.

Boy Dunk while training with HMS St. Vincent.

HMS Royal Oak

The loss of the Royal Oak was the first major catastrophe of this Second World War, which was not yet six weeks old and still in its 'phoney war' phase on land. The battleship was thought to have been stowed safely away from the menacing U-Boats threatening the North Sea convoys in the secure Home Fleet anchorage of Scapa Flow, off the far north of Scotland. But in the event, the sub-mariner ace of the German Navy, Commander Prien, had been able to break through the net barrages and fire several salvoes of torpedoes at the sleeping battleship at 1.30 on the morning of Saturday 14th October. Of the ship's company of 1200, only 414 officers and ratings were known to have been saved. Such was the shock to the nation, that Winston Churchill immediately set up an Admiralty Board of Inquiry.

HMS Royal Oak, Walter's first, and last, ship.

175

Walter's two years in the Navy

The Royal Oak had been Walter's first ship, and he had been at sea less than six months. His last visit home to Priory Street had been back in June 1939, when war was still three months off.

He had been only fifteen when he enlisted straight from school in 1937, as a Wireless Telegrapher.

He went first to the Naval Training School, HMS St Vincent, and while starting his training there also found time for some ocean racing. In 1938, he sailed in the Portsmouth Regatta, and was a member of the crew which won the racing cutter class. The medal he won for that achievement remained in his parents' proud possession, as they were pleased to tell the reporter from the *Sussex Daily News*, who interviewed them just three days after the Royal Oak went down. There would have been many such interviews for that reporter, as there were apparently large numbers of the ship's company from the Brighton and Chichester areas.

His commemoration

Having "no grave but the sea", young Walter is commemorated with most of the other 809 lost from the Royal Oak. Their names are inscribed on the Royal Naval Memorial at Portsmouth (Panel 34, col. 2) and the Sussex men at least are also in the Navy Roll of Honour in Chichester Cathedral. His brother Patrick still lives in Lewes, and I have been much helped by him even though they never met.

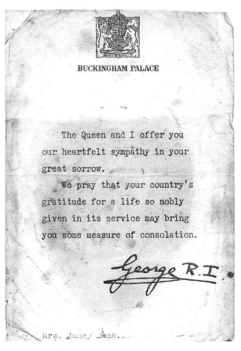

BUCKINGHAM PALACE

The Queen and I offer you
our heartfelt sympathy in your
great sorrow.
We pray that your country's
gratitude for a life so nobly
given in its service may bring
you some measure of consolation.

George R.I.

Mrs. Janey Dunk.

*Letter of Condolence from King George VI
to Walter's mother, Mrs. Janey Dunk.*

Walter Raymond BECK, R.N. 2.02
7th April 1941 aged 23
P/SD/X 1442 Acting Leading Seaman
(Able Seaman/Gunner)
SS Britannia

HOME   2 Windover Crescent, Nevill Estate
COMMEMORATED Royal Naval Memorial, Portsmouth

Family background

Raymond Beck's family had come originally from Alfriston, where they lived until 1914. Several then moved nearer to Lewes. Raymond's uncle, Frederick Joseph, moved into Leicester Road, Lewes, and was both publican and greengrocer there. He had two sons, Frederick and Leonard, who were Ray's cousins. Frederick's son Brian was Ray's second cousin; he continues to live on the Nevill Estate, and has provided much of the information for this biography. It was Frederick Joseph's other son, Leonard A. Beck (also Ray's cousin), who lived in Kingston and started Beck's Taxis.

Boyhood in Lewes

Ray's father was Walter, known to the rest of the family as 'Uncle Wally', and his mother was Violet. Ray was born in 1922; they then had a second son, Terrence Dennis, and several other sons and daughters.

After Primary School, Ray moved on to the Old Central School in Lewes, and the County Boys' Secondary Schools in both East Grinstead and Lewes. He was at the Mountfield Road school in Lewes from 1930-34, and grew up with many Southover people. He became a keen member of the Lewes Crusaders at Castle Lodge, together with several of the others who also lost their lives in this Second World War (see Moppett and Axtell).

On leaving school he went to work in the County Medical Officer's and Public Health Departments, where his work involved accountancy and the licensing laws. He became engaged to Molly Uridge, of Southover Dairy.

Joining the Navy

Ray enlisted with the RNVR at Newhaven in April 1939 when he was 17. He underwent training at the shore establishment, HMS Excellent, and then at the Whale Island Gunnery School, Portsmouth.

By the time of the British Expeditionary Force's evacuation from the Dunkirk beaches in May 1940, he was part of the crew of a motor torpedo boat helping to evacuate soldiers. He also served in the 'Dover Patrol' and on HMS Egret.

He then volunteered for some "important work", which involved sailing for India on a merchant vessel, SS Britannia. They never reached India, so presumably he never accomplished the 'important work', about which nothing is known. They reached only the equatorial waters of the South Atlantic, but were then fired on by the "Thor", an enemy 'commerce raider'. The Britannia went down on 7th April 1941 some 350 miles west of Freetown, Sierra Leone, with the loss of over half of its ship's company of 483.

"LEWES SEAMAN MAKES SUPREME SACRIFICE"

This was the heading of the *Sussex Daily News*' article on 9th May 1941 about Ray's death a month earlier. The first telegram Mr. and Mrs. Beck had had from the Admiralty informed them that Raymond was one of 17 missing, but at the final count 249 were lost. He had been seen in one of the ship's lifeboats, but being very fair-skinned he was probably one of the first to die from exposure.

Ray is commemorated on the Royal Naval Memorial at Portsmouth, Panel 60 column 3.

Those he left behind

His brother Terrence had joined up with the RAF at the outbreak of the war. He survived it, and was to return to Lewes afterwards, continuing to live on the Nevill. An extension was built to his parents' house where the brothers had grown up; it was called "Four Gables" and would have had superb views across Lewes and the Downs from the junction of Windover Crescent with North Way. It must have been one of the early ones to be built on the Nevill estate just after the First World War.

RN Memorial, Portsmouth.

Stanley Frederick JOHNSON, R.N.   2.03
24th May 1941 aged 23
lost with HMS Hood off Greenland
P/MX 58762 Leading Writer
9th Queen's Royal Lancers, 'C' Squadron

HOME   12 Mountfield Road
COMMEMORATED   Royal Naval Memorial, Portsmouth
                      and Lewes Cemetery

Lewes youth

Stanley Johnson was the exact contemporary of Ray Beck (2.02), and they both joined the Royal Navy as career entrants at 17 early in 1939. Stanley was born in 1922, the son of Mr. & Mrs. George Thomas Johnson and his wife Eliza, and he went initially to Southover School from about 1927. In September 1929 his mother had another child, Leslie, who died at only 8 weeks old; this baby Leslie and Stanley were later to be commemorated on the same grave in Lewes Cemetery. Stanley's own headstone is not the official CWGC one, as his official memorial is on the Royal Naval Memorial at Portsmouth; the family have put the words "Sadly Missed" below his name and details of his loss on HMS Hood.

Stanley is remembered from his schooldays by Tony and Jean, the nephew and niece of Alec Richardson (1.39) from St. Pancras Gardens. They also remember Stanley's brothers Roy, Geoffrey and Alan. Stanley is also remembered by Ray Moore, the youngest brother of Fred Moore (2.17), who followed on after him at Southover School. Ray now lives in retirement at Wallasey, Cheshire, and as well as providing a lot of Moore family background on Fred above and on his two uncles lost in the First War, identified for me the commemorative child-size grave the Johnson family had put in Lewes Cemetery, in memory of both Stanley and his baby brother Leslie.

From Southover, Stanley moved at eight or nine to the Pells School. When he left there in 1934 at thirteen he went to work at the High Street solicitors Blaker, Son & Young, and worked there for five years as a clerk. He then decided after the Munich crisis in 1938 to join the Navy the following spring. He made *"excellent progress"* on the clerical and admin. side, and was *"undergoing training for a commission as a Paymaster"*.

Naval rating on HMS Hood

It must have been a very great thrill and honour for Stanley and his family when he was posted to HMS Hood. This massive battlecruiser was the pride of the British Navy, and from her completion on the Clyde in 1920 right through till 1940 was the largest ship in the world. Her length was 860 ft. and her beam was 105 ft. (half as wide as Stoker Axtell's "Fleur de Lys" was long, 205ft - see no. 2.05). She had a displacement of over 42,000 tons, and a ship's company of 1,477 Officers and men. She was known the world over as "The Mighty 'ood", and was widely regarded as "one of the most beautiful warships ever built."

HMS Hood (picture from 1924 in the St.Lawrence River, Quebec).

Her home port was Portsmouth, so the majority of the crew were Sussex and Hampshire men. A friend of Stanley's was on the Hood with him from the autumn of 1940; he was Geoff. Clarke, a journalist on the Worthing Herald. Geoff came from Willingdon where his father was an architect, and the two young sailors spent much of their last leave together in Lewes in the spring of 1941.

Stanley continued with his training on board, and wrote to his parents early in May 1941 that he had just passed his Petty Officer's exams.

Hood versus Bismarck

This was one of the earliest big naval battles of the Second World War, after the Graf Spee in the South Atlantic. The main news item in the *Sussex Daily News* for Monday 26th May 1941 began like this:

> *"HMS Hood, the world's largest battle cruiser, has been blown up by a hit on a magazine during a battle with German naval forces off Greenland, which began early on Saturday morning… few survivors are expected."*

Over the next few days, there was much coverage of the hunt for the Bismarck by the rest of the British fleet, culminating in news on 28th May that she too had finally been sunk the previous day, after a sea chase of some 2,000 miles. Three survivors from the Hood were then landed in Iceland, and it was soon realised they were the only ones to have survived out of the whole company of 1,477.

However, a sequel about Stanley's friend Geoff Clarke mentioned above, shows that he himself was one additional unexpected survivor. The *Sussex Express* records on 30th May 1941 that they had been informed by said Geoff Clarke, to say that he was still at home on leave in Willingdon and had just read their Obituary on him as one of the 1,474 who had been lost with the Hood! He had apparently had an extra spell of shore leave in order to attend a Selection Board interview, presumably for a promotion in the Navy, so escaped the fate of his comrades.

Stanley Johnson is commemorated on his brother Leslie's grave in Lewes Cemetery

Albert Edward WEBB   2.04
17th June 1941 aged 26
in hospital in Libya while a P.O.W.
2660221 Guardsman
3rd Battalion Coldstream Guards

HOME   5 St Pancras Gardens
BURIED   Benghazi Military Cemetery, Libya

Family and friends

Guardsman Webb was one of at least two sons and two daughters born to William Henry Webb and his wife Florence Jane. They lived in the old St. Pancras Gardens area between the Winterbourne Stream and the old Ballards Brewery, where his father was employed. The whole area is now demolished, and has been redeveloped in the sixties. Albert was born at about the time of the outbreak of the First War, and two of his brothers or sisters died in the influenza epidemic then. His father William Henry was known as 'Bob', and is remembered by one of my 'informants' as sporting a very large moustache. He was also a much shorter man than his Guardsman son Albert became; Albert was therefore known in jest as 'Shorty'!

This 'informant' was Jean Davis who was one of the nearby Richardson family. Her uncle Alec was killed in the First War (see 1.39), and she grew up with the younger Webb children between the wars.

Guardsman Albert Webb.

One of Albert's older brothers was Oliver, who served with the Royal Army Medical Corps. throughout the Second War, came back to Lewes and died at the age of 66. One of his sisters was Edna, who worked with Jean nee Richardson in Lewes during and after the war.

Another of the Webb sisters was Elsie, who as far as I know continues to live on in Lewes in her late seventies. Up to 1996 she was living in North Street, and sent me the photographs of her much-missed brother Albert to include in this book, but sadly became ill and moved, leaving no forwarding address.

Albert with his ?Platoon at the ?Cambridge Barracks, Aldershot

Guardsman Webb's war in North Africa

He went for Army training at Caterham and Pirbright, and was then posted to North Africa. He was part of General Wavell's "Forgotten Army", as his sister Elsie told me still with great feeling. She still has some of the letters he sent home, but sadly she was overtaken by illness before she could look any of these out for me to quote from in this book. There was also a diary he kept while in North Africa for his 'young lady', which apparently survived the war and reached her afterwards.

Rommel and his 'Afrika Korps' did not arrive in Libya until February 1941, after reverses for the Italians and the Allied capture of Tobruk. The British then held Tobruk under siege for much of 1941, but had little success under Wavell in the rest of North Africa. Churchill had ordered two small offensives to drive Rommel back in May and June 1941, but with great shortages of both manpower, armour and equipment, both failed.

It was probably in one of those Allied offensives that Guardsman Webb was taken prisoner, probably by Rommel's forces. He was then in hospital as a prisoner of war, needing treatment either for wounds received in action, or for acute illness or disease developed while held by the enemy. He died in hospital on 17th June 1941, and was buried at Benghazi War Cemetery. This is on the main coast road around the Cyranaecean Peninsula, across the Mediterranean to the south from Albania and Corfu. The Cemetery is about five miles to the south east of Benghazi, above the Gulf of Surte, between Tripoli in the west and Tobruk in the east.

His first burial place in North Africa, before Benghazi War Cemetery was developed

Leonard George AXTELL, R.N. 2.05
14th October 1941 aged 25
torpedoed off Gibraltar
P/KX 85771 Leading Stoker
HMS Fleur de Lys

HOME   2 Pump Cottages, Beddingham, then 14 The Course
COMMEMORATED   Royal Naval Memorial, Portsmouth

Sussex family

Leonard Axtell was born on 5th June 1916 at Iford. His parents, Reginald and Elizabeth, lived in a farm cottage there. They had already lost their first baby to poor midwifery, and then twins who were either stillborn or died after only a few days. His father Reginald was serving in the First World War at the time of Lenny's birth, but suffered much for many years later on from head and leg injuries received at Ypres. He had to stay in farm labouring jobs to keep away from too much noise and stress, but even so was often unable to work (yet without any sort of war disability pension).

His mother Elizabeth had been born and bred in Lewes, and his father had come from Wadhurst. Reginald had grown up in some of the big houses around, where his father Charles was the groom and his mother the lady's maid. One of the 'perks' of that job for her was accompanying her lady on the family's annual holiday in Nice. Reginald (the son she and Charles were to have, and who in turn became Lenny's father) would apparently walk into Lewes from Wadhurst for the Sheep Fair and all the big fairs, some 40 miles round trip. It was on one such visit that he met his future wife, who was to become Leonard's mother.

Leonard's sister Margery, and their childhood together

By 1921 when Lenny was six, his younger sister Margery was born. The family was living at Iford by then, but Margery has now been living in Lewes for many years. I was fortunate that my checking- out of Axtells in the phone directory led me to her second cousin Myles Axtell in The Cliffe, who in turn put me in touch with her. She has now lost two husbands, and although surrounded by children, grandchildren and great-grandchildren, is still also very much grieving the loss of her beloved 'big brother' over half a century ago. She was 19 when he was lost at sea, and lived for many years after that in the hope that being "missing presumed dead" meant that he might yet turn up somewhere.

Margery has happy memories of their childhood together in the farms and lanes of East Sussex, from Barcombe and Newick down to Piddinghoe and Beddingham. For several years they were both at Barcombe School together, and this involved walking five miles each way from Longford Farm at Spithurst, where their father was cowman. They had happy days fishing with the farmer's two sons there, and visiting Sutton Hall, the 'big house' nearby. Even being sat on an ant-hill by Lenny and a friend of his, was taken in good humour by the kid sister! She remembers watching him climb a holly tree as part of a dare, and being horror-struck as he slid down to see him being impaled on a strong side shoot which stuck fast in his groin; she remembers running back to mother and the long wait for the doctor, who then opened a bottle of iodine and poured the whole of it straight into the open wound!

'Running away to sea' and seeing the world

Lenny went into the Navy at 16 as a career entrant straight from school in 1932. Margery's memory is that this apparently rather hasty decision was in some way connected to their father's fiery post-First War temper and irascible outbursts. In his nine years in the Navy, seven of them before the war, Lenny had worked his way up to become Leading Stoker, and had seen much of the Mediterranean. There were

Home leave with parents, grandparents and aunts at Piddinghoe

several visits on home leave in the years up to the outbreak of war again in 1939; the family group photograph taken on one of these home leaves shows him with their parents and grandparents, and some of the aunts, at Piddinghoe.

His sister Margery, who was only 10 or 11 when he first joined up, remembers his enjoyment

in recounting some of his shore visits and experiences. She particularly remembers hearing of his great friendship formed while in one of these ports, and kept up over many years, with a young sailor from another ship who happened to be a German. Lenny confided in her, as war seemed to be drawing nearer, his anguish at the possibility of them having to fight each other from opposite sides.

On shore in the Mediterranean or Adriatic before the outbreak of war, with fellow crew members (front row, right)

Wedding and baby son in Southover

At some point in these years up to the war, Lenny met and married a Lewes girl called Irene Patricia Thorpe. She lived with her mother in The Course, and his later Home Leaves were spent there. Their baby Terrance Axtell was born in April 1941. Margery still has the photograph taken of this baby when he was six months old. She has fond memories of the one or two occasions she and her parents were able to meet him, and has been much distressed never to have seen him since. She has no memory of the wedding and thinks Lenny's side of the family was probably not invited. She had gathered Terrance might be still living somewhere in Sussex, but has not felt brave enough to risk attempting any re-making of contact in case the wish for it was not reciprocated.

Grown son re-discovered

However, it has been one of the great joys of researching for this book that I have now been able to meet this long-lost son of Stoker Axtell at his home in Burgess Hill, and put him and his aunt in touch with each other after all these years!

All the following details have now been agreed by both of

On shore in Mediterranean/Adriatic port before the outbreak of war.

them, and some additional photographs have been provided by Terrance, from the remnants of his father's many albums. It is a great sadness for him that none of the actual satin-bound albums remain, nor most of his father's treasured souvenirs from his Mediterranean ports of call. Only a few individual photos came his way when the family split up later on after his mother's re-marriage and move to Kent after the war. He remembers being allowed into his grandmother's front room in The Course on special occasions through his childhood, to pore over all these photographs of faraway places and shipboard life. He remembers being impressed by all the calligraphy in white ink which his father had learned to do in order to write captions on the black pages of the albums under all the photographs. Terrance also treasures the first letter his father wrote his mother from barracks at Winchester in 1935. And he does have a beautiful leather pouch handbag from Egypt, which was one of his father's early presents to his mother.

The Haifa Patrol keeping vital supply and defence routes open across Palestine and down to Suez; Ldg.Stoker Axtell played a part in this Patrol.

Like father, like son

He values the memory of his Auntie Esther, his mother's sister, who kept alive these memories of his father for him. He also remembers going to Southover Church every Sunday with her and his grandmother for many years throughout his childhood. Terrance was given the second name of George after his father, and the third name of Ian after the doctor who delivered him! He is also, judging by the remaining photographs, extraordinarily like his father in appearance and height, and apparently in personality too! Terrance has similarly followed a career in marine engineering.

Terrance still has his father's Certificate of Service in the Royal Navy, which details all his ratings and postings. It also records him as having been "brought up to the trade of Dairyman" , and being 5'3" tall, with black hair, grey eyes, and a fresh complexion. It confirms that Len signed on at the age of 18 on 25th March 1935 for 12 years, with the rating of Stoker 2nd Class. Within a year he became Stoker 1st Class, and by 13th January 1938 he had obtained the Certificate of Qualification from the Auxiliary Machinery Watchkeeping Course. By 12th June 1940 his rating was A/Leading Stoker, and then by 12th June 1941 (just four months before his death) he was promoted to Leading Stoker.

Initially Len served on HMS Icarus out of Portsmouth, and its training units there such as the "Victory" and the "Nelson". He was then also involved in the 'Haifa Patrol', supporting the Army to keep open the important supply routes to and from the rest of the Middle East and the Suez Canal. Trieste was one of the ports he visited that made a great impression on Terrance as a boy when shown his father's photographs of it.

Stoker Axtell's war service

After the outbreak of war he was transferred to HMS Fleur de Lys. Margery has recently discovered that the Fleur de Lys's home port was Devonport (Plymouth), not Portsmouth as she had always assumed. The 'Fleur de Lys' was a brand-new 'Flower Class' corvette of 1020 tons and some 205 feet long, only built in 1940. Some 250 corvettes of this Class were built in UK and Canada between 1939 and 1942. She was in fact originally known as "La Dieppoise", as she was one of four such ships being built for the French Navy at the time of the fall of France. She was taken over by the British Government on 3rd July 1940, after having only been launched on 21st June 1940, and was somehow completed at Middlesborough late in 1940, and brought into service as HMS Fleur de Lys at Plymouth with a pendant number of K.122, for just a few short months. Serving in the same Fleur de Lys Flotilla was HMS Cormorant, on which Stoker Axtell served for some of his last months.

His death and last letter

On 14th October 1941 the Fleur de Lys was some two hundred miles west of Gibraltar, when she was sunk by a torpedo from a U-Boat, number U-206. If he was on duty at the time, Len would have been in the engine room, with much-reduced chances of getting out in time and taking to the lifeboats. Hopefully he had no time to ponder whether his pre-war German naval friend might by then have been serving on the submarine that torpedoed them.

Margery vividly remembers the desolation at home on receiving the telegram from the

Admiralty. But she also remembers the elation a few days later, when she picked up a letter on their front door mat, addressed to them all in Lenny's own hand-writing. Her immediate thought was that he had re-appeared somewhere after being 'missing', and she rushed in to her parents accordingly. It of course only too soon became appar-

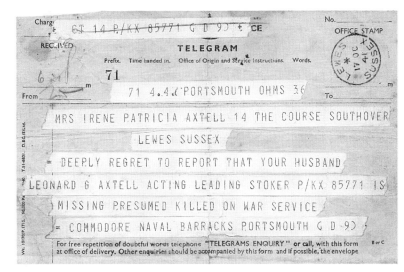

Admiralty Telegram to Len's wife
sent three days after the sinking of HMS Hood.

ent that he had written it some days before the fateful 14th October. Lenny's son Terrance still has the telegram which was sent to his mother, Len's widow at The Course, reproduced here with his permission.

Leading Stoker Axtell's commemoration

In the remaining years of the war, Len's parents put "In Memoriam - On Active Service" notices in the local paper. For example, in the *Sussex Express* on Friday 15th October 1943, the notice read:

> *"In loving memory of our dear Len, Leading Stoker Leonard George Axtell R.N., missing presumed killed on HMS Fleur de Lys, October 1941.*
>
> *From Mum & Dad, 2 Pump Cottages, Beddingham.*
>
> *"You are always in our thoughts."*

After the war, when the Navy added the names of all the Second War losses to the Royal Naval Memorial at Portsmouth, Len's name was there with all his 85 Fleur de Lys comrades grouped rank by rank. It is still there now, on Panel 154 column 2, looking out over the Solent to the Isle of Wight.

Terrance remembers being very proud to wear his father's medals at Remembrance Sunday. This photograph was taken in November 1952 when he was 11 and had just started at secondary school.

Len's son Terrance
wearing his father's medals
on Remembrance Day, 1952,
when aged 11.

Stanley Gordon OLLIVER   2.06
21st October 1941 aged 35
Military Hospital, Aldershot
T/279703 Driver
Royal Army Service Corps

HOME   24 Horsfield Road, Landport
BURIED   Lewes Cemetery

Stanley Gordon (known as Stan) was born at 12 Eastport Lane in 1906 or 1907. He was one of the nine children of Christopher, a house decorator, and his wife Elizabeth Olliver. They were regular attenders at Southover Church, and Stan sang in the choir there. His sister Kath (see below) did so too, but being a girl did not wear choir robes or sit in the choir stalls - girls had to sit in the front pews instead!.

Stan left school at 12 in 1918 and went to work at the Lewes Co-op. stores in West Street. He worked his way up to be in charge of the Provisions Department there, and by the time he was called up in July 1940 had worked a grand total of 21 years there.

His family - old and new

Stan got married at Southover Church on June 11th 1932 when he was 25, to the girl almost next door. His bride, Flossie Henrietta Lee, was a year older and lived at 9 Eastport Lane. She was a domestic servant of some sort, and her father John William Lee was a kitchen hand. Her father was one of the witnesses, and the other was Christopher Alfred Olliver, who was almost certainly one of Stan's brothers. Soon after the wedding, Stan and Flossie moved into the area round St John-sub-Castro. Their son Raymond Gordon was born on 2nd April 1933, and was baptised back at Southover on 28th May 1933 when they were living at White Hill, near the Elephant & Castle between Mount Pleasant and St. John's Terrace. Between then and the outbreak of war, the new little trio moved into their new house at 24 Horsfield Road, Landport.

One of Stan's sisters, Kathleen Maud, then married at Southover on September 1st 1935, her own 24th birthday. This was three years after her brother's wedding, and she was working at the time as a "book folder" at the Lewes Press. The groom was Harold Newman, a bachelor of 28, whose father Albert was a cowman of Southover. Kath lives on in Priory Flats, Southover, and attends the Monday Club at Church End; it was a great pleasure to meet her there, and have her fill in some of the gaps about Stan for me.

Driver Olliver's short war: from the Co-op. Stores to the RASC and Aldershot

Despite being already 34, Stan was called up in July 1940. Flossie his wife would have been 35, and their son Raymond just turned 7. Stan's relatively advanced age gives some indication of the desperate straits this country was in following the evacuation from Dunkirk in May 1940, and while the Battle of Britain was raging over London and the south-east that summer. He was drafted to the Royal Army Service Corps as a Driver; his many years' experience in retailing provisions would doubtless have come in useful in this Army service role.

There is no indication that he ever served abroad, indeed there would hardly have been time for much training then overseas posting, all before being admitted to hospital in Aldershot. Until I met Kath, it was not clear in whether he died from wounds or disease; she remembers being told that it was 'pernicious anaemia' from too much exercise and training, and general exhaustion.

Lewes Cemetery with views to Downs, and the Johnson family grave in the foreground.

His death announcement was in the local paper under the "On Active Service" column, and repeated at least for the next two years in the "In Memoriam" column. One of them each year was put in by his parents:

> *"In loving memory of our dear boy Stan, who fell asleep 21st October 1941.*
> *Sadly missed and loved by all. Mum, Dad, brothers and sisters."*

His wife and son put a similar notice in each year for the rest of the war, also under the "On Active Service" column, for example on 22nd October 1943:

> *"In loving memory of my dear husband Stanley Gordon, who passed away 21st October 1941.   Yet not on this day only, upon our loss we dwell,*
>
> *He is remembered ever by those who loved him well.'*
>
> *From his wife and son."*

His body was returned to Lewes for burial in Section B of the Lewes Cemetery, Grave 85, beside his parents. His name 'Stan' is engraved on the flower plinth, with these words on the headstone above:-

"Not gone dear, only hidden a moment from your eyes,
Not lost but only waiting for you in Paradise."

Kath remembers them shutting the Co-op. stores on the day of his funeral, as a tribute to him. Because he was neither killed in action nor died of wounds, his widow Flossie was never allowed any sort of War Widow's Pension, despite him having a Services headstone and dying in a Military Hospital.

Stan Olliver's grave in Lewes Cemetery.

After the war, Flossie got married again, to one of Stan's old friends; later on still, Stan's son Raymond worked in a furniture shop, then moved with it to Uckfield.

Frederick Francis DUNNE   2.07
15th November 1942 aged 36
in the Middle East
7903863 Trooper/Lance-Corporal
Tank Delivery Regiment, Royal Armoured Corps

HOME   23 then 45 Priory Street, Southover
BURIED   Halfaya Sollum War Cemetery, Egypt

Trooper Dunne came from Liverpool and was born there in 1908. His parents were Frederick and Mary E. Dunne. He had moved south some time before the Second War, and lived in Eastbourne at Enys Road for some years. He then moved to Southover when he met and married one of the Hendy girls of 23 Priory Street. His bride was the youngest, Kathleen Margaret Hendy, who had herself been baptised at Southover Church in March 1911 when she was six months old. Her older sister Agnes Louisa who was nearly two at the time, was baptised with her.

War in the Tank Delivery Regiment

He joined up in the Army during 1940, when he was 34 and she 30. There is no record of them having had any children, or where either of them had worked. He joined the Royal Armoured Corps. and was with their Tank Delivery Regiment. This would have had a key role in 1942 as Italy had joined the Axis powers and was threatening our East Africa and Middle Eastern interests and the safety of the Suez Canal. New supplies of armour and tanks for desert warfare had to be urgently developed and shipped across to North Africa in the attempt to defeat Rommel in the desert.

L/Cpl. Dunne's obituary photo

It was in the autumn of 1942, in the months up to Fred. Dunne's death, that the tide of war began to turn for the Allies. Auchinleck had replaced Wavell, and the Eighth Army came into being, a year earlier. The two objectives in the autumn of 1941 were to relieve Tobruk and destroy Axis armour, by using the considerable reinforcements which had been arriving in the late summer and early autumn. These included the American M3 light tank, known by the British as the 'Honey'. It could well be that Fred. Dunne was involved in the delivery of these tanks, ready for the launch of that autumn offensive on 18th November 1941. There were some massive Allied losses at Sidi Rezegh where the British lost a complete armoured brigade, and for a year all battles were indecisive.

The tide of victory finally turns for Britain at Alamein, and Southover's bells ring

The Allied breakthrough did not finally materialise until Churchill had visited North Africa in the summer of 1942 and put General Montgomery in charge. It was he who was then able to ensure the victory at El Alamein in early November 1942, the last victory of the war to be secured by British forces alone before the input of US forces.

On Friday 20th November 1942, the *Sussex Express* reported the first ringing of Southover Church bells since the wartime ban on their use except as an invasion warning. The peal, on the previous Sunday 15th, was to "celebrate the Eighth Army's victory in Egypt". Little would Kathleen Dunne have known as she heard them from along Priory Street, that her husband died that very day. He apparently died of wounds received in action

But the news must have reached her surprisingly quickly, as the *Sussex Express* carried a brief obituary (from which most of the above has been taken) on December 11th, 1942.

Burial, memories, and moving on

Fred. Dunne's body was buried at the Halfaya Sollum War Cemetery. This is on the main coast road from Mersa Matruh through to Libya; it is on the east side of Halfaya Sollum about nine miles from the Egypt/Libya border. This remains a militarily sensitive area, and there are still some roadside checkpoints.

A year after his death, his widow put the following notice in the "In Memoriam: On Active Service" column of the *Sussex Express*, on 19th November 1943:

"In loving memory of a dear and devoted husband, F.F. Dunn. 45 Priory Street, Lewes."

(N.B. From this point, the *Sussex Express* prints his surname without the letter 'E'.

A year later still, in mid-December 1944, Fred's widow married again. The wedding was at Southover Church, and the new bridegroom was Sapper John William Harrison of the Royal Engineers, only son of Mr & Mrs R. Harrison of Doncaster. The bride was given away by her brother F.W. Hendy of Dover, and her two adult bridesmaids were her niece Yvonne Mitchell from Lancing, and Miss Joan Moody of Dover. They wore green and pink taffeta respectively, and she herself wore white moire silk with a necklace of pearls. She carried a bouquet of red carnations, and the reception was held in 11 Priory Crescent. Her bridesmaids carried chrysanthemums, and Fred Monday was best man. The Rev. D.G. Matthews, the Rector, officiated at the ceremony.

His widow Kathleen re-marries two years later

Ronald Charles BLYTHE   2.08
17th June 1943 aged 20
shot down over Dutch coast
133459 Flying Officer Navigator
RAF Volunteer Reserve, 49 Squadron, Lincs

HOME   5 Manor Terrace, Potters Lane
BURIED   Vlissingen (Flushing) Northern Cemetery
Netherlands

This young servicemen became the first of the six men named on the Southover Memorial for the Second World War who served with the newest 'arm' of the services, the Royal Air Force. These six were among the 'front runners' of those many thousands of young men in the 1940's rushing to join the 'Boys in Blue'; they followed 'The Few' who had, as fighter pilots and gunners of Spitfires and Hurricanes in the Battle of Britain , defended our shores and our land from the threat of invasion in 1940.

His family and childhood

Ronald Blythe was born on 28th February 1923, the second child of Charles Henry and Ada Blythe who were living in Ashford, Kent at the time. His older sister Kathleen had been born there three years earlier, just two years after the end of the First War. That same Kathleen lives on as a widow in Lewes to this day, and has been very helpful in providing much of the detail and photographs for this biography of her much-loved and missed younger brother.

Their family roots were in East Anglia. Their father Charles had been born at Little Snoring Rectory, Norfolk and grew up in the Swaffham and Fakenham area. He was the son of the groom attached to large country houses, and his mother came from a farming family in Essex.

During the First War, he had served with the Artillery; Kathleen remembers seeing some of her father's drawings and diagrams of shells and munitions from his Woolwich days with the Artillery while on a training course there.

When the young Ronnie was two they all moved to Wisbech, Cambs., where his sister continued her schooling. Then in the late 1920's they arrived in Lewes, where their father

Ronald Blythe in Class 3 of St.Anne's School, corner of de Montfort Road and Irelands Lane. He is in the third row back, at the right-hand side of it (c.1930).

Charles became manager of Harper and Edes, the ironmongers in Cliffe High Street. The family lived first at some temporary addresses elsewhere in Lewes, and then moved into their house in Manor Terrace in 1932, beginning a long connection with Southover and its church.

His education and training

Ronald and Kathleen completed their primary education at St. Anne's and Malling Schools. They were then at Central School in Southover Road (where the doctors' surgery now is) as a 'Middle School' for ages 9 to 14. Mr Bowley was the Head Master then and ruled the boys with a caring rod of iron on the ground floor. They were very much segregated from the girls upstairs, who included Ron's sister and were presided over by Miss Flight and her deputy Miss Smith.

Ron did extremely well at the 11+ stage, and won an Exhibition grant towards his schooling at the Lewes County School for Boys. This was in Mountfield Road, and at a later date was to become Priory Upper School. Ronald went there in 1934 and seems to have done very well in all subjects. Several of his contemporaries there were also among those from Southover who were killed in the Second World War, particularly Bruce Tindale (2.09) and Dennis Moppett (2.20).

Ron was also very much a sportsman, and played in all the school teams, culminating in being Captain of Rugby and of Cricket. He also played for the Lewes Priory Cricket Club, and the Lewes Rugby Club at the Stanley Turner ground in Kingston. In his senior years at school he was also a keen member of the Lewes Operatic Society, and also a regular attender at Crusaders which in those years was led at Castle Lodge by old Dr. Nicholl and some of his family. He

Oxford University Air Training Squadron, Trinity College (1941/42)

somehow also found time in among all those other activities both to be School Captain, and to belong to the Air Training Cadets at school; it was that ATC involvement which was to change the course of his life so dramatically.

With Oxford University Air Squadron at Trinity College

The war was nearly two years old by the time Ronald had his 'A' Level results in the summer of 1941. He had gone to work initially at the accountants Oldham Holland Frank & Co. in Lewes High Street until he was old enough to volunteer. While there he applied and was selected for a place at Trinity College Oxford with the Air Training Squadron there for a year from October 1941. He then went straight into more serious flying and officer training with the RAF Volunteer Reserve, involving postings to Eastbourne, North Wales and then to Honeybourne, Gloucestershire. From there, he was posted to no. 49 Squadron which was based at Fiskerton, Lincolnshire, late in 1942 . This was at the time of the major influx of American airmen with their giant bombers to many of the air bases of East Anglia and the east coast, and the early developments in night flights by British bombers.

Commission in the RAF: Navigator with 49 Squadron

Ronald did not start his tragically short flying career with the RAF till early in 1943, around the time of his 20th birthday. He was flying in Lancaster bombers as Navigator, but before the days of radar so relying on earlier methods of taking compass bearings, target finding, and route planning. He was well-equipped for this from his years of maths at Lewes County School. Lancasters were big, heavy droning planes, which carried eight crew members and large amounts of bombs. They were developed particularly for night flying over German industrial and military targets, after the relative failure of many of the earlier daytime bombing raids. They were able to fly sufficiently high over the target areas of Berlin, Hamburg, and the other big industrial centres, to avoid much of the anti-aircraft fire at the time; the problems then often arose on the return journeys when flying lower over the occupied Low Countries, there were greater risks of being picked out by coastal defences or enemy fighter planes. It may well be that Ron was involved in some of the raids on the Krupp iron and steel works on the Ruhr early in 1943.

Flying Officer/Navigator Ronald Blythe,
after obtaining his commission in the RAFVR (c.1942).

His last home leave

Ron was able to have a week at home with his parents and sister in the spring of 1943. In fact, it was a short period of sick leave which happened to coincide with his sister's earlier application for home leave. Kathleen was at that time stationed at Bournemouth with the WAAF, working for the Canadian Air Force on their admin/clerical side. Due to a bombing raid, her actual leave was cancelled at the last minute but she was allowed home just for the weekend. This was to be the last time either she or her parents saw Ron.

Flying Officer Blythe's last flight

He and the rest of his six-man crew took off in their Lancaster from RAF Fiskerton in Lincolnshire on the night of 16th/17th June 1943. They had a full bomb-load and their destination was Cologne, on the Rhine in the industrial north of Germany. At some point on their return journey they were apparently tracked and attacked by German night-fighters. They failed to return to their home base in Lincolnshire at dawn.

Nothing more than those bare facts were known for many weeks. It was of course possible that the damaged plane had been shot down over occupied Europe, with time for any surviving crew to bale out; but the best the family could have been hoping for from that possibility was that Ronald might have been captured by the enemy and interned as a prisoner of war for the duration of hostilities. There might just have been an outside chance of his having been picked up by Belgian or Dutch Resistance workers, and if he had landed relatively uninjured, being helped to escape back across the channel.

In the event, it was early in September 1943 before Mr & Mrs Blythe heard from the War Ministry that their son was now officially 'missing presumed dead'. A letter from his Commanding Officer at Fiskerton followed, confirming the Air Ministry's notification that he was 'believed to have been killed in action'.

Wing Commander P.W. Johnson wrote on behalf of 49 Squadron as follows:-

> *"… I want to offer you my sincere sympathy in your great loss.*
>
> *It is with the greatest regret that I have heard of the death of so many of this very fine crew and while there is so little I can say, I do feel that in your grief you will at least be proud to know that his son has done his duty nobly and well."*

During the autumn of 1943 that year's edition of "The Barbican", which was Lewes County School's magazine, appeared and included with its wartime Obituaries the following notice and tribute:-

> *"We are anxiously awaiting news of two more Old Boys who played a prominent part in School life, both of whom are reported missing:*
>
> *Pilot-Officer Ronald Charles Blythe, R.A.F. (1934-1941) Ronnie Blythe was known to everyone of his generation. Captain of the School, of Rugger and Cricket, winner of the Povey Trophy, Sergeant in the A.T.C., he carried on the tradition of the School at Oxford, where he gained a Freshers' Rugger Trial…*
>
> *Modest to a degree, he was a gentleman in every sense.*
>
> *A brother officer told the writer that Ronnie was one of a "wizard" crew (he was on Lancasters) and one of the best navigators they had ever had on the station.*
>
> *He is missing from a raid on Cologne.*

…We offer our deep sympathy to the parents of these Old Boys in their anxious periods of waiting."

(The other missing Old Boy at that time was Don Stone, also a Pilot Officer in the RAF. He was with Coastal Command, and was also an articled pupil at the same firm of accountants as Ronnie).

It was not until 1st December 1943 that the Air Ministry (Casualty Branch) in Oxford Street, London W.1. wrote again to Mr. Charles Blythe, informing him that his son's body had been washed up on the northern part of the Dutch coast, near Flushing, and was buried in Grave No. 183 of the Vlissingen Cemetery there. The crippled plane had apparently ditched in the North Sea, where the currents and tides had carried his body back to the shore he had last flown over in the small hours of 17th June. His body had been recovered on the shores of Walcheren Island, off Flushing, just over a month later on 19th July 1943. After the war, when the CWGC took over all war cemeteries, they informed the family that his grave was now moved to or incorporated into the Vlissingen

His grave in Vlissingen Northern Cemetery

(Flushing) North Cemetery, Row F, Grave 25. The family then had these words added to his headstone:

"OUR LOVE, OUR HOPE, OUR SORROW IS NOT DEAD"

Those he left behind

When the P.O.W.s were released at the end of the war, it was discovered that there was only one survivor of that Lancaster crew, the wireless operator. He had been able to eject and parachute out into the sea, only to be taken prisoner and interned till the end of the war. It so happened that he was a Canadian, and he was therefore returned to Bournemouth to await repatriation. This was where Kathleen was working, and she was able to meet him. This Canadian survivor told how Ron had turned and waved to him as he jumped from the plane.

It was to be fifty years before Kathleen was able to travel with the British Legion to Holland to visit her brother's grave. She went with her cousin Betty from Stoke Poges who had also lost a brother. They all stayed in a hotel in Nijmegen together, then Kathleen and her cousin were taken by a local Dutch couple who were their generous hosts for the weekend, to the Vlissingen cemetery and the coast. They saw Ron's grave, and that of his Squadron Leader next to him, and laid their wreath of poppies.

Frederick Bruce TINDALE   2.09
17th August 1943 aged 18
lost at sea off East Africa
Cadet, Merchant Navy/Royal Fleet Auxiliary
MV Empire Stanley (Greenock)

HOME   3 Priory Street, Southover
COMMEMORATED   Tower Hill Memorial, London

Lewes childhood

Bruce Tindale was born on 20th October 1924 with a twin sister Freda Beryl. The two of them had an older sister, Evelyn Mary, who was nearly four when they were born. All three children were baptised together at Southover Church on 29th May 1929, when Evelyn was eight and the twins were four. One of the sisters is thought to have been handicapped in some way, such as by Downs Syndrome or Cerebral Palsy. Their parents were William Hall Tindale and his wife Mary. William worked at Lewes Station and in the Southern Region of the railways, as a 'Railway Storekeeper'. He was also for many years a sidesman at Southover Church.

Bruce passed the necessary exams. to go to the Lewes County School in Mountfield Road. He is remembered from those years in the mid-1930s by several of my other 'informants', and those who knew him through Crusaders. Soon after he left school he joined the Merchant Navy, and was a Cadet with the Royal Fleet Auxiliary.

The "Empire Stanley"

The ship he joined, the "Empire Stanley", had only been completed in September 1941. It was one of a fleet of some 50 merchant and cargo ships owned by the Clan Line world-wide, but with strong links with the Greenock Dockyard Company. They were built mainly as refrigerated cargo ships for the frozen meat trade, troop supplies and home consumption. Five of these "Empire" heavy cargo ships were built at Greenock alone in 1940 and 1941, but only one survived the war (though many others were built at other dockyards nationwide). Its dimensions were nearly 450 feet x 56 feet, with a tonnage of nearly 7,000 tons and a ship's company of 53.

Her last voyage

This could conceivably still have been part of her maiden voyage, given the distances and difficulties involved, and the detouring to avoid submarines, minefields and air attack. This last voyage should have been from Durban in South Africa to Aden at the southern tip of the Saudi Arabian peninsula. Its cargo might then have been intended for distribution to troops and colonies in the Middle East, India and the Far East. Or there might have been more cargo to acquire from East Africa or Saudi Arabia to take back home via the Cape again, unless the Suez Canal was safe enough by then to risk getting back through the Mediterranean.

But as it was the "Empire Stanley" never even reached Aden. She had apparently made it to the first port of call on that voyage, which was Lourenco Marques (now Maputo) at the very southern end of Mozambique. But while she was still south of Madagascar in the Indian Ocean on 17th August 1943, she was torpedoed in a submarine attack by U-197.

Cadet Tindale's death

Bruce was one of 25 to go down with the ship. He was last seen helping to launch the ship's lifeboats. The lives of twenty eight men were saved as a result of his action that night. The 25 who were lost included 18 crew, 1 passenger and 8 naval gunners. The crew included the Master, A. J. Pilditch MBE. It is possible that as a Cadet in the Royal Fleet Auxiliary, Bruce was one of the 8 gunners.

It is certain that it took a very long time for any firm news to reach his family. The October 1944 edition of "The Barbican", the school magazine for Lewes County School, has the following entry under its "Old Boys' Notes":

> "No news has been received of Bruce Tindale who, as recorded in our last issue, is missing.
>
> When last seen he was trying to launch one of the ship's boats. The night was black and the vessel had been torpedoed. His death, therefore, can be presumed. We are deeply sorry for his parents. Bruce was an excellent fellow."

After the war Bruce's family moved up to Caburn Crescent on the Nevill Estate. Sadly his father was killed in a car accident soon afterwards, but though it is suggested that others of the family are still around, my attempts to make contact have not been successful.

Bruce's commemoration on the Tower Hill Merchant Navy Memorial

*Merchant Navy Memorial, Tower Hill, London,
with the Tower of London in background,
and mariners' compass set in lawn.*

The twenty Merchant Navy men who were lost with Bruce on the "Empire Stanley" are all commemorated with him on Panel 45 of the Tower Hill Memorial in London. This is a striking Memorial in a premier position beside the Tower of London, on a site already steeped in so much of our nation's history, with the River Thames and Tower Bridge beyond. It is also at a particularly important place in our maritime history, being in the grounds of the Trinity House Corporation (Henry VIII's foundation for the registering and control of all coastal pilotage and lighthouse services).

The Memorial was built originally by Sir Edwin Lutyens in 1927 to commemorate those from 1914-18, the "Twelve Thousand of the Merchant Navy and Fishing Fleets who have No Grave But The Sea."

It was then extended after the Second World War by the creation of a sunken garden beside it, containing a 'pool' of bronze in the centre designed as a mariner's compass, set to magnetic north. Much more of great poignancy and symbolism is included in the design and sculptures.

Memorial Panels for Second War MN men lost at sea, recorded ship by ship.

The whole is surrounded by a wall containing bronze panels, with all twenty four thousand additional names inscribed on the panels. These are displayed in alphabetical order, ship by ship, with no rank or rating indicated except the Master or Skipper. Queen Mary unveiled the first part of the whole Memorial in 1929, and our present Queen the second in 1955, just twenty six years apart.

The inscription for 1939 - 45 reads:

THE TWENTY FOUR THOUSAND OF THE MERCHANT NAVY AND FISHING FLEETS

WHOSE NAMES ARE HONOURED ON THE WALLS OF THIS GARDEN

GAVE THEIR LIVES FOR THEIR COUNTRY

AND HAVE NO GRAVE BUT THE SEA

This eloquent Memorial is beautifully maintained by the Commonwealth War Graves Commission, who provide benches for City office workers and visitors to sit in peace with their sandwiches and their memories.

The 20 crew of the "Empire Stanley" who went down with her, including Bruce Tindale, on Panel 45.

Raymond Clifford SCRASE   2.10
18th September 1943 aged 22
in Assam, N.E. India
1446658 Leading Aircraftman
R.A.F. Volunteer Reserve, R.A.F. Regiment

HOME   22 Valley Road, Winterbourne
BURIED   Gauhati War Cemetery, Assam, India

Ray Scrase was the second of the Southover men in the Second World War to lose his life while with the RAF. His cousin Joan Gurr remembers him having always wanted to be one of the "Brylcreem Boys", and the photograph she has kindly provided shows him as just that (p.202). It was taken for Christmas 1941 when he was mid-way through his RAF training in West Wales.

The Scrase family in Priory Street

Ray and Joan were cousins who were both brought up by their grandparents, Emily and Stanton Scrase at 38 Priory Street. Their mothers, Lil and Sue respectively, were sisters, and were two of the three daughters of Emily and Stanton. Emily their grandmother had a big heart and a big welcome for everyone. She took Ray in as soon as he was born in1920 and raised him as her own. His mother Lil could not manage alone since his father, a Canadian serviceman who had been stationed in Lewes in the First War, had gone back to Canada by that time. Ray then became not just the grandson but also the foster son of Emily and Stanton. Their grandfather Stanton worked in the construction industry and was at Ringmer Building Works; later on, he was part of the construction team that built the County Grammar School down Mountfield Road in the 1930s.

When Joan was born in 1926, when Ray was already six, she too needed her Gran's tender loving care as she was born so prematurely that she was not expected to survive. But her grandmother rose to the challenge and fed her hourly with a fountain pen dropper for as long as it took! Joan's parents, Sue and George Boon lived in Coldstock, and already had one child little more than a year old, so could not cope with such a tiny new baby as well. Joan's parents went on to have no fewer than thirteen children in quick succession, so although she always went back to them for holidays each year, there never was an ideal moment for her to return to her own parents so she stayed on with her grandparents indefinitely. Her father was in the Sussex Police Force.

Ray's childhood and youth

Joan has vivid memories of Priory Street in the early 1930's, and remembers exactly who lived at each house between the Kings Head and Garden Street on both sides of the road, including several of Ray's schoolfriends in that stretch. Dennis Moppett, Cedric Cunnington and Wally Dunk were the other three named on the Southover Memorial who he knew best. His special

200

friend 'Woody' Woodgate, was also a near neighbour in Priory Street. In his childhood Ray was a choirboy at Southover Church for five years. Joan remembers her Gran working occasionally (part-time) at the Jolly Friars, nearly opposite their home. Ray's own mother Lil, also worked there at times through his childhood.

In 1938, when Joan was 11 and Ray already 17, their house and several others on either side had to be demolished to make way for the block of flats called Priory Place (it is still there, and backs onto Urry's Yard off Eastport Lane). Ray had already left Central School but Joan was still there, under the renowned Mr Bowley. One of Ray's early jobs had been at the outfitters' Hugh Rae in the High Street, but from there he moved to another job at Beard's Brewery in Castle Ditch Lane. Joan remembers feeling that Ray was particularly at risk of being 'spoiled rotten' by his doting Gran, who reduced her charges to him for board and lodging rather than insist he wore the protective clogs that Beard's provided for all their Brewery workers; he particularly wanted to wear his own 'proper shoes' but they then got so stained by the brewery spills that they needed to be replaced every few weeks as they rotted - he could not afford to do this as well as pay her the normal full amount for his keep.

The move to Valley Road

Joan remembers her grandmother being very upset at having to leave Priory Street. She was 'getting on a bit' by that time and already had heart trouble, so did not relish the prospect of all the hills and steep front paths in the Winterbourne estate. Being one of the earliest to move into Valley Road, she was able to choose the house with the fewest steps; that was number 22, and that is where her grand-daughter Joan still lives today. The two cousins, Joan and Ray, rounded off their teenage years there. Joan's main memory of Ray in those years up to his call-up was that she was a nuisance to him, or rather that he felt she was a nuisance. The age gap between them was at least five years, which she felt was too wide for her to share at all closely in his life. She remembers him best for the parachute he made and tied to the only doll with a china face she had ever had; he then dropped both doll and parachute from an upstairs window, with the inevitable disastrous result !

Their home became known as 'The Shop' as it was such a focal point and always full of neighbours and friends, particularly young people. Their Gran seemed to have a soft spot for them all, and they all kept flocking there to share a laugh or their woes.

The war years: 1940/41

Ray was not quite 18 when war broke out. He continued at the Brewery initially, while joining the Home Guard as well and doing shifts on Air Raid Precaution duties, firewatching and blackout-checking. By August 1941 he had decided to join up, and was sent by the RAF for traing in Cardiganshire, West Wales. Joan was 15 by this time, and had been very involved at school and at home with the evacuees who came to Lewes from Tooting Bec School in south London. They had had two billeted with them, as well as a Commando. Since the war, this Commando has given the family great pleasure by coming back to see them again. Joan's attempts to trace their evacuee John have not so far had any success, much to her disapppointment.

In June 1942 Ray was posted overseas. His grandmother found it particularly hard to take that he was apparently rushed off at the last minute, without time even to complete some final parts

201

of his training. The war in the Far East was opening up dramatically after Pearl Harbour in 1941 and the eventual fall of Singapore in 1942. Ray's rank of Leading Aircraftman qualified him in all aspects of aircraft maintenance, but not directly in flying as such. On being posted to the Indian sub-continent at this crucial time, Ray was attached to the RAF Regiment. With them he had a largely maintenance and servicing role, and was involved in the building of landing strips in the jungle. The area he was in was the distant border country between the north eastern corner of India across the Brahmaputra River from the far eastern end of the Himalyas, and between what is now Bangladesh and Burma. Then it would have been in the area under Mountbatten's command, closely involved in the behind-the-lines planning, preparations and execution of the war against Japan in the jungles of Burma.

Meanwhile, back home in Valley Road, his grandfather Stanton Scrase was failing fast. He died in the early summer of 1943, almost certainly without Ray

Raymond Scrase, taken in 1941.

having heard the news even of his illness. The CWGC had him listed as Ray's next of kin, identified on their papers as being both his grandfather and his foster-father. Joan's memory is that her Auntie Lil, Ray's own mother, had also died by then. Their grand-mother Emily was suddenly very alone, after years of having had such a full house.

Then early in September, Ray was selected for a slot in one of the Forces Broadcasts sending messages back home. Joan does not remember the family getting any advance notice of this, so they never heard it themselves. It was in fact broadcast over here on what turned out to be the last Sunday morning of his life, and according to the obituary in the *Sussex Express* on 15th October 1943:

> *"Several of his friends heard his voice on the wireless on the Sunday morning previous to his death, he having been selected as one of the members of the Forces to broadcast a message home."*

Illness, death and burial in September 1943

Ray himself was then suddenly taken ill in mid-September 1943. He was admitted to the Assam Military Hospital, near Shillong the then capital of Assam in N. E. India. It was eventually found that he was suffering from a waterbourne infection due to contaminated water supplies;

it was thought that rats had somehow got into the wells from which his supplies came. There was sadly neither the time, and possibly not the medication either, for any effective treatment to be provided. He died in hospital after only a few days of acute illness, just a few days short of his 23rd birthday.

He was buried immediately in the local cemetery of Silghat, Assam. The CWGC later incorporated his grave after the war into the Gauhati War Cemetery nearby, where it is carefully maintained today among tall tropical trees and lush plants in the fertile valley of the Brahmaputra River. It is on the eastern banks of this great river, about 400 miles east of Calcutta. The early photographs suggest there were paddy fields nearby, but now it is surrounded by residential area on the road out to the Nabagraha Hindu Temple past the Brahmaputra Hotel.

His first burial place, at Silghat, Assam.

Report of his death in the local paper, October 1943

The *Sussex Express*, by that time amalgamated with both the *County Herald* and the *East Sussex News*, reported Ray's death on the front page of their issue of Friday 15th October 1943, under the title:

Lewes Aircraftman's Death

"News has been received that Leading Aircraftman Raymond Scrase… has died abroad after a few days' illness… He was well known in Lewes where he had many friends… His father (sic) died a few months ago, and Mrs.Scrase has received many expressions of sympathy in her double bereavement. One of the letters was from the Rev. D. G. Matthews (Rector of Southover) on behalf of himself and the organist and choir. Another was from Messrs. Beard & Co., Brewers, on behalf of the directors and staff, he having been in the employ of that firm before he joined the R.A.F…"

Those he left behind

The family marked the first anniversary of his death by putting an announcement in the *Sussex Express*, under the "In Memoriam - On Active Service" column on September 22nd 1944. It read:

SCRASE: In loving memory of our dear Ray, R.A.F., who died in India on September 18th 1943; from Mum, Joan, Doll and Evelyn.

> *"Gone from us but not forgotten,*
> *Never shall thy memory fade;*
> *Loving thoughts shall ever linger*
> *Round the spot where you are laid."*

By 1947 his cousin Joan had married one of the R.A.F. men who did return. Their second son was born on what would have been Ray's birthday, and they named him Raymond. They lived in the same Valley Road house, and Joan soon had to nurse her grandmother Emily through her last illness in 1948.

Joan's father had served with Sussex Police for 32 years, and her husband was for many years with Every's Iron Foundry in Lewes, then the Haven Foundry at Newhaven, until he died in 1986. By then there were seven children, and now there are ten grandchildren. Joan is very pleased to have been able to stay on at the same house, and now to own it with one of her sons and to have it extended by one of the others.

His final resting place in the Gauhati War Cemetery, marked by a white cross.

Frederick Jasper SMITH   2.11
17th November 1943 aged 28
in the Middle East
1331800 Sergeant (Navigator/Bomber)
100 Squadron, R.A.F. Volunteer Reserve

HOME   3 St Pancras Gardens, Southover
BURIED   Ramleh War Cemetery, Lod (Lydda)
near Tel Aviv, Israel

Fred Smith is one of those Southover men about whom I have unfortunately not been able to find out very much at all. His parents were Albert William Smith and his wife Harriet, and they lived at 3 St. Pancras Gardens, long before the present flats were there. It is thought that Fred had at least one sister, ?Emily, who married a Mr. ?Rogers and lived on in St. Pancras Road before ?moving to Seaford.

He did also have a distant second cousin or great nephew by the name of Jim Smith, who is still living in Southover. Jim also grew up in the old St. Pancras Gardens area, and has many war-time and early post-war memories of other local families, but nothing on Frederick Jasper.

Some of my 'informants' about other men remember hearing of Fred at Central School in Lewes, and then of him moving on to Brighton Grammar School. It is thought he then worked for some while at Lewes Post Office. He presumably joined up before the war, as he was already in the Reserve with the RAF.

With the RAF in the Middle East

When Fred arrived in the Middle East in the early part of the war, he would have found it a simmering melting-pot of conflicting interests of Arab and Jew, not to mention Christian, of Britain and Commonwealth and of Europe, and of Allies versus Axis. For Britain, there was the major need to keep the Suez Canal open for the Empire out east, for the Jews there was the increasingly desperate need for a homeland in the face of Hitler's atrocities, and for the Arabs particularly in Palestine who also were without a homeland and suffering much from anti-Christian and anti-British folk memory going back to the Crusades. As throughout history, this little corner of the world seemed to have the conflicting interests and problems of the whole world compressed into it.

1943 had begun with Churchill and Roosevelt having their Casablanca Summit. By May the Axis forces in North Africa had surrendered in Tunis. Between July and September, the Allies were landing in Sicily and eventually establishing themselves enough to begin their invasion of mainland Italy. Mussolini was overthrown, and Italy changed sides to join the Allies. Fred Smith's 100 Squadron could well have been involved in any or all of these ventures. November 1943, when Fred. Smith was killed, was the month of the Teheran Summit of all the Allied leaders, with Stalin as well. Though that was in some ways the beginning of the end of World

War Two, the whole Middle East remained in particular turmoil.

Further north in Palestine, there was the strategic importance of Haifa on the Mediterranean coast beside Mount Carmel, to be maintained. Even the Navy had been involved before the war, in manning the "Haifa Patrol". Haifa was at the junction of the two big trade and supply routes, one to Damascus in Syria to the north, and the other down to Qantara on the Suez Canal via the Sinai Military Railroad. Fred and his 100 Squadron were almost certainly involved in defending these routes.

His death and burial

Fred was killed on 17th November 1943, and the news reached Lewes in little over a week. There was the briefest of entries in the Deaths Column of the *Sussex Express* for Friday 26th November, merely announcing the death on active service in the Middle East of Sgt. F.J. Smith, R.A.F.

Later on, when the CWGC could again get access after the war to their First War Military Cemeteries in the region, he was buried alongside many RAF servicemen in the Ramleh Military Cemetery. Although this is now almost encroached on by motorways to Tel Aviv airport, and a large prison and land-fill rubbish dump, it does still have a beautiful distant view across the Jordan valley into the deserts and hills of Jordan through the eucalyptus trees. It is beautifully maintained, with a profusion of semi-tropical plants and shrubs. *"Unto the hills will I lift mine eyes"* are the words inscribed on the great Memorial Tablet at the entrance tablet.

This is the very same Cemetery in which lies Alec Richardson, one of the Southover men from the First War. Please see 1.39 for further details about the Cemetery and my attempts to visit their graves; and strangely enough also about life in St. Pancras Gardens, which is where Alec too was raised.

General view of Ramleh War Cemetery.

Kenneth Arthur PIPER
18th November 1943 aged 19
in hospital at Birmingham
14416980 Private/Driver
Royal Army Ordnance Corps

2.12

HOME   21 Dale Road, Winterbourne Estate, Lewes
BURIED   Lewes Cemetery

His family and pre-war youth

The Piper family lived in Keere Street before moving to Dale Road in the early 1920s. Kenneth was the middle of three sons born to Bert and Annie Piper. His father was a well-known Lewes cricketer and footballer, and was also a football referee for the Sussex County Football Association. He was also something of a pigeon fancier, and is still remembered for that by the now elderly neighbour whose husband shared that hobby through the 1930s with Bert.

Kenneth was born on 18th November 1922, just around the time the family moved to the new Winterbourne Estate. His older brother was Bob, and the younger one was Alan. Ken went to the Pells School, and sang in the choir at St Michael's Church. They grew up next door to Fred Moore, who was seven years older than Kenneth; Fred went into the Royal Engineers, and was away serving in Italy by the time Kenneth joined up.

Before the war Ken had worked at the Belgrave Supply Depot (Motor Accessories) in Lansdown Place as their Assistant Storekeeper. He also played cricket for the St. Anne's Team, and was a member of the Lewes Air Training Corps. From the outbreak of war in 1939 he also worked in off-duty hours as an Air Raid Precaution (ARP) messenger.

His brief war service

Once he had turned 18, he volunteered for the Army. In January 1943, he was posted with the Royal Army Ordnance Corps. He was a Driver with them, presumably driving ammunition trucks or involved with a Bomb Disposal Squad. While 'on active service' in the Midlands in mid-November 1943, he was involved in a road traffic accident. He was admitted to the Central Hospital, Birmingham, where he subsequently died of his injuries. This was on 18th November, his own 19th birthday. As far as is known, he died without ever having been out of the country.

Funeral at Southover

This was held on Wednesday afternoon 22nd November, with a Guard of Honour from the Lewes A.T.C. and the coffin was draped with the Union Jack. The service was followed by interment at the Lewes Cemetery, and the account in the local paper two days later lists no fewer than 20 family mourners and over 30 wreaths. Besides his parents, and his uncle and aunt Mr and Mrs A. Piper from Nottingham, his sister-in-law Mrs John ('Bob') Piper was there. She was presumably the wife of his older brother who was away serving in Italy at the time. There is no mention of his younger brother, who was still at school, having been there. Then there were three sets of Holder uncles and aunts, presumably on his mother's side, and another uncle and aunt Mr and Mrs F. Footitt with their son Tony, his cousin. His former employers, Mr and Mrs F. Gibbins, were there, as were half a dozen other friends or relations. There were also various representatives of the British Legion and from the Civil Defence No. 6 Post.

A year later the Dale Road heard of the loss of Fred Moore, from next door to the Pipers. Kenneth's family put a notice in the 'In Memoriam' column of the *Sussex Express*, on 17th November 1944:

> PIPER, K.A. *Cherished memories of our Ken, called home November 19th 1943.*
>
> > *"Sleep on dear Ken and take your rest,*
> > *We needed you but God knows best.*
> > *Your death came, a blow we can never forget,*
> > *But your life is a sweet memory that is with us yet."*
> >
> > 21 Dale Road, Lewes.

On the lower part of Ken's CWGC headstone in Lewes Cemetery, the family then had these words engraved:

"LOVE'S LAST GIFT: REMEMBRANCE."

Kenneth Piper's grave in Lewes Cemetery.

PTE. K. A. PIPER

On his 19th birthday Kenneth Arthur Piper, son of Mr. and Mrs. R. Piper, of 21, Dale-road, was killed in a road accident while on duty in the Midlands. He volunteered for the Army in February this year and was a driver in the R.A.O.C. He was employed as assistant storekeeper at the Belgrave Supply Depot, Lewes, until he joined up, and was a member of the choir at St. Michael's Church and of the Lewes A.T.C., and played in St. Anne's cricket team. In 1939 he joined the A.R.P. as a messenger and continued to work with them until early this year. He has an elder brother serving in Italy and a younger one at R.A.O.C. His father is well known as a cricketer and footballer, and has been a referee for the Sussex County Football Association.

The funeral service was held in Southover Church, Lewes, on Wednesday afternoon, a guard of honour from the Lewes A.T.C. being present. At the interment in the cemetery, Messrs. H. C. Wheeler and W. Huggett attended with the Lewes British Legion standard. Civil Defence personnel from No. 6 Post were also present. The coffin was enveloped by a Union Jack. The family mourners were: Mr. and Mrs. R. Piper (father and mother), Mr. and Mrs. A. Piper, of Nottingham (uncle and aunt), Mrs. John Piper (sister-in-law), Mr. and Mrs. S. Holder, Mr. and Mrs. J. Holder and Mr. and Mrs. G. Holder (uncles and aunts), Mr. and Mrs. F. Footitt and Tony (uncle, aunt and cousin), Mrs. Loder, Mrs. Grace and daughter, Mr. G. Lee and Mr. D. Southey. Among those also present were Mr. and Mrs. F. Gibbins, deceased former employers. The floral tributes numbered over 30 and included wreaths from deceased's commanding officer, his comrades in the unit and numerous other friends.

The funeral arrangements were carried out by Mr. W. Weller of Malling-street, Lewes.

Pte. K.A. Piper, in local paper obituary

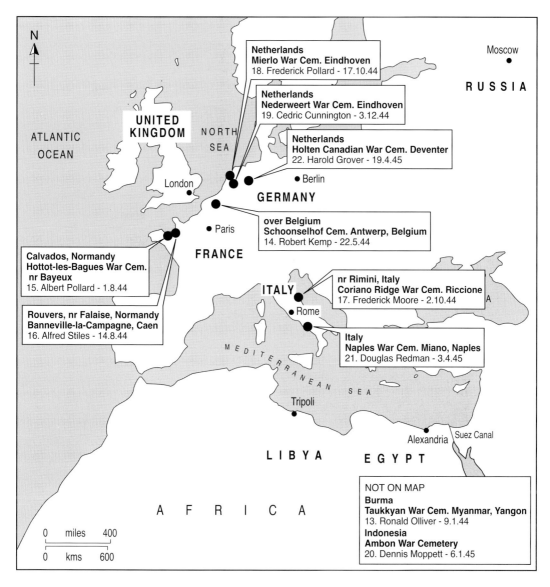

Netherlands
Mierlo War Cem. Eindhoven
18. Frederick Pollard - 17.10.44

Netherlands
Nederweert War Cem. Eindhoven
19. Cedric Cunnington - 3.12.44

Netherlands
Holten Canadian War Cem. Deventer
22. Harold Grover - 19.4.45

over Belgium
Schoonselhof Cem. Antwerp, Belgium
14. Robert Kemp - 22.5.44

Calvados, Normandy
Hottot-les-Bagues War Cem.
nr Bayeux
15. Albert Pollard - 1.8.44

Rouvers, nr Falaise, Normandy
Banneville-la-Campagne, Caen
16. Alfred Stiles - 14.8.44

nr Rimini, Italy
Coriano Ridge War Cem. Riccione
17. Frederick Moore - 2.10.44

Italy
Naples War Cem. Miano, Naples
21. Douglas Redman - 3.4.45

NOT ON MAP
Burma
Taukkyan War Cem. Myanmar, Yangon
13. Ronald Olliver - 9.1.44
Indonesia
Ambon War Cemetery
20. Dennis Moppett - 6.1.45

Place of death and cemetery/memorial of Southover men killed 1944-45 (nos 13 - 22)
(number before name refers to order of death)

Ronald OLLIVER   2.13
9th January 1944 aged 19
in Burma
6411955 Private
Queen's Own Royal West Kent Regiment

HOME   6 Priory Place, Southover
BURIED   Taukkyan War Cemetery, Rangoon, Burma

The Ollivers of Southover

Both the men named Olliver on the Southover Second War Memorial were from the same wider family; they lived two streets apart and died two years apart, across the world from each other. Ronald was only 19 and had not yet left home, but his Uncle Stanley who had died on active service two years earlier was already 35 and the father of an 8 year old son (see 2.06). Ronald's grandparents thus lost not only him their grandson, but also their own son as well, all within three years.

Ronald was born in 1925 and then adopted by Christopher Alfred Olliver and his wife Dorothy. They lived at 6 Priory Place, and later had a second son Norman. Their father was one of the sons of Christopher Olliver, house decorator, and his wife Elizabeth, who lived round the corner at 12 Eastport Lane. Ronald's uncle was Stanley Gordon Olliver, his father's brother who was the other son of the same grandparents. His father's sister, his aunt Kath, who still lives in Priory Flats, remembers Ronald having a mass of blond curls as a little boy. Ronald would have been a boy of seven when his Uncle Stanley had got married at Southover Church on 11th June 1932, and was probably there too as his father Christopher Alfred was one of the witnesses.

By the time Ronald reached the age of enlisting at 17 or 18 in 1943, that same Uncle Stan had been dead for two years. Ronald was up to that time working in London with a firm called Stewarts & Grays, in one of the South West districts, probably commuting from Lewes station.

He then joined up with the Queen's Own Royal West Kent Regiment, though one newspaper report (below) refers to him having been with the Royal Sussex Regiment. At any rate, he was soon sent out to Burma, where the needs were very great.

Ronald Olliver

Ronald's war in Burma

The first of the Chindit operations had begun in Burma early in 1943, but the big fighting there did not come until 1944. Mountbatten became Supreme Commander of Southeast Asia Command at the end of August 1943. Up to then South East Asia had been felt by some of those serving there to have been a somewhat neglected theatre of war, but Mountbatten was able to attract a greater share of manpower and resources, with the aim of driving the Japanese out of Burma.

The capture of its occupied capital, Rangoon, was a necessary pre-requisite, and that was not achieved until May 1945. In the meantime, the British advance in the Arakan in the north of Burma began successfully enough in December 1943, but was driven back by a new Japanese attack early in February 1944. It was just at that point that the *Sussex Express* reported on February 4th 1944 under the heading "LEWES SOLDIER KILLED" that:

> *"Mr. & Mrs. C. A. Olliver of 6 Priory Place, Southover, received notification last Friday that their son Private Ronald Olliver (19) has been killed in action while serving with the Royal Sussex Regiment (sic) in Burma."*

His Aunt Kath remembers hearing that he was shot by a sniper in a rice field.

A year later the family put this notice in the In Memoriam column, in January 1945:

> *"In never-forgotten memory of our beloved son Private Ronald Olliver of Lewes, killed in action in Burma on 9th January 1944.*
>
> > *'Deep in our hearts your memory is kept*
> > *By those that love you and will never forget'."*

It was not till long after the atomic bomb had ended the war in the Far East that the Commonwealth War Graves Commission could start giving a decent burial or commemoration to the tens of thousands of British servicemen who gave their lives in Burma, as near as possible to where they fell.

Ronald Olliver's last resting place is in the War Cemetery at Taukkyan in Myanmar, some 25 miles north of Rangoon. His grave there is no. E.24 in Plot 4.

Robert William KEMP   2.14
22nd May 1944 aged 22
while on operations over Belgium
1801055 Flight Sergeant/Engineer
626 Squadron, R.A.F. Volunteer Reserve

HOME   45 Priory Street, Southover
BURIED   Schoonselhof Cemetery, Antwerp, Belgium

'Robbo' Kemp was born to Robert and Flossy Kemp, who lived in North Street. He grew up there, and saw a lot of relatives on his father's side, Mr and Mrs Wing who also lived in North Street. They lived at no. 28 North Street so escaped the worst of the air raid damage in 1943.

'Robbo' went to the Pells School. When he first left school at 16 he was employed at Ringmer Building Works, and once he was 17 he joined up with the RAF.

He did his training at RAF Northolt, and was then posted to RAF Wickenby in Lincolnshire. He was flying Lancaster bombers, known colloquially as the 'Heavies', and was promoted Flight Sergeant/Engineer.

RAF Wickenby was one of those airbases in the East Anglian front line for the big bombing raids over Germany in 1943 and 1944. By the end of March 1944 a series of major setbacks for the Allies' Combined Bomber Offensive (such as the loss of 96 bombers out of 795 in one night) led to some policy changes. Then there was the threat to London and the south east from the rocket launch sites of Peenemunde on the Baltic Coast, and the RAF was instrumental in crippling these.

Robert Kemp

Marriage and family

At some point in all this, probably in 1940, 'Robbo' had got married and moved to Priory Street. His bride was Mary Louise Andrews, and their first son was also called Robert. He was born in April 1941, and their second son Kenneth followed only just over a year later in May 1942. These two boys still live in Lewes over half a century later; Robert is in Hill Road, and Kenneth on the Nevill. Their father's medals and some photographs are still in the wider family, and Kenneth responded to my postcard advertisement in the window of the Nevill Post Office and Stores window about this book last year.

Kenneth only ever saw his father on a few occasions. Those were only in his first two years of life so he has no memory of them, but he knows that photographs of himself and his older brother were sent to his father.

His death and burial

It may perhaps be that when Flight Sergeant Kemp was shot down in May 1944, he was on one of these Peenemunde operations. There must have been some difficulty in tracing his body and his plane, as it took a full six months for any news of his even being missing to appear in the *Sussex Express*. It then appeared on 17th November 1944, under the heading "Flight Sergeant's Death":

> *"… in addition to his wife, Flight Sergt. Kemp leaves two little boys. He was a grandson of Mr & Mrs Wing of 28 North Street Lewes, and much sympathy has been expressed with the family in their loss."*

He was eventually buried in Schoonselhof Cemetery at Wilrijk, a suburb of Antwerp, about 40 miles north of Brussels. The Commonwealth War Graves Commission seem to have opened up some extra plots at the far end of the Municipal Cemetery. Flight Sergeant Kemp's grave there is number E. 25 in Plot IVa.

After the war

The fatherless family moved from Priory Street down Mountfield Road, where his widow could be nearer her parents who had themselves moved there. She then later re-married and they moved up to St. John's Street, where the boys were brought up by her and their step-father. She died in 1991.

Albert Edward POLLARD   2.15
1st August 1944 aged 27
in Normandy
6403842 Rifleman
12th Battalion King's Royal Life Corps
(2nd Battalion The Queen's Westminsters)

HOME   18 Landport Road, Lewes
BURIED   Hottot-les-Bagues War Cemetery, near Bayeux, Normandy

Rifleman Pollard was the first of the Southover men to die for the liberation of Europe, at the beginning of the end of this Second World War. He may have been actually part of the 'D' Day landings on 6th June 1944, and have been fighting his way inland from Gold or Juno Beach since then, or he may have only arrived in Normandy after the first wave of the invasion.

Southover childhood

Albert was born on 19th November 1916, before the First World War was even halfway through. His parents were Private Horace Thomas Pollard, who was then in the 15th Battalion Royal Sussex Regiment, and his wife Phoebe. Their home then was at 8 St Andrews Lane, and Albert was the youngest of the family at the time. He was baptised at Southover when he was four months old on 11th March 1917. He then had a younger sister Elsie Violet born on 20th March 1920, who was baptised at Southover when she was two months old, on 16th May 1920. By then, they had moved to 8 St. Pancras Lane, Southover, and their father Horace had been invalided out of the Army.

Albert went to Western Road School, and then went to work at the Home & Colonial Stores in Cliffe High Street. After a spell there he moved to Ringmer Building Works.

The war years

It was while he was working at Ringmer that he was called up in March 1940 when he was 23. Shortly after that his older brother was invalided out of the Army after the evacuation of the BEF at Dunkirk. His younger sister was also serving with the ATS.

Two years later Albert married a girl called Lucie Vera Joan Botwood in March 1944. She was then from Church Road, Heston, Middlesex, but had come originally from Stoke Heath, near Shrewsbury. This was an area with several army training establishments and rifle ranges, and RAF Turn Hill remains there. It could be that he had been sent up there for training, which could account for how she came to know this young Southover Rifleman. I am in contact with a member of the Botwood family in the Stoke Heath area, and am hoping he may be able to discover any

Rifleman Pollard

remaining contacts with the family Albert married into, as it seems his widow returned there after the war.

Rifleman Pollard proceeded inland with his unit in this historic Battle of Normandy. British forces were not able to liberate Caen until 9th July, and from there they swept round in a wide arc through Tilly-sur-Seulles, Hottot-les-Bagues and Villers Bocage to meet the Americans coming in from the Cherbourg peninsula. This culminated in the liberation of Vire, some thirty miles further inland, early in August.

Albert's death and burial

It was on 1st August 1944 that Albert was killed, somewhere in the now peaceful Normandy countryside, or in one of the farming villages in the area as outlined above. They met much resistance from the occupying German forces, so unfortunately much damage was done to the villages and farms they went through.

After the war, the Commonwealth War Graves Commission took responsibility for collecting up and re-burying those of the dead who had been buried where they fell or buried in small local cemeteries. Rifleman Pollard's grave is now in the Hottot-les-Bagues War Cemetery, Calvados, on the D9 road from Caen westwards towards Caumont l'Evente. He is among 965 British soldiers, in a total of 1137 in the whole cemetery. His grave is no. E.11 in Plot X11. His young widow Lucie has had these words inscribed on the headstone, under the official inscription:

"In memory of my dearly beloved husband who died that I might live

R. I. P."

Albert Pollard's grave at Hottot-les-Bagues War Cemetery, near Bayeux, Normandy

2.16

Alfred James Wade STILES
14th August 1944 aged 33
in Normandy
772577 Sergeant
1st Lothians & Border Horse/Royal Scots Greys (Royal Armoured Corps)

HOME   "Eastport House", Eastport Lane, Southover, then Offham, then Rutland
BURIED   Banneville-la-Campagne War Cemetery, Troarn, Calvados, Normandy

Family and friends in Southover

It is very fortunate that this man's widow Mollie and daughters Diane and Janet still all live in Lewes, and they have been most helpful in compiling this biography and supplying some of the photographs. I am most grateful to them for answering my Nevill Post Office window advertisement.

Alfred Stiles was born on 8th January 1911 in Brighton to Henry William Stiles and his wife Kate Mary. He had an older brother James, and three sisters Gladys, Peggy and Phyllis. His father had come from Brighton originally, and was for many years a tobacconist running the shop now known as 'Full o' Beans' in Lewes High Street. The family later moved to Eastport House, the large double fronted house with a raised front step, probably the house now known as 23 Eastport Lane. It was next door to what was the Salvation Army Hall (probably now 'The Old Meeting') between the Bell Inn and the Southover High Street end of Eastport Lane.

Alfred (or 'Smug' as he came to be known to his friends) was at Central School, Lewes, from 1921 to 1925. He left there with Standard VIII and a high commendation from the Headmaster, Mr Bowley, in the form of a character reference for work, from which the following phrases are quoted:

> "…his school work reached a high level… excelled in English and Maths… high moral character… personality most pleasing… he will be found very trustworthy, regular and punctual."

He was best friends while there with Fred Moore, also of Eastport Lane, who was also to be killed in 1944 (see 2.17). Alfred then worked briefly as a butcher's boy for Mr Cosham at the London & Provincial Meat Stores in Lewes High Street, before deciding to sign on with the Regular Army for six years from the age of 17 in the late 1920's.

"A most exceptional horseman" with the Royal Scots Greys

He joined the Royal Scots Greys, and was based at the Mooltan Barracks, Tidworth, Hants. Then from July 1929 to May 1930 he was sent on an Army School of Equitation course at Weedon. He was awarded a Special Certificate from this, and again had some pretty exceptional references afterwards. For example, Major Dudgeon wrote that he was:

Alfred Stiles in training with the Royal Scots Greys, Dreghorn, May 1929.

" *a most exceptional horseman in every branch, and has acquired an exceptional knowledge in Equitation... All horses go kindly with him and he has a great horse sense... I have always found him honest, sober and trustworthy...*"

Lieutenant-Colonel Piggott-Moodie wrote:

"*...smart, intelligent, hard-working man... a good horseman and trainer of young horses, with varied experience... an excellent Instructor of Equitation.*"

Lt.-Col. A. C. Brooks and Major-General A. W. Harman, the Commandant of the School of Equitation, who awarded the Special Certificate, wrote:

"*...nice quiet rider with nice hands... has endless patience and tact, and being a good horseman produces excellent results... Came late on the Course but has put it all in in every branch, and has done exceptionally well. A very promising N.C.O.*"

He must have quickly made his mark with the Royal Scots Greys, as by 1933 he was appearing in the Royal Tournament with them. His six years' service was completed in 1935, but he remained in the Reserve. He then found a new post as groom/chauffeur at Coombe Place, Offham

New groom marries 'childhood sweetheart'

By the late summer of 1938, as the war clouds were gathering around the Munich crisis, he got married back home in Southover. The wedding was on 14th September at Southover Church, when he was 27 and his bride (Winifred) Molly Standing was 25. She had been friends for years with Alfred's sisters, and was also a dressmaker as was one of them. Her father Albert was chauffeur for Mr Verrall of Southover Manor, and the Standing family lived at 28 Southover High Street on the way out to Kingston, next door to "Brookside" (where the Glover family had grown up through the First War, see 1.09 and 1.12). Alfred's father was not still alive by the time of his son's wedding, but his best friend Fred Moore, was best man. Fred was also from Eastport Lane, but had by the time of Alfred's wedding moved to the Winterbourne estate. Fred was only to last another two months longer in the war than was Alfred, as he was to be killed in Italy in

October 1944 (see 2.17). After the wedding, Alfred and Mollie moved away to Rutland, where Alfred had found a new groom/chauffeur post.

From grey horses to gun turrets of tanks

Then less than a year later, the next war started. When war broke out, Alfred was recalled to the colours from the Reserve. The great irony, after all that School of Equitation training only ten years earlier, was that the 1st Lothians & Border Horse/Royal Scots Greys were now being mechanised, and were in the process of becoming the Royal Armoured Corps.

In the years before he was sent to Normandy, Alfred was able to see at least one of his two little girls. Diana Patricia was born in March 1940 and Janet Muriel followed in March 1944. Both were baptised at Southover Church when a month old, but Alfred was not able to get to his younger daughter's baptism because his unit was stationed on the south coast by then, in training for the 'D' Day Landings. Janet was barely three months old when her father had to set off for Normandy.

In back garden of Eastport House, 23 Eastport Lane.

Alfred in Normandy

Alfred was participating in a rare moment of history, by being part of this Allied invasion of France in order to free it from its earlier invader. There is now an inscription round the base of the Bayeux Memorial to the 2,000 British and Commonwealth soldiers who died in Normandy but have no known grave, which translated from the Latin reads:

> *"We, once conquered by William, have set free the Conqueror's native land."*

There are over 22,000 British war dead buried in the other eighteen CWGC Cemeteries of Normandy.

The three British and Canadian landing beaches in Normandy on and from 6th June 1944 were those most to the east, Gold, Juno and Sword. The Americans landed further west and on the Cherbourg peninsula. Once Caen and Bayeux had been secured, and the enemy flushed out from the hinterland, the two forces were to meet up inland and together break through the 'Falaise Gap', making for the Seine and eventually Paris. This is exactly what happened, but it all took longer than expected because of the intense resistance from the occupying forces. Paris was not finally reached and liberated until 24th August.

Death at Rouvers

Alfred was killed on 14th August, just three days before British tanks and infantry met up with the Canadians and together stormed through the Falaise Gap. His tank was hit while going through an un-cleared village, and was set on fire. While climbing out of the gun turret, Alfred was shot dead by a sniper. He was buried initially by the Padre in the countryside of rolling downland he would have been so happy to ride in, near the village of Rouvers between Caen and Falaise.

The Padre and Alfred's commanding officer, Lt.-Col. James Dalmeyer both wrote to his widow Mollie in the next few days, explaining the details of the burial in which the Padre had *"dedicated his soul to the Almighty"*. His Commanding Officer referred to Alfred's great "ability and likeableness", and described him as the *"best N.C.O. in the Regiment"*, who had been Acting Squadron Sergeant Major for the ten days before his death. In another of those amazing feats of wartime communication, news of Alfred's death in France on 14th August had reached his old friend and best man Fred Moore in Italy within a week; Alfred's widow still has the letter of condolence written to her by Fred on 21st August.

Burial at Banneville

After the war, the CWGC grouped together many of the men previously buried in little local cemeteries, and created some particularly beautiful larger ones but still in the area each man fell in. The cemetery at Banneville-la-Campagne is, as its name suggests, in softly rolling and wooded pastoral countryside, now with restored Normandy farmhouses and fields full of cattle and sheep again. It is two-thirds of the way eastwards from Caen to Troarn, fortunately left in peace by the new motorway a little to the south. It is beautifully kept, with plants replenished as necessary from the CWGC's own Nursery nearby. There are 2,175 British and Commonwealth graves there, and Alfred's is in Plot V, Row E, Grave 5. Below the official inscription on his headstone, the family have added the words:

"LOVE'S LAST GIFT: REMEMBRANCE."

Sgt. Stiles grave at Banneville-la-Campagne War Cemetery,
Calvados, Normandy (4th along in front row).

Frederick Martin MOORE   2.17
2nd October 1944 aged 27
died of wounds in Italy
2014352 Sapper
207 Field Company, Royal Engineers

HOME   23 Dale Road, Winterbourne, then 23 Brunswick Place, Hove
BURIED   Coriano Ridge War Cemetery, off Rimini-Riccione road. Italy

The Moores of Southover

Fred Moore came from the same large Moore family in Southover that lost two of its sons in the First War, Jesse (1.08) and George (1.31 and see comment below). Fred was the eighth of ten children born to Daniel and Edith Moore of Hamsey then Southover. His father Daniel worked on the railways, as a plate-layer and 'ganger'. Fred shared the same Moore grandparents, Henry and Eliza, as his First War cousins Jesse and George above, who had been the sons of Harry and Mary Anne, ?known as Polly. Fred's eldest sister was already 27 by the time his youngest brother was born!

(The family was so large and each generation spanned so many years, and was inter-twined with other local families such as the Fellows, that Fred's remaining brother, sister and cousin have accumulated a great deal of family history details, which are available to any who might wish; they are summarised in the Family Tree following this biography. It should be added that the family themselves has no record of George Moore, as at 1.31 above, having been one of them; it is only the CWGC whose Casualty Details and next-of-kin lists place him in the same family. I am much indebted to Fred's youngest brother Ray in Cheshire and his three surviving sisters particularly the oldest, Mabel, in Lewes; and to his niece Jacque in Norfolk, who is the daughter of Tom & Rene Fellows nee Moore, for all their help.)

Eastport Lane was where they all hailed from in this century, after a short stay in Priory Street. Fred was born on 13th October 1916 just after his parents moved into 15 Eastport

Daniel and Edith Moore, c.1919, with eight of their children at home in Eastport Lane, with Fred the youngest in the picture.

Lane with their four older children still at home, the three eldest having already moved out to work. Up to his birth they had all been living next door at no. 16, looking after Grandad Moore and handicapped Aunt Lucy. Despite the fact that eight people were already living there, the Billeting Officer had decided in 1914 that he would billet no fewer than three soldiers there as well! It was four to a bed and the babies in a cot - family togetherness we don't see the like of any more. Harry and Mary Ann and all the cousins lived along the road at no. 20.

Schooling and friendships in Lewes

Fred was baptised at Southover Church on 29th April 1917 when he was six months old. He went to Southover School, and sang in the church choir. He then went to Central School, from where he won a scholarship for Grammar School in 1928, but as Lewes County School was not yet ready he had to start at Uckfield Grammar School and move back to Lewes when the County School opened in Mountfield Road in 1930. Being one of the original pupils at the County, he helped to dig the hole that was to become the school's Swimming Pool - all good practice for a would-be Sapper!

His best friend from his earliest years was Alfred 'Smug' Stiles, who also came from Eastport Lane and lived in the large house next to what was the Salvation Army Hall, towards the Southover High Street end of the Lane. Many years later it was Alfred who invited Fred to be his best man. The two friends were then killed within a few weeks of each other in 1944 (see 2.16 above).

Another special friend he grew up with was killed in 1943, Kenneth Piper (see no. 2.12 above). Kenneth had grown up in Keere Street, but he and Fred were then to be next door neighbours in Dale Road after 1935. The other special friend from Southover School days was Alma Birdsey, who he was to marry in 1940 (see below).

Scouting and work before the war

Throughout Fred's life his main interests and activities were involved with the Scouting movement. He was closely involved with the 1st Lewes Troop which met at the Old Naval Prison, as a boy member and later helped to run it as Assistant Scoutmaster. The Scoutmaster in charge was a Mr. Smith, who for many years was also the butcher in Southover. Both Fred and Mr. Smith are in a 1934 picture featured by the *Sussex Express* for the Troop's 75th Anniversary in 1985.

While he was still at school he helped out at the newspaper 'cabin' outside Lewes Station. He helped the Wholesale Newsagent in 'batching up' the newspapers etc. for onward delivery to other Newsagents in the area. Once he left school he started working for W. H. Smith in the Lewes Station bookshop, and later at some of their other shops too, including New Cross Gate in S.E. London.

There was a big family event in 1931 when Fred's grandfather Henry Moore died on 30th October at the age of 94. He had lived next door at 16 Eastport Lane for many years looking after his crippled sister Lily, and Fred at sixteen would most likely have gone to his funeral at Southover Church early in November. There had already been newspaper articles at the time of the old man's 90th birthday in 1927, acclaiming him as a "Nonagenarian of Lewes"

(Fred's grandfather had come from Beddingham where he started out as a shepherd boy on the Downs, and then as a carter's boy. In his nineties he could still recall harrowing Mr Ellman's fields at Church Farm, Beddingham, with a team of 8 oxen working four abreast, and just a boy helping. He then joined the railways locally, and moved into Lewes after his wife Eliza died in 1882.)

Eastport Lane to Winterbourne Estate and call-up

It was just four years later in 1935 that Fred's branch of the Moore family left 15 Eastport Lane. Their landlord, Mr. J. Urry the coal merchant, needed the house and yard behind it for re-development, having already built the flats and garages occupying the yard behind the site. This coincided with the Council's development of the Winterbourne Estate, so Daniel and Edith with their three youngest still at home, became the first occupants of 23 Dale Road in 1935

*June 1940: Fred at home
23 Dale Road.*

Then came the war, and Fred was called up in May 1940. His brother Ray remembers hearing in those early days of Fred's training in anti-gas warfare, and of Fred on weekend leave at home telling them about having to ride about on a bright yellow bicycle, the danger warning colour for gas. Daniel and Edith were by now glowing with pride that three of their sons and a further three sons in law were 'serving their country'. The Express featured them all one week in a photo-gallery of all six early on in the war, but later on it became eight rather than six actually in H.M. Forces, with a further two older sons-in-law in the Home Guard - "quite a family record!" as Ray says.

Southover wedding

Fred's childhood sweetheart, Alma Birdsey, continued to play an important part in his life from days in Southover School onwards. He moved on to Central School in Lewes a year or two ahead of her, and she stayed there when he moved on to Uckfield Grammar in 1928 at the age of 11 or 12. They would always walk to school together, with Fred pushing his bike; having dropped Alma off at Southover and later at Central, he would then ride on to Uckfield.

By the time the war came, Alma was living in Priory Street and working as a hairdresser, and her parents had moved to Hove. Fred and Alma were 24 and 22 when they decided to get married. The wedding was at Southover Church on 16th November 1940. The *Sussex County Herald* described it thus:

> *"…The bride wore a full-length dress of ivory satin, and veil held in place by a coronet of silver flowers, and she also wore silver shoes. She carried a bouquet of dark red carnations. She was attended by Miss Violet Moore, sister of the bridegroom, who was*

*10 November 1940: Fred and Alma's
wedding at Southover Church.*

*attired in a full-length dress of powder blue
taffeta, with halo to tone, and silver shoes. She
carried a bouquet of pink carnations, and
wore a gold pendant which was a gift from the
bridegroom. Mr. H. E. Blaber (brother-in-
law of the bridegroom) was best man.*

*A reception was held at Mr. C. P. Holloway's
restaurant in High Street, Lewes. There was
no honeymoon owing to the bridegroom
having to return to his unit. The bride and
bridegroom received many useful presents."*

In the event, there were to be less than two years
for them together in this country, and another two
years with him serving overseas.

North Africa with the First Army

Fred was sent to North Africa with 270 Field Coy. of the Royal Engineers in the summer of
1942. The war in the desert against the Axis powers under Rommel was at its height then, and
it was not until Montgomery's famous victory at El Alamein that November/December 1942
that the tide began to turn for the Allies. His brother Ray remembers hearing that Fred had been
able to write home in 1943 after being in action at Bizerta and the fall of Tunis. By July 1943,
Fred was involved in the landings on Sicily, then in September at Salerno on mainland Italy.
Throughout 1944 the Allies pressed on into Italy, with Anzio in January, Monte Cassino in
May, and the liberation of Rome in June.

Fred's death in Italy

Then on the night of 29th/30th September 1944 Fred was
on guard duty at his unit H.Q. somewhere further on up
into Italy. As his Company Sergeant Major was to write to
Alma later:

> *"…The billet area was heavily shelled in the early hours
> of 30 Sept and your husband was wounded by shrapnel
> while on Guard Duty. He remained cheerful throughout,
> and after immediate attention from H.Q. personnel he
> was taken to hospital. He was fully conscious throughout
> and appeared to be in no danger, his last words being
> 'I'll soon be back - cheerio!'*
>
> *It was therefore a great shock to learn that he had died
> from his wounds in hospital on 2 Oct., and on behalf of
> myself and all the men, especially HQ Platoon, I offer
> you my sincere sympathy and hope that you will be given*

June 1943: Fred in Tunis.

223

added strength to bear such a heavy burden."

October 13th would have been Fred's 28th birthday, and it was on that very day that Alma received the first news of his death. The letter above did not reach her until well into January 1945, as CSM F. G. Walton had decided to defer writing until the first shock and grief had passed. He added:

> *"On behalf of the men of the unit, I feel I must offer you my deepest sympathy in the great loss you have sustained.*
>
> *A registered parcel containing a wristlet watch was returned to you via the normal channels some weeks ago now. Several gift parcels containing soap, cigarettes, sweets etc., I have taken the liberty of distributing to personnel of HQ Platoon.*
>
> *I do hope that this was your wish.*
>
> *May the coming year bring peace and happiness to the world, and may God help and guide you in the days ahead. With sincere best wishes for the future…"*

Fred's sister Mabel, wife of his best man, was asked by Alma's parents to go to Dale Road and break the sad news to his parents. She remembers then also being the one to write and tell their younger brother Ray while he too was serving overseas.

The *Sussex Express* printed their obituary notice on Sapper Moore on 20th October 1944, under the title "Sapper's Death from Wounds". In the same edition there was an entry in the 'Return Thanks ' column as follows:

> *"MOORE: Mrs Frederick Moore and Mr & Mrs Daniel Moore of Lewes wish to thank all kind friends for their messages of sympathy in their very sad loss."*

Burial overlooking the Adriatic

Coriano Ridge is one of the mountain ridges of the Apennines running up through Italy, and the CWGC used it as the name for one of its War Cemeteries, near the village of Coriano. Originally it was known as the Coriano Ridge British Empire Cemetery. This Cemetery is high up above the road between Rimini and Riccione, two resorts above the Adriatic coast. Fred Moore's grave is in Plot XV, Row A, Grave 10. The fact that there are fifteen plots suggests a larger than average Cemetery, as does the fact that it has its own full time local gardening staff.

Family dispersal after the war

Alma then spent many years divided between Priory Street and her mother's in Hove once Fred. had been sent overseas. They had no children, and she did not re-marry for many years. She did much later marry a widower and settle happily in Hove, and stays in occasional correspondence with some of Fred's family. His parents both lived to a great age, and eventually agreed to move to a residential care home in Peacehaven. His father died there in 1969 and his mother in 1975.

For movements of other family members, please see Family Tree following.

This family tree is added as a sample of the size of some of the Southover families in this book, and the span of years covered by each generation; of the way they go back many generations, and the way different families of the same name interweave with each other, and marry into other Southover families, e.g. Fellows.

Family Tree for Frederick Martin Moore, 1916-1944

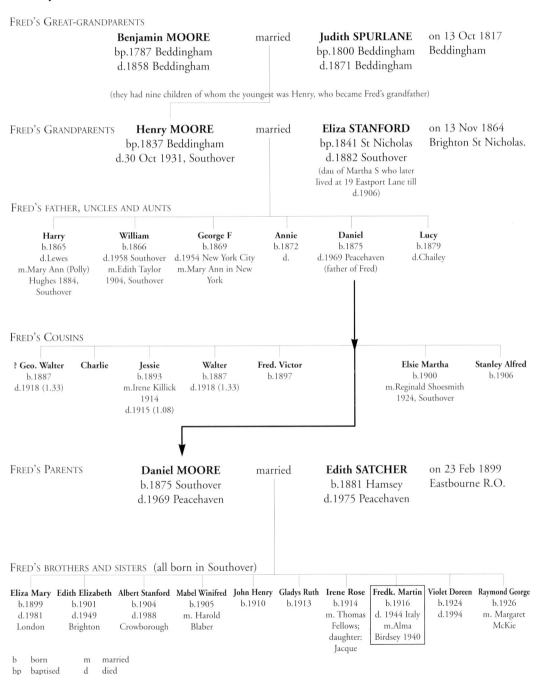

FRED'S GREAT-GRANDPARENTS

Benjamin MOORE   married   **Judith SPURLANE**   on 13 Oct 1817
bp.1787 Beddingham   bp.1800 Beddingham   Beddingham
d.1858 Beddingham   d.1871 Beddingham

(they had nine children of whom the youngest was Henry, who became Fred's grandfather)

FRED'S GRANDPARENTS   **Henry MOORE**   married   **Eliza STANFORD**   on 13 Nov 1864
bp.1837 Beddingham   bp.1841 St Nicholas   Brighton St Nicholas.
d.30 Oct 1931, Southover   d.1882 Southover
                                  (dau of Martha S who later
                                  lived at 19 Eastport Lane till
                                  d.1906)

FRED'S FATHER, UNCLES AND AUNTS

Harry	**William**	**George F**	**Annie**	**Daniel**	**Lucy**
b.1865	b.1866	b.1869	b.1872	b.1875	b.1879
d.Lewes	d.1958 Southover	d.1954 New York City	d.	d.1969 Peacehaven	d.Chailey
m.Mary Ann (Polly)	m.Edith Taylor	m.Mary Ann in New		(father of Fred)	
Hughes 1884,	1904, Southover	York			
Southover					

FRED'S COUSINS

? Geo. Walter	Charlie	Jessie	Walter	Fred. Victor		Elsie Martha	Stanley Alfred
b.1887		b.1893	b.1887	b.1897		b.1900	b.1906
d.1918 (1.33)		m.Irene Killick	d.1918 (1.33)			m.Reginald Shoesmith	
		1914				1924, Southover	
		d.1915 (1.08)					

FRED'S PARENTS   **Daniel MOORE**   married   **Edith SATCHER**   on 23 Feb 1899
b.1875 Southover   b.1881 Hamsey   Eastbourne R.O.
d.1969 Peacehaven   d.1975 Peacehaven

FRED'S BROTHERS AND SISTERS   (all born in Southover)

Eliza Mary	Edith Elizabeth	Albert Stanford	Mabel Winifred	John Henry	Gladys Ruth	Irene Rose	Fredk. Martin	Violet Doreen	Raymond George
b.1899	b.1901	b.1904	b.1905	b.1910	b.1913	b.1914	b.1916	b.1924	b.1926
d.1981	d.1949	d.1988	m. Harold			m. Thomas	d. 1944 Italy	d.1994	m. Margaret
London	Brighton	Crowborough	Blaber			Fellows;	m.Alma		McKie
						daughter:	Birdsey 1940		
						Jacque			

b	born	m	married
bp	baptised	d	died

Frederick Arthur POLLARD   2.18
17th October 1944 aged 32
in N.W. Europe
14663626 Private
2nd Battalion King's Shropshire Light Infantry

HOME   11 Horsfield Road, Landport, Lewes
BURIED   Mierlo War Cemetery, North Brabant, Netherlands

The intricacies of the Pollards of Southover

Frederick Pollard was born at 5 Spring Gardens, Southover two years before the First War started.

Spring Gardens was at the end of the old St. Pancras Gardens where it went down to the spring feeding the Winterbourne Stream, long before all the old cottages there were demolished to make way for the post-war flats. His parents were Horace Pollard, a gardener, and his wife Harriet, who was known as 'Harty'. They had two other children at least, a daughter Dorothy Alice and a much older son Horace.

While they were all still at home, they moved across the road into 10 St Pancras Gardens. Fred went to Central School, and played football for the school team. He then became a gardener like his father and many other Southover men. In 1935 when he was 23, he and his sister Dorothy who was 26 and a 'domestic servant', got together to have a double wedding at Southover Church on 23rd March.

Dorothy married Frederick Charles French, a diamond worker from Barcombe (of all unlikely combinations!). Fred married Elsie Millicent Gurr, who was just 20 at the time, and they soon moved into their own home at 11 Horsfield Road, Landport.

Fred and his nephew Albert on the same Memorial

Fred and Dorothy's older brother Horace Thomas Pollard had long since left home, in fact he had been to and come back from serving with the Royal Sussex Regiment in the First War, and had been invalided out. Horace T. had set up his own home in St. Andrews Lane originally, and then moved back to the St. Pancras area when his wife gave birth to their youngest child Elsie in 1920. Up until then, their youngest had been Albert E. Pollard (see no. 2.15). Later on still, Horace Thos. and his wife Phoebe moved up to Landport, and moved into the new 18 Landport Road, where they would be conveniently near to both nephew Albert and his wife Lucie, and brother Fred with his wife Elsie.

Fred Pollard

So these two Southover servicemen with the same surname, were in fact the Uncle Fred. and the nephew Albert. Surprisingly perhaps, there is no known connection between them and Edie Pollard, the daughter of the other Pollard (another Fred.) on the Southover World War 1 Memorial (see no. 1.41). Strangely enough, Edie has returned to live in retirement in the 'new' flats in the rebuilt St. Pancras area.

Private Pollard and the war

As war drew nearer, Fred gave up gardening and switched to being a lorry driver for the East Sussex War Agricultural Executive Committee. This was the body that, among much else, dealt with food production and the Women's Land Army. Fred was then called up in March 1940 when he was 28.

Initially he was with the Oxford Light Infantry, but was later transferred to the Kings Shropshire Light Infantry from 1943. This transfer probably happened on returning to active service after being wounded, but at least it meant that after a spell back home their only child could be born nine months later. Their daughter Cynthia Joy was born on 27th January 1944, and although they were settled in Landport, she was taken back to Southover to be baptised exactly a month later.

That summer saw the D-Day landings and the Normandy campaign, and the beginnings of the liberation of western Europe. In September Holland began to be re-taken by the Allies, but then there was the Arnhem debacle. In mid-October the King was given a tour of the north west Europe battlefields by the Generals Eisenhower, Montgomery and Bradley. In the week up to 20th October there was the battle for Aachen in N.W. Germany, and the first surrender of German territory to the Allies. How much of all that Fred Pollard was directly involved in is not known, but he was killed on 17th October and buried just in Holland at Mierlo War Cemetery near Eindhoven.

The *Sussex Express* for 3rd November 1944 reported Fred's death a fortnight previously, and gave many of the biographical details already referred to. It continued:

> *"Much sympathy will be expressed with Mrs. Pollard in her great loss, particularly as she is the mother of a baby nine months old. Pte. Pollard was well-known in Lewes…"*

A week later on 10th November, the family put an entry in the 'Return Thanks' column:

> *"Mrs. Frederick Pollard (widow) and Mrs. Horace Pollard (mother) of Lewes, also brothers and sisters, wish to thank their many friends for the expressions of sympathy they received following the death in action of a beloved husband and loving Daddy of baby Cynthia."*

Cedric Augustus CUNNINGTON   2.19
3rd December 1944 aged 26
died of wounds in action, N.W. Europe
2042346 Corporal
279 Field Company, Royal Engineers

HOME   3 South Place Flats, St John's Street, Lewes
BURIED   Nederweert War Cemetery, Netherlands
(between Eindhoven and Roermond)

Cedric Cunnington remains one of those Southover men about whom least is known. It seems his father had died or separated before the war. His mother Mrs A. Cunnington was then given as next of kin by the CWGC, with his step-father as Mr F. Taylor. He is remembered by the families of some of those who went to Lewes Crusaders with him. There are also several who went to Central School with him and remember him from those days, but nothing since. It is thought he had two brothers, Leslie and Stanley, but nothing is known of them either.

Cedric apparently worked for Mr. Colbourne, the old-established Family Butchers in Lewes High Street, between leaving school and the outbreak of war, when he would have been 20 or 21.

At some point, presumably after that, he got married to a girl from Barcombe called Beatrice May. Whether it was then that he moved into South Place Flats with her, or whether that was his mother's home anyway, is not known.

War with the Royal Engineers

Nor is anything known about when he joined up with the Royal Engineers, or in which theatres of war he served with them earlier on in the war. All is known that he was with his unit in the inexorable Allied advance through north west Europe after the liberation of France. "Operation Market Garden" was designed to liberate the Low Countries and break through into Germany. They reached Nijmegen in September 1944, but the parachute landings at Arnhem met much heavier resistance than had been expected. Allied hopes of ending the war by the end of 1944 were dashed. But in that process Cedric Cunnington sustained the injuries from which he was to die over there on 4th December.

He was buried at the CWGC's Nederweert War Cemetery, where his grave is no. 9, in Row B and Plot I. The Cemetery lies between the village church of Nederweert, and the road from Weert to Helmond on which the village lies. It is 15 miles south east of Eindhoven, and 25 miles north west of Roermond.

It was apparently his widow Beatrice who ensured he was also commemorated on the Southover Memorial with so many of his friends, but sadly nothing is known of where she then went after the war.

Dennis George MOPPETT   2.20
6th January 1945 aged 24
while Japanese P.O.W.
1281149 Leading Aircraftman
R.A.F. Volunteer Reserve

HOME   Abinger Place, Lewes
BURIED Ambon War Cemetery, Moluccas Islands, Indonesia

Dennis Moppett was born on 28th November 1920, and was baptised at Southover Church. He was confirmed at Southover in his teens, and went to the County Grammar School in Mountfield Road. He was a keen member of Lewes Crusaders during this time.

Dennis was only 18 when the war broke out, but volunteered in its early days. He was with the R.A.F. Volunteer Reserve and proceeded to serve with them in the Far East. He then had the misfortune to be in Singapore when it fell to the Japanese in February 1942, and it was there that Dennis was taken prisoner.

His family having had no news for three years, eventually received a telegram to state that Dennis had died in the Camp Hospital on 6th January 1945.

Douglas George REDMAN   2.21
3rd April 1945 aged 24
in flying operations over Italy
610728 Corporal
Royal Air Force

HOME   "Green Bank", Rotten Row, Lewes
BURIED Naples War Cemetery, Italy

Douglas Redman was the second son of his family, who also had two older daughters. Their parents were Henry John and his wife Edith Olive Redman. By the end of the war Henry Redman had become head of the auctioneers Messrs. J. R. Thornton of Lewes Cattle Market. They had lived at several different addresses in Southover High Street over the years the children were at home, first "The Croft" then "Newlyn", and ending up in Rotten Row during the war.

Douglas went to Roborough School, Eastbourne. He left school at 17, and after a short spell in training as a surveyor, joined up with the RAF in April 1938. Later that same year both his sisters got married in a double wedding at Southover Church on 26th October 1938. Like

Alfred Stiles (see 2.16) whose wedding was also at Southover just a month earlier, this was at the height of the Munich Crisis. The older sister was Margaret Irene, a nurse of 29, who married John Curtis Gosling who was an agricultural engineer of 31. The younger one was Beatrice Mary, a secretary of 25, who married George Horton, a farmer of 34.

Douglas Redman

The Redman parents must have wondered what had hit them after all that, particularly when their older son announced he was joining the Royal Artillery. Hopefully they were happy about Douglas getting married to a girl called Sheila on 12th October 1942, and making them into proud grandparents a year later when a baby boy was born. Presumably there was ample opportunity for Douglas to return home on leave and get to know his son during the only two years their lives overlapped.

But sadly no other information about either the family or Douglas' war service with the RAF, or the whereabouts of his son, has been forthcoming. All that is known is that Douglas was killed in action while on flying operations over southern Italy, within just five weeks of the end of the war in Europe. He was then buried in the Naples War Cemetery at Miano off the Rome - Naples Highway, four kilometres north of the town centre. It is situated on high ground at Via Vincenzo Ianfolla; but it is sad to continue to read the CWGC description of this Cemetery and find a warning to would-be visitors that "it is located in an area where there have been a number of robberies from individuals".

Perhaps not surprisingly, the Redman parents decided to move away from Lewes at the end of the war. They went to Hove, but there were to be many more years of sadness to follow. Douglas's older brother Sgt. Geoffrey Henry Redman, Royal Artillery, had been seriously injured in the Allied landings at Anzio in January 1944. He was returned to this country for prolonged medical treatment and surgery at both Catterick and Roehampton Military Hospitals, but he never recovered. He finally died of his war injuries at Kings College Hospital, London, just before Christmas 1950, on 22nd December.

His brother's body was later returned to Lewes for interment in the family grave in Lewes Cemetery.

"Greenbank", Douglas Redman's parents' wartime home in Rotten Row.

Harold Russell GROVER
2.22

19th April 1945 aged 24
Dutch/German border
G/4268 Bombadier/Gunner
6th Field Regiment, Royal Canadian Artillery

HOME   14 St James' Street, Southover
BURIED   Holten Canadian War Cemetery, Deventer, Netherlands

Canadian childhood

Harold Grover was born and brought up in New Brunswick, Canada. His father's forbears go back many generations there, with some American connections over the border in Massachusetts as well (details available). His parents were Herbert Russell Grover and Margaret Katherine Grover of North Devon, New Brunswick, and he was their eldest son. It is thought he was one of twins but that his twin died; one other son had married and moved away before the war.

When his unit was posted to Europe, Harold Grover was among those many Canadians to be stationed and billeted in Lewes. Southover Manor School was his first billet, but at some point he was also lodged with the Verger of Southover Church. At the time, this was a Mrs. Ethel Ada Head and she lived down at the bottom of St. James's Street, almost opposite the church. She lived there with her husband, William Horace Head (who had been the uncle of Arthur Henry Head, one of the Southover men killed in the First War, see 1.17), and their only daughter Phyllis.

Southover wedding

Phyllis was just 18 when the Canadians first arrived. She was doing war work at the old Needlemakers' Factory in Lewes, as it was then, making needles for use in the Services' hospitals and casualty units. She remembers having to avoid the other group of Canadian servicemen when they were out from their billets at Claydon House on the dark streets of Lewes once the blackout was in force. The group at Claydon House apparently had a lot of

Lewes Bride for Canadian": wedding at Southover Church of Harold Grover and Phyllis Head, on 18th February 1944.

volatile French Canadians among them, and were reputed to be "a bunch of ex-convicts".

As might have been expected, Phyllis and Harold Grover, who was from the much more sedate Southover Manor group, fell for each other, and by 1944 had decided to get married. They were married by the Revd. D. G. Matthews. The two adult bridesmaids were a friend, Molly Hoad, and a colleague from the Needlemakers, who also married a Canadian. One of the two child bridesmaids was the daughter of another friend, and the other was a little evacuee from the bombing raids on London. The wedding was reported in the *Sussex Express* on 18th February 1944, with a glamorous picture suggesting clothing coupons were not in such short supply by then.

> *"The bride who was given away by her father, wore a dress of white silk taffeta with veil and wreath, and carried a bouquet of red carnations and fern. The bridesmaids, each of whom wore a chain and cross given to them by the bridegroom, were the Misses Molly Hoad and Josephine Holder (wearing blue silk), and the children the Misses Maureen Taylor and Ann Farrell (wearing net and pink silk).*
>
> *Gunner Clarence Albert Whitman of the Royal Canadian Artillery, was best man. A reception held at All Saints Parish Room was followed by a Dance in the evening. The honeymoon is being spent in Edinburgh."*

Harold Grover was better off than many of the wartime bridegrooms, as he was able to get leave for a whole two weeks either side of the wedding. And it was his only opportunity to visit Scotland; little did he know that he only had little over a year of his life left. It is his bride, now his widow, Phyllis that has been my main source of information about her young soldier husband, but sadly she has been overtaken by illness before we could have the next session together that I had hoped for.

Death and burial in newly-liberated north west Europe

There must have been a bitter irony in getting so nearly to the end of the war without even being wounded, only then to go down within sight of the finish. It must have been all the worse that Harold's death was, although on active service, not in action but rather accidental and as it were under 'friendly fire'. Harold's Artillery unit had crossed into north Germany, and were enjoying a rest period while on the way to Berlin. He was by all accounts on a motor cycle making his way to his unit's session at the local bath-house, when he was in collision with one of their own armoured cars, and died shortly after.

His burial was later on arranged at the Holten Canadian War Cemetery. This is along woodland tracks in a forest area on higher ground in the Netherlands but near the German border, fifteen miles from Deventer on the main road from Amsterdam to Bremen. His grave is in Plot X, Row E, Grave 1.

Bombardier Grover's grave in Holten War Cemetery, Edeventer, Holland.

After the war

Harold may sadly have died without having heard the news that Phyllis was already expecting their first, and in the event, only child. The baby was born on 15th November 1945, and was baptised in Southover Church at the end of January 1946. Phyllis decided to call her Haroldene Lorraine, in memory of Harold. She was then able to have a whole year in Canada with the baby, meeting all Harold's family, who neither of them had met before. She remembers it as a time of great warmth and generosity, which must have been quite a tonic for them both.

They returned to live with her parents at the bottom of St. James' Street again. When Haroldene was about ten they moved along the street towards the church, into Rose Cottage, 4 St. James' Street.

Once Haroldene was a teenager in the early 1960s, they decided it was time to go to the Netherlands and visit the Cemetery together, which was memorable for them both.

Phyllis still lives at Rose Cottage, in the street where she has spent her whole life. Haroldene has married and had two children, one of whom married in Newhaven in 1995, and is presenting her with grandchildren. Haroldene herself lives in Somerset, and has her mother to stay several times a year.

The Canadian Government's commemorative tribute to Harold Grover.

Men lost in the Second War

REGIMENTS/UNITS IN WHICH THE SOUTHOVER MEN SERVED

Regiment/Service.	Battalion/Unit	Name	Number in text
Coldstream Guards	3rd Bn.	Albert E. WEBB	4
King's Shropshire Light Infantry		Frederick A. POLLARD	18
Merchant Navy / R.Fleet Auxiliary	M.V. Empire Stanley	Bruce F. TINDALE	9
Queen's Own Royal West Kents		Ronald OLLIVER	13
Queen's Westminsters	2nd	Albert E. POLLARD	15
Royal Air Force		Douglas G. REDMAN	21
Royal Air Force	RAF Regiment	Raymond C. SCRASE	10
RAF Volunteer Reserve		Dennis G. MOPPETT	20
RAF Volunteer Reserve	49 Squadron	Ronald C. BLYTHE	8
RAF Volunteer Reserve	100 Squadron	Frederick J. SMITH	11
RAF Volunteer Reserve	626 Squadron	Robert W. KEMP	14
Royal Armoured Corps		Frederick F. DUNNE	7
Royal Armoured Corps		Alfred J. W. STILES	16
Royal Army Ordnance Corps.		Kenneth A. PIPER	12
Royal Army Service Corps.		Stanley G. OLLIVER	6
Royal Canadian Artillery	6th Field Regt.(Saskatchewan)	Harold R. GROVER	22
Royal Engineers	270th Field Coy.	Frederick M. MOORE	17
Royal Engineers	279th Field Coy.	Cedric A. CUNNINGTON	19
Royal Navy	HMS Fleur de Lys	Leonard G. AXTELL	5
Royal Navy	HMS Royal Oak	Walter Wm. DUNK	1
Royal Navy	HMS Hood	Stanley F. JOHNSON	3
Royal Navy Volunteer Reserve	M.V. Empire Stanley	Walter R. BECK	2

CONCLUSION

The words of King George V on visiting the war graves in Flanders in 1922 provides a fitting conclusion to this book.

COMMONWEALTH WAR GRAVES COMMISSION

"We can truly say that the whole circuit of the earth is girdled with the graves of our dead... and, in the course of my pilgrimage, I have many times asked myself whether there can be more potent advocates of peace upon earth through the years to come, than this massed multitude of silent witnesses to the desolation of war."

King George V   Flanders 1922.

INDEX

Entries in **bold type** are those men whose biographies appear in the book.